Performance Tuning using SQL Server Dynamic Management Views

By Louis Davidson and Tim Ford

First published by Simple Talk Publishing 2010

Editor: Tony Davis
Technical Review and Additional Material: Glenn Berry
Cover Image: Tim Ford
Typeset & Designed: Matthew Tye & Gower Associates

Table of Contents

Chapter 3: Query Plan Metadata _____ **75**

About the Authors

Louis Davidson

Louis has been in the IT industry for 16 years as a corporate database developer and architect. He has been a SQL Server Microsoft MVP for six years and has written four books on database design. He is currently the Data Architect and sometimes DBA for the Christian Broadcasting Network supporting offices in Virginia Beach, Virginia and Nashville, Tennessee. He graduated from the University of Tennessee at Chattanooga with a Bachelor's degree in Computer Science, with a minor in mathematics.

For more information, visit his website at HTTP://DRSQL.ORG/ or email him at LOUIS@DRSQL.ORG.

Tim Ford

Tim is a SQL Server MVP, and has been working with SQL Server for over ten years. He is the co-founder of SQL Cruise, LLC, a training company for SQL Server specializing in deep-dive sessions for small groups, hosted in exotic and alternative locations throughout the world. He is also a Senior SQL Server Professional for Next Wave Logistics, Inc. and is the owner and Lead Consultant for B-Side Consulting, LLC. He's been writing about technology since 2007 for a variety of websites and maintains his own blog at HTTP://THESQLAGENTMAN.COM/ covering SQL as well as telecommuting and professional development topics.

Tim is an established SQL Server Community Speaker and long-term volunteer in the technical community, having held positions in the Professional Association for SQL Server (PASS) since 2002. He has also been leading the West Michigan SQL Server User Group (WMSSUG) since 2008.

When not neck-deep in technology, Tim spends his time travelling with his wife, Amy and sons, Austen and Trevor, be it to Alaska or simply to one of Trevor's tennis practices or Austen's Boy Scout meetings. Tim is passionate about photography, cooking, music, gaming, and exercise, and either experiences or writes about them often.

Glenn Berry (technical review and additional material)

Glenn Berry works as a Database Architect at NewsGator Technologies in Denver, CO. He is a SQL Server MVP, and has a whole collection of Microsoft certifications, including MCITP, MCDBA, MCSE, MCSD, MCAD, and MCTS, which proves that he likes to take tests. He is also an Adjunct Faculty member at University College, University of Denver, where he has been teaching since 2000, and he has completed the Master Teacher Program. His blog is at HTTP://GLENNBERRYSQLPERFORMANCE.SPACES.LIVE.COM/ and he is GlennAlanBerry on Twitter.

Acknowledgements

Louis Davidson

To acknowledge all the people who made my part of this book possible would take forever (plus, I don't think I could just cut and paste the entire list of SQL Server MVPs, the Microsoft employees, and all of the bloggers out there who blogged about DMVs in here, and get away with it).

However, I do want to mention three particular people on the technical side. First, Tony Davis who is both one of the best editors around and one of the most annoying (*you take that back! – Ed*). The results he gets from an amateur like me never cease to amaze me, even if his super attention to detail makes him "fun" to work with.

Next, Glenn Berry, who is a heck of a guy and has done some awesome work with the DMVs on his website, during his technical review of this book, and in his contributions to the text and scripts herein.

Finally, Tim Ford, without whom I doubt I would ever have finished this book. It was our conversations with Tony at the 2008 PASS conference that really got the book started on the path to completion.

On the less computer-oriented side, I want to thank my wife and daughter for just being there. After five books, I don't think they even notice I am doing this anymore, but they do give me strength to keep going at times. And my granddaughter, who didn't even exist when I first started this book, three years ago; and boy, does that put it all into perspective!

Tim Ford

I dedicate this book to Amy, Austen, and Trevor. I could (and should) have spent with you all the hours devoted to working on this book – missing sporting events, school activities, and just those quiet moments that add up to make a life. Thank you for your patience, love, and understanding in letting me fulfill a commitment made – and a goal I had set for myself since I was 13 years old: to write a book. Unfortunately, there are no aliens, car chases, or explosions in the pages that follow; no dashing young man that gets the girl. (To my adolescent self I offer my sincerest apologies.)

To my co-author, Louis, who said, "I told you it would be great if you *wrote* a book, not if you *write* a book!" while I was in the midst of writer's block, and to our editor Tony Davis: to think this all started with a fondness for a decent pint of beer!

To Dad, Pop, Grandma Conrad, and Grandma Ford. I miss not being able to share this and my many other proud moments with you.

Introduction

With the advent of the Dynamic Management Objects (DMOs) in SQL Server 2005, Microsoft vastly expanded the range and depth of metadata that could be exposed regarding the connections, sessions, transactions, statements, and processes that are, or have been, executing against a database instance. These DMOs provide insight into the resultant workload generated on the server, how it is distributed, where the pressure points are, and so on, and are a significant and valuable addition to the DBA's troubleshooting armory.

In order to see a full list of the individual DMOs, from within SSMS, we can run a query against the **sys.objects** system catalog view.

```
SELECT   [name] ,
         CASE [type]
            WHEN 'V' THEN 'DMV'
            WHEN 'IF' THEN 'DMF'
         END AS [DMO Type]
FROM     [sys].[sysobjects]
WHERE    [name] LIKE 'dm_%'
ORDER BY [name] ;
```

In SQL Server 2005, this returns 89 DMOs and, in SQL Server 2008, 136. Alternatively, we can view the all of the system catalog views, system compatibility views, **INFORMATION_SCHEMA** views, and DMOs through the SSMS object explorer. Navigate to Databases | System Databases | master | Views | System Views to see the Dynamic Management Views (DMVs), or ...| master | Programmability | Functions | System Functions | Table-valued Functions to see the Dynamic Management Functions (DMFs). In each case, the relevant objects will be prefixed with **sys.dm_**.

In short, if you look hard enough, you will find an almost overwhelming amount of data regarding user activity on your SQL Server instances, and the CPU, I/O, and memory use and abuse that results. The focus of this book is squarely on core engine activity, and on those objects that, as DBAs, we find most useful in periodic to day-to-day troubleshooting. We'll describe the most important columns that these DMOs return, and provide a core set of scripts that can be saved and adapted for your own environment, to shine some light on previously dark corners of SQL Server performance optimization.

In the process, we'll cover about a third of the total number of available DMOs, spanning 6 of the available 19 categories of DMO, outlined below.

Execution related – *Chapters 2* and *3* show how to investigate the activity generated by SQL statements executed against our SQL Server instances, and how to establish a chain of ownership, from the user connections, to the sessions they spawn, to the resulting requests that generate the SQL workload. *Chapter 2* focuses on activity that is occurring right now, on a given instance, and *Chapter 3* takes a more historical perspective, examining CPU, I/O, and memory use by statements for which a plan exists in the cache, and also investigating critical issues such as plan reuse.

Transaction related – *Chapter 4* steps down to the transaction level, showing how to pinpoint locking and blocking issues, expose open but inactive transactions, and investigate transactions that are causing substantial transaction log writes. It also covers those DMOs dedicated to snapshot isolation level, and use of the version store in `tempdb`.

Index related – Defining an effective indexing strategy is the best way to ensure that the most significant and frequent queries in your workload are able to read *only* the required data, and in a logical, ordered fashion, thus returning that data quickly and efficiently, with minimal I/O. The DMOs in this category, covered in *Chapter 5*, are among the most frequently used by DBAs, and we'll provide scripts for investigating index use, missing indexes and index fragmentation.

Database related and **I/O related** – A critical aspect of SQL Server performance is how the engine uses the disk I/O subsystem, and the ability of that subsystem to cope with the I/O throughput (I/Os per second) demanded by the system workload. *Chapter 6* investigates those DMOs that expose I/O activity at the file, database, and even table level, and also return valuable statistics regarding the size and structure of tables and indexes. It also has a section dedicated to investigating the use of the critical `tempdb` database.

SQL Operating System related – This is the largest of all DMO categories, currently containing 29 DMOs for investigating CPU, I/O, and memory usage from the point of view of the SQL Server Operating System (SQL OS). *Chapter 7* covers ten of the most useful DMOs in this category, including those that expose where and why user sessions have had to wait (and have thus been delayed in the execution of their task), and those that expose SQL Server performance counters, as well as possible resource latching issues.

While this list describes the basic structure of the book, you'll find that certain DMOs crop up in several places throughout the book. For example, the `sys.dm_exec_query_text` DMF, which returns the associated T-SQL command corresponding to the supplied identifier (`sql_handle` or a `plan_handle`), appears in more or less every chapter. In conjunction with the `sys.dm_tran_locks` DMV, it allows us to find out which commands are causing blocking; used with `sys.dm_os_waiting_tasks`, it reveals the T-SQL commands whose execution is delayed due to a particular type of wait, and so on.

The ability to join a range of DMOs to return, in a single result set, exactly the information needed to diagnose an issue, makes these objects a highly flexible and versatile way to investigate SQL Server performance issues.

By illustrating and explaining the various patterns and techniques used to retrieve this metadata and turn it into useful information, we hope to convince the skeptical DBAs among you that the added initial complexity of querying the DMOs, compared to using "old favorite" tools such as `sysprocesses` and `sp_who2`, pays huge dividends in terms of the depth and granularity of the data returned, and the ease with which it can be analyzed and acted upon.

Code Examples

Throughout this book are code examples, demonstrating how to return troubleshooting data from the various DMOs. All the scripts have been tested on both SQL Server 2005 and SQL Server 2008. In cases where a given script is only relevant to SQL Server 2008 and later, this will be noted in the text.

To get the most out of this book, you will need, as a minimum, access to any edition of SQL Server 2005 or later, except Compact Edition (which is a totally different engine). A free 2008 copy of SQL Server Express Edition, plus associated tools, can be downloaded free from: WWW.MICROSOFT.COM/SQLSERVER/2008/EN/US/EXPRESS.ASPX.

Bear in mind, however, that those scripts that investigate current activity will only return results when run against an active SQL Server instance. In such cases, the authors present results taken from live SQL Server 2005 and 2008 Standard and Enterprise Edition production servers (with all sensitive information omitted or disguised, of course).

To download all the code samples presented in this book, visit: WWW.SIMPLE-TALK.COM/REDGATEBOOKS/DAVIDSONFORD/DMV_CODE.ZIP.

Chapter 1: Using Dynamic Management Objects

Dynamic Management Objects (DMOs) are a set of SQL Server objects, referenced in the system (**sys**) schema, which provide the SQL Server DBA with a window into the activities being performed on their SQL Server instances, and the resources that these activities are consuming. In other words, these DMOs expose valuable information concerning the connections, sessions, transactions, SQL statements, and processes that are (or have been) executing against a database instance, the resultant workload generated on the server, how it is distributed, where the pressure points are, and so on. Having revealed a particular pressure point on their SQL Server, the DBA can then take appropriate steps to alleviate the problem, perhaps by tuning a query, adding an index, improving the disk subsystem, or simply "killing" a blocking session.

The term "dynamic" refers to the fact that the information reflected in these DMOs is generated dynamically from a vast range of "instrumentation" points in memory structures throughout the SQL Server engine. This data is then exposed in tabular form via these DMOs, either in views, in which case they are referred to as **Dynamic Management Views** (DMVs), or in table-values functions, in which case they are referred to as **Dynamic Management Functions** (DMFs).

***

Too many acronyms

The objects, collectively, should be referred to as DMOs, but since this tends to cause some confusion with the entirely unrelated "Distributed Management Objects," it's still very common for DBAs to refer to the Dynamic Management Objects, collectively, as "DMVs."

***

So, DMVs and DMFs are simply system views and system functions and you use them just like you use any other view and function within SQL Server: querying them, joining to them, passing parameters when needed, and ultimately returning a single result set containing the data you need, to investigate a particular issue regarding the state or health of your SQL Server instance.

The goal of this short first chapter is to provide a brief, high-level overview of the following topics:

- how metadata is exposed through DMOs, as well as compatibility views and catalog views

- permission required to view data in the DMOs

- how and where the DMOs can be used, and the sort of data they provide

- how to use the DMOs strategically, to diagnose SQL Server performance bottlenecks

- where they fit alongside the number of other performance tools available to the DBA.

Compatibility Views, Catalog Views, and DMOs

In addition to the DMOs that are the focus of this book, SQL Server exposes a range of metadata through other system views, notably the **system compatibility views** and the **system catalog views**. For the most part, the catalog views and the DMOs have rendered the compatibility views obsolete. However, the catalog views will frequently be needed in conjunction with our DMO query because, most of the time, "name" data simply isn't returned by the DMOs (for example, the name, rather than just the ID, of a given table or database).

It's worth briefly reviewing the history of the transition from system tables to compatibility views, to system views and DMOs, as it provides some interesting insights into the different ways in which the metadata is exposed and presented.

In releases prior to SQL Server 2005, SQL Server exposed metadata in a range of physical system tables, stored or referenced in the `master` database (e.g. `master.dbo.sysobjects` or `dbo.sysprocesses`). Microsoft warned SQL DBAs and developers not to code against the system objects, as they could not guarantee that they would not be changed, or that they would even continue to be supported in future releases. However, most DBAs did just that, and the `sysprocesses` system table, in particular, became the "go-to" source of information when troubleshooting performance concerns in SQL Server. This single table gave the DBA access to the `spid` (unique identifier for the user session), cumulative CPU usage, memory, and I/O consumption, client connectivity information (host name, host program name, login information, and process id) and a myriad of other important columns that identified, at a quick glance, what was transpiring on the SQL instance at any given time. Many of us rolled our own management solutions and queries, based on `sysprocesses`, allowing us to dig into the guts of SQL Server.

Microsoft realized the importance of these scripts, and knew that many DBAs relied on them but, at the same time, wanted to introduce a layer of abstraction between the user and their metadata. So, starting in SQL Server 2005, they moved the system tables from the `master` database into the new `resource` database that is inaccessible to the end-user, and even the DBA (there are techniques to access the `resource` database, if it is really necessary, but we won't cover them here).

In their place, in the `master` database, Microsoft created a set of compatibility views, based on the data in these, now hidden, system tables. These compatibility views are structured identically to the original system tables they were replacing (column names, data types, and column order remain constant), but they are now owned by the `sys` schema. They were provided purely for backwards compatibility purposes; they do not reflect any new features and functionality added in SQL Server 2005 and later. However, with a simple schema change in any applicable code, they allowed DBAs to keep using their existing set of troubleshooting scripts and tools.

At the same time, with SQL Server 2005, Microsoft introduced a new set of system catalog views, as well as the DMOs, both of which also live in the `master` database, but source their actual data from the `resource` database. These catalog views and DMOs would be fully supported and reflect all new functionality, and Microsoft began encouraging DBAs to make the switch.

In some cases the switch is fairly subtle; for example, the `sys.sysobjects` compatibility view becomes the `sys.objects` catalog view; `sys.sysindexes` becomes `sys.indexes`, and so on. In other cases, the switch is slightly more complex; for example, `master.dbo.sysprocesses` became the `sys.sysprocesses` compatibility view, but was officially superseded at the same time by the `sys.dm_exec_requests` DMV. In reality, however, the rather complex `sys.sysprocesses` compatibility view has been normalized to deal with several new constructs such as support for MARS connections, and so on. The net result is that the information previously found in the single `sys.sysprocesses` view is now scattered across `sys.dm_exec_connections` and `sys.dm_exec_sessions`, as well as `sys.dm_exec_requests`.

With the introduction of the catalog views and DMOs, Microsoft took the opportunity to simplify naming conventions and standardize them across both sets of new views. So, for example, the `uid` column in the compatibility views is universally represented as `schema_id` in the catalog views and DMOs. Likewise, `spid` becomes `session_id`; `dbid` becomes `database_id`; `indid` becomes `index_id`, and so on. What DBAs appreciate most is the consistency. For example, we know that if we wish to obtain the name of an object, database, index, column, and so on, from a catalog view or DMO, we need to query for the `name` column, regardless of the specific target view.

And so to the DMOs; rumor has it that Microsoft never intended to release them to the general public. The story goes that they were created internally to allow developers, technicians, and testers at Microsoft to analyze and troubleshoot issues during the design phase of SQL Server 2005, and for post-deployment troubleshooting during support calls. The exact truth of this story is open to debate, but ultimately, and thankfully, the DMOs were exposed to the end-users, though one could argue that the sometimes sparse documentation and the confusing interfaces that some of the objects provide, hint strongly at an original intention to keep them a deep, dark secret, for use only by the Microsoft CAT, CSS, and PSS teams.

The DMOs expose a sometimes dizzying array of information; the original **sysprocesses** system view, for example, has essentially been normalized, many new DMOs have been added, and many new columns made available. As the database engine becomes better and better instrumented, so the amount of data available about the engine and the work it is doing, will continue to grow.

The added complexity of stitching together data from a disparate array of DMOs, coupled with initial confusion regarding which columns are exposed where, has led some DBAs to liken querying DMOs to "collecting mystic spells." It's certainly true that DMO queries look a lot more complex and tend to have many more joins than equivalent queries against **sysprocesses**, but the problem with the latter was that, because of changes to the engine, a huge number of rows could be returned for a single **spid**, making the data very hard to interpret. The big payback with the DMO is that, for a little added querying complexity, the "normalization" process has made the data that the DMOs return much easier to analyze and understand, as we hope this book will prove.

Furthermore, catalog and compatibility views are generally siloed by object type: **sys. tables**, for example, is the catalog view that pertains to information specifically (and narrowly) restricted to table objects in a database. The DMOs, on the other hand, relate to specific *ranges* or *topics* about which we may need to obtain information. Need to know what sessions are currently active? Go to **sys.dm_exec_sessions**. Need to know what requests they are currently running? Go to **sys.dm_exec_requests**.

In some ways, it helps to think of DMOs as "system views of system views." They pull together into a logical unit columns sourced from multiple catalog and compatibility views, plus others, in order to provide insight into specific activities that are occurring on a SQL Server instance at any point in time.

DMO Security and Permissions

As noted in the previous section, from SQL Server 2005 onwards, the `master` database is no longer the main system database for storing all metadata and operational system data. All system metadata (except that relating to backups and SQL Agent) which was, and still is, hosted in the `msdb` database, is now sourced from the `resource` database. Incidentally, the fact that metadata on SQL Server Agent jobs and backups is still stored in `msdb` explains why you won't find DMOs related to these areas.

The `resource` database is completely shielded from even those who are granted the system administrator role rights. It exists as two files, `mssqlsystemresource.mdf` and `mssqlsystemresource.ldf`, stored in the default data folder of any SQL Server 2005+ instance. The `resource` database can't be queried, nor can it be backed up by anything other than a file copy. It is completely shielded from use.

In the process, the `master` database has been transformed into a sort of abstraction layer, housing the compatibility views, catalog views, and DMOs that ultimately expose this metadata to the end-user, in a controlled and secure way. In order to view the data in these views and DMOs, unless you are the system administrator of the server, you will need to be granted one of two privileges, depending on the scope of the object you are querying:

- **server scoped objects** require the `VIEW SERVER STATE` privilege to be granted to the relevant login; most DMOs covered in this book required this privilege

- **database scoped objects** require the `VIEW DATABASE STATE` to be granted to the relevant login.

Note that these privileges allow a DBA to view the state of the server without having system administrator rights. Using these permissions for all users who only need to access the DMOs, rather than giving them system administrator privileges, could save you from the "Oops, I dropped a database by accident" phone call late one evening.

Performance Tuning with DMOs

In simplistic terms, performance problems are caused by excessive demands on some shared resource of the SQL Server system, leading to bottlenecks and poor response times. The biggest problem for most DBAs is in pinpointing the exact cause of the problem. There are many "shared resources" in SQL Server, from CPU to memory (such as buffer cache or plan cache), to the disk subsystem, to process schedulers and so on. Furthermore, a single piece of performance data, considered in isolation, can often lead the unwary DBA to misdiagnose a performance problem.

Too often, slow query performance is diagnosed as a need for more CPU, or faster disks, without knowledge of the exact cause of the slow performance. If, on your SQL Server instance, 90% of the total response time consists of I/O waits and only 10% of the time is spent on the CPU, then adding CPU capacity or upgrading to faster CPUs won't have the desired impact.

The really big win with the DMOs is that they allow us to narrow the focus of tuning and troubleshooting quickly, and adopt a more systematic approach to performance troubleshooting. Wait statistics are a prime example. Each time a worker needs to wait for a resource, it is recorded in SQL Server. This information is cached and incremented until the next SQL Server service restart. We can query and aggregate these metrics via `sys.dm_os_wait_stats`, as shown in Listing 1.1.

```
SELECT   wait_type ,
         SUM(wait_time_ms / 1000) AS [wait_time_s]
FROM     sys.dm_os_wait_stats DOWS
WHERE    wait_type NOT IN ( 'SLEEP_TASK', 'BROKER_TASK_STOP',
                            'SQLTRACE_BUFFER_FLUSH', 'CLR_AUTO_EVENT',
                            'CLR_MANUAL_EVENT', 'LAZYWRITER_SLEEP' )
GROUP BY wait_type
ORDER BY SUM(wait_time_ms) DESC
```

Listing 1.1: Performance troubleshooting based on wait times.

As will be discussed in detail in *Chapter 7*, aggregating and sorting upon `wait_type` and `wait_time_ms` will allow us to prioritize our troubleshooting, by identifying what type of waits the SQL Server instance is encountering. From there, we can use other DMOs to further narrow our tuning scope. Depending upon the results of queries against `sys.dm_os_wait_stats`, we will probably investigate further the particular issue indicated, be it CPU, Memory, I/O or other specific concerns, with the DMOs, correlate the data with that obtained from PerfMon, run Profiler traces, use third-party monitoring tools, and so on, until the exact cause is diagnosed.

For example, if the top waits consisted of `CXPACKET` and `SOS_SCHEDULER_YIELD`, we'd need to look at CPU concerns, specifically parallelism settings. By default, SQL Server allows all processors to partake in parallel queries. However, it is unusual for OLTP queries to benefit much from parallel execution. We recently saw behavior identical to this on one of the nodes that host 50 of our databases that had been consolidated onto a two-node cluster. On changing the instance's Max Degree of Parallelism setting from 0 (dynamic) to 4 (this was an eight-core server), the `CXPACKET` waits associated with parallelism dropped off the top of the list. If we had attempted the same analysis with PerfMon, we would have had to play that game we DBAs used to always have to play in the past: Pick a Counter. The `SQLServer:Wait Statistics` Performance Object has a dozen counters associated with it. If someone were to ask why we recommend using the DMOs as a starting point when an instance is performing badly and the cause is unknown, then this is a prime example.

Of course, `SOS_SCHEDULER_YIELD` waits, indicating that the SQL OS Scheduler is experiencing pressure and regularly swapping out a running session in order to allow another session to proceed, could indicate that you are running a lot of CPU-intensive queries, which are getting assigned to the same scheduler. An issue of this type can be investigated further using a DMO such as `sys.dm_exec_query_stats`, to isolate the most CPU-intensive cached queries.

This ability to analyze a potential issue from several different perspectives is one of the great advantages of the DMOs (although the flip side to this is that the sheer amount of data can be overwhelming), and it applies to investigation of CPU, Memory, I/O, or other specific concerns, as we will demonstrate throughout the book.

Navigating through the DMOs

In some ways, working through the DMOs for the diagnostic data you need is a process of "peeling back layers." At the outer layer, we can find out what and who is **connected** to our SQL Server instances, and how; what **sessions** are running against them, and what **requests** are being performed by these sessions. From here, we can find out the details of the **SQL statements** being executed by these requests, the **query plans** that are being used to run them, and so on (*Chapters 2 and 3*).

Dropping down a layer, we have the **transaction** level, where we can find out what **locks** are being held as a result of these transactions, investigate any potential **blocking**, and so on (*Chapter 4*).

A critical aspect of optimizing SQL Server is minimizing the amount of I/O that the engine has to perform (fetching data to and from the disks or, preferably, the data cache). An effective indexing strategy is fundamental to the drive to minimize I/O, and DMOs are provided to investigate which indexes are and aren't being used by the query optimizer, plus details of indexes that optimizer would find useful but are missing (*Chapter 5*). Furthermore, DMOs are provided to investigate disk I/O activity directly, at the file level (*Chapter 6*) allowing the DBA to assess whether the disk subsystem is providing sufficient I/O throughput capacity to cope with the demands of SQL Server, as well as any other applications that may share the use of that subsystem.

Dropping down another layer, we can find how the workload represented by the submitted requests translates into actual work in the operating system (*Chapter 7*).

We can find out, for example:

- what actual tasks (threads) are being executed in order to fulfill the requests

- what work they are performing in terms of I/O, CPU, and memory usage

- how I/O is distributed among the various files

- how long threads spend waiting, unable to proceed, and why.

It is the job of the DBA to join together all the pieces of data from the various different layers, to provide the results needed to highlight the specific problems in the system.

As you can probably gather from this discussion, you'll only occasionally use a given DMO in isolation. You'll need to join to other DMVs and DMFs, in order to pull together the set of data you need to diagnose the problem. Many DMOs have useful "foreign keys" that can be used to join to data in their parent objects, or to other DMOs and system catalog views.

Other times, we will need to pass correlated parameters to a DMF to return a certain column, then join it to our existing data set. For example, several of the execution-related DMVs, `sys.dm_exec_requests`, `sys.dm_exec_query_stats` and `sys.dm_exec_cached_plans` store tokens, called handles, that are used to uniquely identify the batch or stored procedure to which a query belongs (a `sql_handle`), or the cached query plan for a batch or stored procedure that has been executed (a `plan_handle`). We can retrieve a handle from one of these DMVs and then supply it as a parameter to another, function-based DMV, `sys.dm_exec_sql_text` in order to extract information about a specific SQL statement or query plan.

Fortunately, once you start to write your own scripts, you'll see the same tricks, and similar join patterns, being used time and again. This means that a relatively small core set of scripts can be readily adapted to suit many requirements.

Point-in-time versus cumulative data

We can query data held on the DMOs just as we would any other table, view, or function. However, always remember that the data returned is "dynamic" in nature. It is collected from a range of different structures in the database engine and represents, in the main, a point-in-time "snapshot" of the activity that was occurring on the server at the time the DMO query was executed.

Sometimes, this is exactly what is required; we have a performance issue right now, and want to find out what sessions and queries are running, right now, on the server that could be causing it. Bear in mind, though, that this point-in-time data can, and likely will, change each time you query it, as the state of the server changes. You should expect to occasionally see anomalous or non-representative results, and you may need to run a script many times to get a true picture of activity on your instance.

Also, it is quite difficult to query the data in these point-in-time DMOs in the hope that the problem will simply "jump out at you." If, for example, you have a performance problem and you want to check for any "unusual" locking patterns, then it's unlikely that a "*select [columns] from [locking DMV]*" will tell you much, unless you're already very familiar with what "normal" locking looks like on your system, and you can therefore easily spot anomalies.

In other cases, the DMOs are cumulative. In other words, the data in a given column is cumulative and incremented whenever a certain event occurs. For example, every time a session waits a period of time for a resource to become available, this is recorded in a column of the sys.dm_os_wait_stats DMV. When querying such a DMV, you will be seeing, for instance, the total amount of time spent waiting for various resources, across all sessions, since SQL Server was started or restarted. While this will give you a broad overview of where time has been spent waiting, over a long period, it will make it hard to see the smaller details. If you want to measure the impact of a certain change to the database (a new index for example), you'll need to take a baseline measurement, make the change, and then measure the difference.

For example, in *Chapter 6*, we use a DMO named **sys.dm_io_virtual_file_stats** to return, amongst other things, the number of reads in a database file. This value returned reflects the total number of cumulative reads on the file since the server was started. In order to measure a "time slice" of activity, we take a baseline measurement, inserting data into a temporary table, as shown in Listing 1.2.

```
SELECT   DB_NAME(mf.database_id) AS databaseName ,
         mf.physical_name ,
         divfs.num_of_reads ,
    --other columns removed in this section. See Listing 6.14 for complete code
         GETDATE() AS baselineDate
INTO     #baseline
FROM     sys.dm_io_virtual_file_stats(NULL, NULL) AS divfs
         JOIN sys.master_files AS mf ON mf.database_id = divfs.database_id
                                 AND mf.file_id = divfs.file_id
```

Listing 1.2: Taking the baseline measurement.

Next, after an appropriate time lag, we use a Common Table Expression (CTE) to capture the current values, then join it to the temporary table and calculate the difference in the readings, as shown in Listing 1.3.

```
WITH   currentLine
       AS ( SELECT   DB_NAME(mf.database_id) AS databaseName ,
                     mf.physical_name ,
                     num_of_reads ,
           --other columns removed
                     GETDATE() AS currentlineDate
            FROM     sys.dm_io_virtual_file_stats(NULL, NULL) AS divfs
                     JOIN sys.master_files AS mf
                       ON mf.database_id = divfs.database_id
                          AND mf.file_id = divfs.file_id
          )
  SELECT   currentLine.databaseName ,
           currentLine.physical_name ,
       --gets the time difference in milliseconds since the baseline was taken
           DATEDIFF(millisecond,baseLineDate,currentLineDate) AS elapsed_ms,
       --gets the change in time since the baseline was taken
           currentLine.num_of_reads - #baseline.num_of_reads AS num_of_reads
```

```
        --other columns removed
FROM    currentLine
     INNER JOIN #baseline ON #baseLine.databaseName = currentLine.databaseName
     AND #baseLine.physical_name = currentLine.physical_name
```

Listing 1.3: Returning accumulated file reads since the baseline measurement.

This basic pattern is applicable to obtaining time slice measurements from any of the accumulating counters covered in this book.

In some cases, it is possible and useful to manually clear out the accumulated statistics. A classic case in point, described in detail in *Chapter 3*, is when analyzing activity associated with cached plans. If a server has been up and running for a long period of time, it is very hard to compare the relative expense of each plan because it will not be a "level playing field." Different plans will have been in the cache for different periods of time, executed different numbers of times, and the stats will have been accumulating for different periods of time. Unless you are able to flush the cache, thus removing all plans and their associated statistics, the results will be heavily skewed towards plans that have been cached for a long period. Of course, many DBAs would be wary of doing this, as it means all the plans will have to be recompiled, but others, mainly those blessed with modern, high-power processors, feel that the benefits outweigh the costs.

Finally, always bear in mind that much of the data you're seeing in the DMOs is aggregate data, collected across many sessions, many requests, and many transactions. The previously mentioned `wait_stats` DMV, for example, will show you at an instance level where SQL Server spent time waiting, aggregated across all sessions. You cannot track the wait times at an individual session level, unless you happen to be working on an isolated server and you are the only session on there!

Beware of the watcher effect

Generally, running DMO queries will require far fewer server resources than, for example, capturing Profiler traces. Nevertheless, the DBA should exercise due caution when capturing DMO data, in order to avoid the "watcher" effect, whereby the collecting of performance data adversely affects the performance of the server.

If your DMO queries are complex, and collect and aggregate data from many databases, look out for expensive sorts, hashes and spools while they are running, and for any possible performance impact on the server.

Using DMOs with other performance tools

As useful as they are, DMOs are not a replacement for other tools such as PerfMon, Profiler, and so on; they are complementary tools and, in fact, it's not always wise to reach a conclusion as to the required action, based on a DMO measurement, without first correlating it with evidence gathered from these other tools.

Profiler, for example, is an invaluable tool for tracing a defined set of actions (events) that are occurring in SQL Server in response to a certain SQL workload. It is a powerful tool for diagnosing poorly performing queries, locking, blocking, and a lot more. Indeed, DBAs ought to continue to use Profiler regularly, alongside the DMOs. The DMOs tell you a great deal about the state of your instance and provide, as you'll see early in the book, significant information about the sessions, requests, and transactions that comprise the activity in your SQL Server instance. However, Profiler is unequalled in its ability to offer real-time insight into the activity on your instance. It is not a lightweight tool, though, and you will need to have the most concise set of filters, and to return the correct columns and rows for your trace, in order to prevent the "watcher" effect mentioned in the previous section. In this respect, the DMOs are often useful in providing initial detailed, rapid insight into where we should apply the magic sponge to the injured athlete that is our SQL Server instance.

DMOs do offer further advantages over Profiler. One of the limitations of Profiler is that it can only collect performance statistics while it is running, actively capturing query activity. If a "bad query" suddenly executes on the server, causing performance issues, the DBA will usually find out about it after the event. He or she will need to run a trace, and hope the problem occurs again so that it can be captured and analyzed. With the DMOs, as long as the query plan is still in the cache, you can retrieve it and find out what resources the queries used when it ran, and who ran it. Another advantage is the fact that running DMO queries will, in general, have a much lower impact on the server than running Profiler traces. Finally, for certain issues, DMOs offer a much more granular level of detail than Profiler. For example, with DMOs, we can investigate I/O activity at the file system level, whereas Profiler will only summarize it at the drive level.

Performance Monitor (PerfMon) allows us to graphically identify a large number of metrics, but primarily at the server level. Remember that PerfMon is first and foremost a Windows troubleshooting tool. There are Microsoft SQL Server Performance objects that you can utilize to look at SQL-centric metrics but, again, they are not at the same level of granularity that you get from the DMOs. Note that we can also get SQL Server-centric PerfMon counters from the DMOs, as will be demonstrated in *Chapter 7*.

Nevertheless, PerfMon is a valuable tool and it is common for DBAs to correlate evidence gathered from various counters with that obtained from the DMOs. An excellent white paper, *SQL Server 2005 Waits and Queues*, HTTP://TECHNET.MICROSOFT. COM/EN-US/LIBRARY/CC966413.ASPX, explains a powerful performance-tuning method-ology, based on correlating data regarding the points where SQL Server is spending a lot of time waiting (the waits, obtained from the DMOs), with the resource "queues" indicated by tracking various PerfMon counters.

Activity Monitor is one native tool, built into SSMS, which uses DMOs (as well as PerfMon counters) "under the covers." Graphical representations of % CPU Time, Waiting Tasks Count, Database I/O MB/sec, and Batch Requests/sec – counters you would typically enlist first in PerfMon – are included along with output from queries against `sys.dm_exec_sessions`, `sys.dm_exec_requests`, `sys.dm_os_wait_stats`, `sys.dm_exec_query_stats`, and many others. These are segregated into categories for Processes, Waits, Data File I/O, and Recent Query Costs. Activity Monitor is not a bad place to start a performance investigation, but just doesn't offer the same degree of control and filtering that you'll get from using DMOs and good old T-SQL.

Some DBAs still use tools such as **sp_who2**, or some of the DBCC commands, to extract similar information to that which you can get from a few of the DMOs. Again, these former tools are simply rather limited in the information they return, compared to the DMOs. For example, DBCC OPENTRAN can return some of the information that you can get from the transaction-related DMOs, with regard to active transactions in the system. However, the DBCC command fails to give a complete picture, missing, for example, "sleeping" transactions that may still be holding locks, and also not providing valuable information such as how many log records or how many bytes have been written by a given transaction, which is very useful when diagnosing a rapidly filling transaction log file.

Finally, many **third-party monitoring tools** have dashboards that will tie directly in to the DMOs, along with functionality to allow for Profiler tracing activity, because Profiler and the DMOs are so vital for rapid, successful identification and remediation of performance issues in Microsoft SQL Server. Such tools can remove some of the pain of having to construct and maintain custom scripts, schedule them, and collate the results in meaningful form, and so on. They will scrape the data out of the DMOs under the covers, present it to the DBA in a digestible form and, critically, warn in advance of impending problems. Of course, the DBA will still want to know how things work under the covers, and will still need to occasionally write their own custom queries directly against the DMVs, because what you lose with a tool, inevitably, is the exact granularity and control of the data returned that you get when writing your own queries.

Summary

Ultimately, it is the granularity of the data, and level of programmatic control, which makes the DMOs such an important addition to the DBA's performance tuning toolkit. DMOs do not necessarily replace other performance tools, but they do offer a level of detail that is largely unavailable elsewhere, or at least from the native tool set. Furthermore, you don't need to master a new GUI, or a new language in order to use them; it's all done in a language every DBA knows and mostly loves – T-SQL.

Hopefully, this chapter has provided a brief, broad overview of the sort of data that the DMOs covered in this book can offer. It is up the rest of the book to provide the scripts, explanations and details that will allow you to collect the information you need to troubleshoot SQL Server problems on your servers.

Chapter 2: Connections, Sessions and Requests

Within the outer layers of our investigation into SQL Server performance monitoring using the DMOs, the logical hierarchy of user interaction within SQL Server is broken down into:

- the **connections** that are accessing our database instances and who/what owns them

- the **sessions** that are spawned inside these connections

- the **requests** that are executed by these sessions, for work to be performed by SQL Server; these requests can comprise a single query, a batch, a call to a stored procedure, and so on.

As this hierarchy suggests, there is more to user interaction with SQL Server than just query execution. An entity, be it an application or, perhaps, a DBA using SQL Server Management Studio, must first make a connection to the SQL Server instance. Consequently, a session, or multiple sessions, can be established in the context of that user connection. Only then can the user submit requests and retrieve information from the database.

The Dynamic Management Objects (DMOs) and scripts presented in this chapter will allow DBAs to paint a very clear picture of the activity that is occurring *right now* on their SQL Server instances, from the point of view of the sessions and connections that instigated the activity. We'll examine how users are connected to a SQL Server instance, how many sessions each connection has and the attributes of these sessions, which requests are running on the server right now, and what SQL they are running. We'll gather some raw performance data, in terms of CPU, I/O, and memory being used by the SQL queries and batches executed by these requests, to show which currently executing queries are the most expensive. In this way, we can create a trail leading from the current expensive queries to the sessions, connections and users that own them. All of this is accomplished via the following DMOs, which belong to the "Execution-related" category of objects, and therefore all start with `sys.dm_exec_`.

- **sys.dm_exec_connections** – provides information about network traffic and protocols, as well as user attributes from the calling source of the connection. Additional details are available from Microsoft Books Online: HTTP://MSDN. MICROSOFT.COM/EN-US/LIBRARY/F006BD46FE1-417D-452D-A9E6-5375EE8690D8.ASPX.

- **sys.dm_exec_sessions** – returns information about each user and internal system session on a SQL Server instance including session settings, security, and cumulative CPU, memory, and I/O usage. More on this DMV is available from Microsoft Books Online: HTTP://MSDN.MICROSOFT.COM/EN-US/LIBRARY/MS176013.ASPX.

- **sys.dm_exec_requests** – provides a range of query execution statistics, such as elapsed time, wait time, CPU time, and so on. It returns one row for every query currently executing. More information about this DMV is available in the following Microsoft KB: HTTP://TECHNET.MICROSOFT.COM/EN-US/LIBRARY/MS177648(SQL.90). ASPX.

- **sys.dm_exec_sql_text** – returns the text of the SQL batch identified by a sql_handle; see HTTP://MSDN.MICROSOFT.COM/EN-US/LIBRARY/MS181929.ASPX.

- **sys.dm_exec_query_plan** – returns, in XML format, the query plan, identified by a plan_handle, for a SQL batch (this DMO is covered in more detail in *Chapter 3*).

Of course, the journey does not end there. In *Chapter 3*, we'll delve deeper into query execution and, in particular, into the **execution plans** that SQL Server generates, stores and, hopefully, reuses, during this process. This allows a broader analysis of your query workload, from the point of view of what is in the plan cache, rather than just those queries that are executing right now. In *Chapter 4*, we'll step down to an even lower granularity, to look at the **transactions** that are initiated once a query is assigned a plan and sent on to the engine for processing. Transactions do (hopefully) complete and requests are fulfilled, yet the associated user can, and usually does, still maintain connectivity to the SQL Server instance.

Sysprocesses versus DMOs

Before we get started in earnest with the **sys.dm_exec_connections**, **sys.dm_exec_sessions**, and **sys.dm_exec_requests** DMOs, it's worth saying a few words about the system compatibility view that these DMOs have superseded, namely **sys.sysprocesses**.

As was noted in *Chapter 1*, the **sys.sysprocesses** system compatibility view was, for a long time, the "go to" source of information regarding activity on a SQL Server instance, and it is hard for some DBAs to get out of the habit of using their "old standby." It provides a nicely concise picture of what is going on with the server, and it is arguably quicker to query than the DMVs when you just need a quick ad hoc view of server activity.

Many of the columns available in these three DMOs are also represented in **sys.sysprocesses**. However, the scope of each of the three DMOs, along with the ability to return, for each session, command text and query plan information, through relationships with **sys.dm_exec_sql_text** and **sys.dm_exec_query_plan**, make the querying of the DMVs far more powerful and detailed than relying on **sys.sysprocesses** alone.

Aside from some of the naming convention differences between **sysprocesses** and the DMOs, as discussed in *Chapter 1*, another issue DBAs struggle with initially is where certain columns are, and aren't, exposed. To give a brief, simple example: open two tabs in SQL Server Management Studio (SSMS) and target them both at the same database (**SimpleTalk**, in this example). In Tab #1, interrogate the **sysprocesses**. Leave Tab #2 empty. For the sake of our discussion here, the **session_id** (spid, in pre-SQL Server 2005 parlance) is 54 for Tab #1; 56 for Tab #2 (results may differ in your environment).

```
SELECT   spid ,
         cmd ,
         sql_handle
FROM     sys.sysprocesses
WHERE    DB_NAME(dbid) = 'SimpleTalk'
```

	spid	cmd	sql_handle
1	54	SELECT	0x01000900B11FC12AE8D3C1260000000000000000
2	56	AWAITING COMMAND	0x010009000A54CB0778D1C1260000000000000000

Listing 2.1: Running the query against **sysprocesses.**

Now, also in Tab #1, run the equivalent query against **sys.dm_exec_requests.**

```
SELECT   session_id ,
         command ,
         sql_handle
FROM     sys.dm_exec_requests
WHERE    DB_NAME(database_id) = 'SimpleTalk'
```

	session_id	command	sql_handle
1	54	SELECT	0x02000000B11FC12AA5DAD69C36FDCF0EB83ED2325F1B90AE

Listing 2.2: Running the query against **sys.dm_exec_requests.**

In **sysprocesses**, the **sql_handle** is available at session-scope and so we see an entry for the "empty session" (Tab #2) as well as for the query being executed in the current session. With **sys.dm_exec_requests**, a request is only observable while the query engine is processing each transaction associated with it. Once the final commit for the last transaction associated with the request is made, the request is no more. Thus, the second idle session is invisible to **sys.dm_exec_requests**, since no requests are currently being processed.

Furthermore, **sql_handle** is not available from **sys.dm_exec_sessions**, so we could not run the equivalent query against that view. Both **sysprocesses** and **sys.dm_exec__requests** will, of course, detect currently executing queries, but, interestingly, if the second session (56) contained, for example, a modification that had completed, but not committed (or rolled back), then it would *not* be detected by a simple query against **sys.dm_exec_requests**.

In addition, there are a couple of key fields from `sys.sysprocesses` that are not included in any of the `sys.dm_exec` DMVs covered in this chapter:

- **kpid** – identifies the Microsoft Windows thread on which the session is executing; this is not exposed in the DMVs we cover here, but it can be discovered through additional joins back to the `sys.dm_os_threads` DMV

- **physical_io** – a combined metric for cumulative disk reads and writes for the session; this column is handled better within the DMVs, however, in that reads and writes are separated into individual columns in both `sys.dm_exec_sessions` and `sys.dm_exec_requests`.

All other columns of interest provided by `sys.sysprocesses` exist within at least one (and often more) of the Dynamic Management Objects, often by a different name. For example, `spid` in `sys.sysprocesses` is referred to throughout many of the DMVs and DMFs as `session_id`.

Connections and Sessions

Over the course of this chapter and the ones that follow, we will drill down through the layers of user interactivity within our SQL Server instances. That journey starts at the "outside" with the **connections** that are being established to our SQL Server instances, and then the **sessions** that are associated with them.

The `sys.dm_exec_connections` DMV returns server-scoped information about physical connections into SQL Server and is "network-centric" in the information it returns. The `sys.dm_exec_sessions` DMV is server-scoped; it returns a row for every session on your SQL Server instance, and provides a vast array of information regarding session ownership, the state of these sessions, and the work they are performing. It is rare to query either of these DMVs in isolation and, in fact, you will often join them to other

DMOs to get an initial, session-level view of the work currently being executed on your instances, and from which connections this work originated.

Let's first take a brief overview of each of these DMVs, and then we'll get to the set of diagnostic scripts that use them.

sys.dm_exec_connections

The **sys.dm_exec_connections** DMV uses the following three identification columns, to uniquely identify a connection and to facilitate joins to the information in related DMOs:

- **connection_id** – uniquely identifies the connection at the instance level; use this column when joining to **sys.dm_exec_requests**

- **session_id** – identifies the session associated with this connection; it is the foreign key referencing **sys.dm_exec_sessions** and is used to join **sys.dm_exec_connections** to that DMV

- **most_recent_session_id** – the session_id for the most recent request associated with the connection; when dealing with SOAP (Simple Object Access Protocol) sessions, it's possible for a session to outlast a connection to SQL Server (connections may span several sessions, in fact); coverage of SOAP is outside the scope of this book, but Microsoft TechNet offers a good primer: HTTP://TECHNET.MICROSOFT. COM/EN-US/LIBRARY/MS187904(SQL.90).ASPX.

Rows in **sys.dm_exec_connections** correlate to the session information exposed in **sys.dm_exec_sessions** via the session_id and most_recent_session_id. It is appropriate to use the most_recent_session_id column on joins between these two DMVs as sessions will reuse open connections as seen fit, and the most_recent_session_id column will store the more accurate information to complete the join.

The most_recent_sql_handle column returned by this DMV is the handle associated with the last request executed against SQL Server on this connection. This column is always associated with the most_recent_session_id column, and not necessarily the session_id column. The text of this sql_handle can be returned by passing the handle to the **sys.dm_exec_sql_text** Dynamic Management Function, as will be demonstrated a little later.

The **sys.dm_exec_connections** DMV returns detailed information regarding the physical connections to SQL Server, including the protocols and security used, network packet information, and so on. The following columns represent a small selection of the more commonly-used ones:

- **encrypt_option** – Boolean column that identifies whether encryption is used on this connection

- **auth_scheme** – authentication scheme for the connection; Windows authentication (NTLM, KERBEROS, DIGEST, BASIC, NEGOTIATE) or SQL, for SQL Server authentication

- **num_reads** – number of *packet* reads that have occurred across this connection; note that this is not the same as **sys.dm_exec_session.reads**

- **num_writes** – number of *data packet* writes that have occurred over this connection; note that this is not the same as **sys.dm_exec_session.writes**

- **last_read** – time that the last read occurred over this connection

- **last_write** – time of the last write occurring over this connection

- **client_net_address** – IP address of the client connecting to the SQL Server instance.

sys.dm_exec_sessions

The `sys.dm_exec_sessions` DMV is server-scoped and returns a row for every session on your SQL Server instance. Microsoft recommends using `sys.dm_exec_sessions` to initially identify "sessions of interest," then performing more detailed analysis on these sessions via queries utilizing the other DMVs, which is a pretty accurate description of the approach we'll take in this book.

An interesting point to note is that the values in the `sessions` DMV are updated only when their associated requests have finished executing, whereas the `requests` DMV (covered later) provides a real-time view of what is happening right now on your system.

As was the case with `sys.dm_exec_connections` we will be working with just a subset of the columns available in `sys.dm_exec_sessions`. There is a full list of the columns available with this DMV at HTTP://MSDN.MICROSOFT.COM/EN-US/LIBRARY/MS176013.ASPX, and here we'll include a summary of only the most important columns for the DBA in the text that follows.

The DMV provides a unique identifier for the session on a given instance (`session_id`). This column corresponds to the `spid` column from the `sys.sysprocesses` system compatibility view. Based on this `session_id`, the DMV can reveal such information as the client program that initiated it (`program_name`), the status of the session (`status`), and the SQL Server login under which the session is executing (`login_name`), which may, due to context switching via such commands as `EXECUTE AS`, be different from the login that initiated the session (available from `original_login_name`).

The `status` column is worthy of special mention, as it relates to SQL Server wait time analysis, which will be discussed in detail in *Chapter 7*. If the "work" owned by a session is currently being executed (i.e. is "on the CPU") then the session's status is listed as `running`. If none of the session's requests are currently running, then the status is `sleeping`. There is also a third status value of `dormant`, indicating a session that "has been reset due to connection pooling." A `status` column also appears in the `sys.dm_exec_requests` DMV, and provides a slightly more detailed view of the current state of a request.

The *sessions* DMV also provides a host of columns that reveal the value, for each session, of various session-level settings. Again, these are self-explanatory and include the value of `DATEFORMAT` (`date_format`), `ANSI_WARNINGS` (`ansi_warnings`), the transaction isolation level for the session (`transaction_isolation_level`), how long the session will wait for a lock to release before timing out (`lock_timeout`), and the deadlock priority of the session (`deadlock_priority`), which determines how likely it is that the session will be chosen as a deadlock victim.

Perhaps most interestingly for the DBA, this DMV provides a number of columns that reveal the workload and activity at the session level, as follows:

- **total_elapsed_time** – time in milliseconds since the session was initiated
- **last_request_start_time** – start time of the most recent request to execute on this session (the current request, if the session is in a running state)
- **last_request_end_time** – a DATETIME column that shows the time that the most recent request completed
- **cpu_time** – amount of CPU time, recorded in milliseconds, used by all of the requests associated with this session
- **memory_usage** – number of 8 KB pages of memory used by all requests associated with this session
- **total_scheduled_time** – total time in milliseconds that the requests associated with this session were scheduled for execution
- **logical_reads** – number of reads *from the data cache* performed by all requests associated with the session
- **reads** – total number of reads *from disk* performed by all requests in the session
- **writes** – total number of writes performed by all requests in the session.

Note that many of the columns in this DMV may have a NULL value associated with them if the sessions are internal to Microsoft SQL Server (those with session_id < 51).

Who is connected?

The most immediately obvious use for these DMVs is to help identify who and what is connecting to an instance of SQL Server, and to gather some useful information about each connection. While it is not necessary for DBAs to know the intimate details of every application, application server and workstation in the environments they support, they do at least need some way of knowing which ones are accessing their SQL Server instances, when, and how often. The query in Listing 2.3 identifies sources of multiple connections to your SQL Server instance and so will allow the DBA to identify where the bulk of the connections originate, for each of their instances.

```
-- Get a count of SQL connections by IP address
SELECT  dec.client_net_address ,
        des.program_name ,
        des.host_name ,
      --des.login_name ,
        COUNT(dec.session_id) AS connection_count
FROM    sys.dm_exec_sessions AS des
        INNER JOIN sys.dm_exec_connections AS dec
                        ON des.session_id = dec.session_id
-- WHERE    LEFT(des.host_name, 2) = 'WK'
GROUP BY dec.client_net_address ,
        des.program_name ,
        des.host_name
    -- des.login_name
-- HAVING COUNT(dec.session_id) > 1
ORDER BY des.program_name,
        dec.client_net_address ;
```

	client_net_address	program_name	host_name	connection_count
1	63.38.39.148		WK2095	2
2	63.12.41.139	.Net SqlClient Data Provider	WK7085	2
3	63.12.43.145	.Net SqlClient Data Provider	WK7001	2
4	63.8.33.168	Scan Capture App	WK6146	2
5	63.8.33.168	Scan Capture DataMods	WK6146	2
6	63.8.43.12	Scan Capture DataMods	WK9922	2
7	63.8.47.115	Scan Capture DataMods	WK6062	2
8	63.8.43.12	HelpsoftModuledule	WK9922	2
9	63.8.43.12	Helpsoftviewview	WK9922	2
10	63.8.47.115	Helpsoftviewview	WK6062	2
11	63.97.13.249	Microsoft SQL Server Management Studio	WK1062	2
12	63.11.100.53	Microsoft SQL Server Management Studio - Query	WK3387	3
13	63.3.83.240	Helpsofton 2on 2	WK9661	24
14	63.3.37.27	Transport View	WK1190	3
15	63.3.47.98	Transport View	WK6783	3

Listing 2.3: Who is connected?

This particular query provides the IP address and name of the machine from which the connection is being made, to a given SQL Server instance, the name of the program that is connecting, and the number of open sessions for each connection. This query, in our environment, is limited to workstation-class clients only. However, you can easily manipulate the **WHERE** clause of the statement to fit the naming conventions of the hardware in your environment.

I find this to be extremely useful information in several ways. It lets you see which middle-tier servers are connecting to your server, and how many sessions each one of them has, which is very helpful when you are trying to help your developers debug application or connectivity issues. It lets you see if anyone is using SSMS to connect to your instance.

From these results, I would immediately review the possibility of an issue relating to the **Helpsofton 2on 2** application, at address 63.3.83.240, as it is a workstation-class box generating 24 connections on software I know does not require such activity. Likewise, I would review the activity associated with the **Transport View** application to determine whether or not multiple connections, and multiple sources of said connections, are appropriate.

It is quite common that many, if not most, of the Application Servers in your environment will be generating multiple connections into your SQL Server boxes. However, if you observe the same behavior from a workstation, you may need to investigate the usage patterns of the application with the application analyst or vendor representative, to determine if this is an architectural issue or a result of misuse by the end-user (opening multiple instances of the application in an attempt to increase productivity).

Who is connected by SSMS?

Closely related to the previous script, Listing 2.4 focuses on those who are directly connected to the SQL Server instances I support, via SSMS. If I see results that reference a server-class box, I would be apt to question the activity. Red flags would also be generated if I encounter rows that are not associated with workstations assigned to DBAs, developers, or other authorized SQL Server professionals in my environment.

```
SELECT   dec.client_net_address ,
         des.host_name ,
         dest.text
FROM     sys.dm_exec_sessions des
         INNER JOIN sys.dm_exec_connections dec
                    ON des.session_id = dec.session_id
         CROSS APPLY sys.dm_exec_sql_text(dec.most_recent_sql_handle) dest
WHERE    des.program_name LIKE 'Microsoft SQL Server Management Studio%'
ORDER BY des.program_name ,
         dec.client_net_address
```

	[No column name]	host_name	text
1	63.97.13.249	WK1062	use [master]
2	63.97.13.249	WK1062	SELECT db_name() AS [Database_Name], SCHEMA_...
3	63.11.100.53	WK3387	select @@spid; select SERVERPROPERTY('Product...
4	63.11.100.53	WK3387	--Identify all connections to the instance using SQL man...
5	63.11.100.53	WK3387	SELECT SDEC.[client_net_address], SDES.[host_na...

Listing 2.4: Who is executing what via SSMS?

Notice the use of the **CROSS APPLY** operator to join to the results returned by the **sys. dm_exec_sql_text** table-valued function (discussed later). The function is invoked once for each row in our "outer" table, and we pass in to the function the **most_recent_ sql_handle** parameter so that we can return the text of the most recently-executed query in our result set. The use of **CROSS APPLY** (as opposed to **OUTER APPLY**) means that a row will only be returned from the "outer" table if the function produces a result for that row.

You will see this **CROSS APPLY** pattern repeated many times in DMO queries, though there are a few DMOs, for example **sys.dm_db_index_operational_stats** (see *Chapter 5, DMOs for Indexing*), which do not allow joins to table-valued functions in this manner.

Session-level settings

Listing 2.5 is really just a "dump" of some useful columns from the **sys.dm_exec_ sessions** DMV for the current session, via the **@@spid** system variable. Nevertheless, it is useful as a quick, one-stop source for determining the session settings for the current connection, or when troubleshooting a specific session. You could easily supply a **session_id** in place of **@@SPID** if diagnosing a performance issue on an identified **session_id**.

```
SELECT   des.text_size ,
         des.language ,
         des.date_format ,
         des.date_first ,
         des.quoted_identifier ,
         des.arithabort ,
         des.ansi_null_dflt_on ,
         des.ansi_defaults ,
         des.ansi_warnings ,
         des.ansi_padding ,
         des.ansi_nulls ,
         des.concat_null_yields_null ,
         des.transaction_isolation_level ,
         des.lock_timeout ,
         des.deadlock_priority
FROM     sys.dm_exec_sessions des
WHERE    des.session_id = @@SPID
```

	text_size	language	date_format	date_first	quoted_identifier	arithabort	ansi_null_dflt_on	ansi_defaults
1	2147483647	us_english	mdy	7	1	1	1	0

	ansi_warnings	ansi_padding	ansi_nulls	concat_null_yields_null	transaction_isolation_level	lock_timeout	deadlock_priority
1	1	1	1	1	2	-1	0

Listing 2.5: Return session-level settings for the current session.

The various session settings determine, not only how the session handles requests and transactions that flow along its ownership chain, but also how the session interacts with other sessions running concurrently on the SQL Server instance. Sessions with elevated deadlock priority, for example, are able to run roughshod over any other sessions with which they may conflict in a deadlock situation. This may be by design, but it may be indicative of a user manipulating their session settings to "play the bully." It's also useful to know if any sessions are running transactions using the READ UNCOMMITTED isolation level, meaning that the requests running on the session may return data compromised by dirty reads.

Logins with more than one session

The simple query in Listing 2.6 reports on the number of sessions being run by each login on your SQL Server instance. It's especially useful for seeking out those logins that own more than a single session.

```
SELECT   login_name ,
         COUNT(session_id) AS session_count
FROM     sys.dm_exec_sessions
WHERE    is_user_process = 1
GROUP BY login_name
ORDER BY login_name
```

	login_name	session_count
1	DBA	6
2	sa	1
3	Sauron\Timothy	4

Listing 2.6:   Logins with more than one session.

Note that much published code uses `WHERE  session_id > 50` to filter out system processes. However, certain system features, such as Database Mirroring or Service Broker can, and will, use a `session_id` of greater than 50 under certain circumstances, such as when a large number of tasks are involved. Hence the use here of `is_user_ process = 1`.

This can be useful, especially if you use application level logins for different applications that use your database instance. If you know your baseline values for the number of connections per login, it is easier to see when something has changed. While not an indicator of a problem in its own right, multiple open sessions may be an indicator of either poor design or improper usage habits by the end-user, such as running multiple instances of an application or, impatient with the performance, clicking a link or command button repeatedly and expecting the application to respond quicker.

Identify sessions with context switching

Context switching is the act of executing T-SQL code under the guise of another user connection, in order to utilize their credentials and level of rights. While full coverage of context switching is outside the scope of this book (and is explained in greater detail in Books Online at HTTP://MSDN.MICROSOFT.COM/EN-US/LIBRARY/MS181362.ASPX), the simple script in Listing 2.7 will at least allow DBAs to identify its occurrence.

```sql
SELECT   session_id ,
         login_name ,
         original_login_name
FROM     sys.dm_exec_sessions
WHERE    is_user_process = 1
         AND login_name <> original_login_name
```

	session_id	login_name	original_login_name
1	54	login1	DBA

Listing 2.7: Identify sessions with context switching.

Identify inactive sessions

The query shown in Listing 2.8 identifies all sessions that are open and have associated transactions, but have had no active requests running in the last *n* days. The script joins to the `sys.dm_tran_session_transactions` DMV, which will be discussed in *Chapter 4, Transactions*. In the script, we extract the "day" portion of the `last_request_end_time` and use it to hunt down any sessions where the last request completed more than five days ago and where there are no requests currently running. We achieve the latter simply by returning sessions with any `Status` other than `Running` (i.e. `Sleeping`, `Dormant` or, in SQL Server 2008, `Preconnect` sessions).

```
DECLARE @days_old SMALLINT
SELECT  @days_old = 5

SELECT  des.session_id ,
        des.login_time ,
        des.last_request_start_time ,
        des.last_request_end_time ,
        des.[status] ,
        des.[program_name] ,
        des.cpu_time ,
        des.total_elapsed_time ,
        des.memory_usage ,
        des.total_scheduled_time ,
        des.total_elapsed_time ,
        des.reads ,
        des.writes ,
        des.logical_reads ,
        des.row_count ,
        des.is_user_process
FROM    sys.dm_exec_sessions des
        INNER JOIN sys.dm_tran_session_transactions dtst
                    ON des.session_id = dtst.session_id
WHERE   des.is_user_process = 1
        AND DATEDIFF(dd, des.last_request_end_time, GETDATE()) > @days_old
        AND des.status != 'Running'
ORDER BY des.last_request_end_time
```

	session_id	login_time	last_request_start_time	last_request_end_time	status
1	186	2009-06-28 15:13:42.570	2009-06-28 15:13:42.587	2009-06-28 15:13:42.587	sleeping
2	429	2009-06-28 15:50:43.937	2009-06-28 15:50:44.157	2009-06-28 15:50:44.157	sleeping
3	436	2009-06-28 15:50:46.280	2009-06-28 15:50:46.483	2009-06-28 15:50:46.483	sleeping
4	431	2009-06-28 15:50:49.953	2009-06-28 15:50:50.157	2009-06-28 15:50:50.157	sleeping
5	443	2009-06-28 15:50:50.547	2009-06-28 15:50:50.750	2009-06-28 15:50:50.767	sleeping
6	407	2009-07-02 11:55:10.100	2009-07-02 12:11:36.580	2009-07-02 12:11:36.580	sleeping

	program_name	cpu_time	total_elapsed_time	memory_usage	total_scheduled_time
1	SQLAgent - Email Logger	0	2	2	2
2	HAL 3000 Data Mod	0	18	2	13
3	HAL 3000 Data Mod	31	12	2	12
4	HAL 3000 Data Mod	16	17	2	12
5	HAL 3000 Data Mod	16	28	2	13
6	AustenPro	5736	11342	2	6870

	total_elapsed_time	reads	writes	logical_reads	row_count	is_user_process
1	2	0	0	0	1	1
2	18	0	1	154	0	1
3	12	0	1	142	0	1
4	17	0	1	144	0	1
5	28	1	1	151	0	1
6	11342	13	29	72526	0	1

Listing 2.8: Sessions that are open but have been inactive for more than 5 days.

I included the workload/activity columns in the query in order to determine whether the application may hold a session for a long period of time, perhaps permanently, or if the session is truly idle and possibly stagnant.

If cumulative activity is high, as indicated by the values of `cpu_time`, `total_elapsed_time`, `total_scheduled_time`, and so on, but the session has been inactive for a while, then it may be an application that keeps a more-or-less permanent session open, and therefore there is little to be done about it. From this perspective, the **AustenPro** session in the sample data may be "acceptable," and I would proceed to identify possible issues with the first five rows in the results.

From these results, I can surmise that there may have been an event on 6/28/2009 at 15:13 that interrupted connectivity to the server and resulted in a number of "orphaned sessions." In this case, this event was a scheduled downtime in our environment for monthly server patching. The transactions associated with these orphaned sessions should have been rolled back as part of the undo portion of recovery, when bringing the instance back online after the patching. I killed these sessions, based upon the knowledge of the environmental activity and the fact that the sessions were currently not running any requests (as evidenced by the value of the `status` column being `sleeping`).

As always, it's not enough just to understand the metadata values for the DMOs; before acting on this data, you must also know and understand your *environment*, your *data*, and your *users*.

Identify idle sessions with orphaned transactions

The following query joins **sys.dm_exec_sessions** to **sys.dm_exec_requests** and **sys.dm_tran_session_transactions**. The **requests** DMV will be discussed in more detail shortly, and the **session_transactions** DMV will be introduced fully in *Chapter 4*.

The inner join to **sys.dm_tran_session_transactions** returns all sessions with corresponding open transactions. By performing a left join to **sys.dm_exec_requests** and returning results where a **NULL** foreign key is encountered, we limit the results to only those sessions that have open transactions, yet no corresponding request associated with the session.

```
SELECT  des.session_id ,
        des.login_time ,
        des.last_request_start_time ,
        des.last_request_end_time ,
        des.host_name ,
        des.login_name
FROM    sys.dm_exec_sessions des
        INNER JOIN sys.dm_tran_session_transactions dtst
                    ON des.session_id = dtst.session_id
        LEFT JOIN sys.dm_exec_requests der
                    ON dtst.session_id = der.session_id
WHERE   der.session_id IS NULL
ORDER BY des.session_id
```

	session_id	login_time	last_request_start_time
1	83	2009-06-30 03:18:38.080	2009-07-10 03:23:09.373
2	217	2009-07-10 13:39:14.390	2009-07-10 23:58:30.430
3	307	2009-06-30 03:18:40.300	2009-07-04 03:19:33.290
4	371	2009-06-28 15:20:38.340	2009-07-10 23:58:30.150

	last_request_end_time	host_name	login_name
1	2009-07-10 03:23:09.373	TST12345	trevor_ford
2	2009-07-10 23:58:30.430	WKS23112	TEST_DOMAIN\amyf
3	2009-07-04 03:19:33.290	TST12345	trevor_ford
4	2009-07-10 23:58:30.150	SRVR54321	TEST_DOMAIN\timf

Listing 2.9:   Identifying sessions with orphaned transactions.

Microsoft offers a version of this query in Books Online, but I have a few issues with their version. It returns all columns from `sys.dm_exec_sessions`, which is completely unnecessary, and its join structure is, in my opinion, convoluted.

Requests

Now we reach the level of the requests that are made against the SQL Server engine, and the batches, queries, and stored procedures that are executed within these requests.

Query tuning is the heart and soul of optimizing SQL Server performance. If your typical workload consists of ill-designed, inefficient queries then, for a number of reasons, you will have performance and scalability issues. If your queries are longer, more numerous, and more complex than necessary, they will require more CPU resources during execution, and so will take longer to run. Ill-designed queries, along with a failure to make proper use of indexes (see *Chapter 5, DMOs for Indexing*), will cause more data to be read more often than is necessary. If this data is read from the buffer cache, this is referred to as logical I/O, and can be an expensive operation. If the data is not in memory, and so needs to be read from disk (or, of course, if data needs to be written), this is physical I/O and is even more expensive. In addition, if you have many queries that return huge amounts of data, it could cause memory pressure on the buffer cache, and result in SQL Server flushing data out of the cache, which will affect the performance of other queries.

The problems do not even end there; as your SQL workload executes, it will need to obtain locks or latches on various shared resources (a data page, a plan in the cache, and so on). Poorly-designed SQL will acquire more locks/latches than necessary and hold them for longer than necessary, thus forcing other requests to wait longer than necessary before proceeding, and so limiting the scalability of the system.

The set of DMVs in the "Execution-related" category, including those in this chapter and the next, will help you to track down the sessions, requests and queries that are the most resource intensive, and take the longest time to execute. Central to this task are the two DMOs we'll discuss next: `sys.dm_exec_requests`, a DMV that returns one row for every request currently executing and provides a range of execution statistics for that request, such as elapsed time, wait time, CPU time and so on; and `sys.dm_exec_sql_text`, which is a DMF that returns the text of the SQL batch or procedure identified by a `sql_handle`, obtained from `sys.dm_exec_requests` (or from another DMO) and passed in as a parameter.

Overview of sys.dm_exec_requests

The `sys.dm_exec_requests` DMV supplies a row for each user and system request currently executing within a SQL Server instance. Of the three DMVs discussed in this chapter, `sys.dm_exec_requests` is undoubtedly the workhorse. It provides much of the same information that we find in `sys.dm_exec_sessions` but that information was cumulative for all the requests that have been satisfied from the time the session was opened. The `sys.dm_exec_requests` DMV shows us what is *currently* running on the SQL Server instance, its impact on memory, CPU, disk, and cache. The previous two DMVs we've discussed in this chapter may only be updated with this cumulative information once the queries complete and the requests running on the associated connections and sessions are satisfied. The information returned from `sys.dm_exec_requests` is real time; it's not returned after the fact.

SQL and plan handles

As noted, the `sys.dm_exec_requests` is one of the DMOs that expose the `sql_handle` column, which identifies the currently executing batch or procedure (or one that is in the cache – see *Chapter 3*). We pass this handle to the `sys.dm_exec_sql_text` DMF, to obtain the SQL text of the executing batch. This batch or procedure may consist of tens or even hundreds of SQL statements, so we'll get back the text for all those statements. A common pattern is to use the `SUBSTRING` function and the byte offset columns (`statement_start_offset` and `statement_end_offset`), supplied by `sys.dm_exec_requests`, to extract the text for only that statement within that batch that is currently executing.

> ### The changing data type of `sql_handle`
>
> In SQL Server 2005, the `sql_handle` is a `binary(20)` value, but in SQL Server 2008 it is documented as a `varbinary(64)`.

Also exposed is the `plan_handle` column, which identifies the execution plan for the procedure or batch. We will use this column briefly in this chapter, when exposing the graphical execution plan associated with sessions of interest, but it is covered in detail in *Chapter 3*.

Identification columns

The primary key of the `sys.dm_exec_requests` DMV is the `request_id` column, which uniquely identifies a request within a session. However, this value is very rarely used in practice. More useful are the three foreign keys:

- **session_id** – session on which the request is run; used to join to _sessions

- **connection_id** – connection associated with the request; used to join to _connections

- **transaction_id** – transaction associated with the request; used in several objects including the complete suite of **sys.dm_tran...** Dynamic Management Objects, as well as tools such as Profiler; this column is often used to join to **sys.dm_tran_ active_transactions** to get more detailed information about the transaction(s) associated with a given request detailed in **sys._dm_exec_requests**.

The **sys.dm_exec_requests** DMV offers a huge amount of information regarding the currently executing requests and the work they are performing. As usual, we'll refer you to the relevant page on Books Online (HTTP://MSDN.MICROSOFT.COM/EN-US/LIBRARY/ MS177648.ASPX) for the full listing, and only review here those columns we use most often.

Blocking and locking columns

The _requests DMV exposes columns that describe the blocking state and the wait status of the active requests (if waiting on a resource before it can be fulfilled). As you'll see in *Chapter 7* of this book, much of performance tuning and system performance review begins with the information that comes from wait stats analysis.

The **status** column of this DMV reveals the status of a given request within a session. If a request is currently executing, its status is **running**. If it is in the "runnable" queue, which simply means it is in the queue to get on the processor, its status is **runnable**. This is referred to as a **signal wait**. If it is waiting for another resource, such as a locked page, to become available in order to proceed, or if a running request needs to perform I/O, then it is moved to the waiter list; this is a **resource wait** and the waiting request's status will be recorded as **suspended**.

The following columns can reveal details of the nature of such waits:

- **`blocking_session_id`** – lists the `session_id` that is blocking the request; if no blocking exists, the value will be `NULL`; there are three other possible values for this column besides `NULL` and the `session_id` of the blocking session (per Books Online)
  - -2 – the block is owned by an orphaned distributed transaction
  - -3 – the block is owned by a deferred recovery transaction
  - -4 – the `session_id` of the blocking latch owner could not be identified.
- **`wait_type`** – identifies the wait type for a request that is currently waiting for a resource being used by another process; this column also appears in the `sys.dm_os_wait_stats` DMV, covered in *Chapter 7*, where there is an in-depth discussion of wait analysis as a key initial indicator of resource pressure on a SQL Server instance
- **`wait_time`** – the amount of time the request has been waiting, in milliseconds, cumulatively, for all waits encountered during the request processing to date
- **`wait_resource`** – the last resource that the session waited on; this column can contain various different types of items, from pages in a table, to a `session_id` on a different server for a distributed transaction.

Activity and workload columns

Finally, we have a number of useful columns that report on the work being performed, and resources used, by a given request:

- **`percent_complete`** – can be used as a metric for completion status for certain operations; a partial list of the operations includes:
  - database backups/restores
  - dbcc checkdb / checktable / etc.

- `dbcc shrinkdatabase` / `shrinkfile`

- `dbcc indexdefrag` / `alter index reorganize`

- transaction rollbacks.

- **cpu_time** – the total amount of processing time spent on this request (in milliseconds)

- **row_count** – the number of rows that were processed for the request

- **granted_query_memory** – number of pages allocated to the execution of the request; since this metric is measured in 8 KB pages, you'll need to convert accordingly; I tend to want to review my metrics in MB, therefore I perform the following conversion from pages to MB: MB = (Number of 8 KB Pages)/1024 * 8

- **reads** – total physical disk reads performed for this request

- **writes** – total physical writes performed for this request

- **logical_reads** – total number of reads from the data cache for this request.

Overview of sys.dm_exec_sql_text

Having retrieved the `sql_handle` from the **sys.dm_exec_requests** DMV (or any other DMV that exposes it), we can then provide it as a parameter into the **sys.dm_exec_sql_text** function, in order to retrieve the SQL text for a given batch/procedure.

The **sys.dm_exec_sql_text** table-valued function returns two columns that are only interesting if the `sql_handle` refers to an object, such as a stored procedure, rather than ad hoc SQL statements:

- **dbid** – the identifier (or surrogate key) for the database, if applicable; (note that this is usually `database_id` in other objects)

- **objectid** – identifier/surrogate key for the object in a database, if applicable; (note that this is usually spelled object_id in other objects).

And two other columns that are always interesting:

- **encrypted** – 1 if plan is encrypted, which will prevent viewing of the query text, 0 otherwise

- **text** – the text of the query, unless the object is encrypted, in which case it will be NULL.

In the following sections, we will demonstrate returning the text of ad hoc SQL batches, then show how to "dissect" the sql_handle so that we see only the text of the currently executing statement within the batch or procedure.

Returning the SQL text of ad hoc queries

As a simple example, the query shown in Listing 2.10 uses the sys.dm_exec_requests DMV and sys.dm_exec_sql_text function to retrieve the text of the statement that the current session is executing.

```
SELECT  dest.text ,
        dest.dbid ,
        dest.objectid
FROM    sys.dm_exec_requests AS der
        CROSS APPLY sys.dm_exec_sql_text(der.sql_handle) AS dest
WHERE   session_id = @@spid ;
```

Listing 2.10: Retrieving the text for a currently executing ad hoc query.

If no other statements are executing in the same session, this will simply return the text of this very same query. If you modify this query to return the dbid and objectid, columns, you'll see that they are both NULL. Of course, with this WHERE clause, it isn't a tremendously useful query, but the intent was really just to show that you get back the exact query you ran. Usually, the equality operator in the WHERE clause would be replaced with a not equal operator (<>) because you want to see the other queries.

Using sys.dm_exec_sql_text to retrieve the text of the commands currently being executed is a tremendous leap forward compared to the rather limited view available with DBCC INPUTBUFFER from early versions of SQL Server, where we could only get the first 256 characters.

Consider the case where you want to find all executing batches that contain some specific construct or text. In this example, we'll look for all currently executing queries that contain a WAITFOR command (a very useful command when demonstrating DMVs since it gives you enough time to start a query, and then switch to a different connection and search for it). So, on one connection (in tempdb, ideally), execute the following batch:

```
DECLARE @time CHAR(8) ;
SET @time = '00:10:00' ;
WAITFOR DELAY @time ;
```

Then, on a different connection, just execute a "naked" WAITFOR command:

```
WAITFOR DELAY '00:10:00'
```

Within ten minutes of executing the first batch, you can retrieve the text of this batch, plus the second WAITFOR command, using the code shown in Listing 2.11.

```
SELECT   dest.text
FROM     sys.dm_exec_requests AS der
         CROSS APPLY sys.dm_exec_sql_text(der.sql_handle) AS dest
WHERE    session_id <> @@spid
         AND text LIKE '%waitfor%' ;
```

Listing 2.11: Retrieving the text for a currently executing batch.

We can perform a similar trick to retrieve the text of a stored procedure; create the following small object in **tempdb**, as shown in Listing 2.12 (note that I access some data, just to make sure that the plan has a cost).

```
CREATE PROCEDURE dbo.test
AS
    SELECT  *
    FROM    sys.objects
    WAITFOR DELAY '00:10:00';
```

Listing 2.12: Creating the test stored procedure.

Then, execute the procedure (**EXEC dbo.test;**), which will also ensure a plan gets cached and, while it is still running, execute, from a second tab, the script shown in Listing 2.13.

```
SELECT   dest.dbid ,
         dest.objectid ,
         dest.encrypted ,
         dest.text
FROM     sys.dm_exec_requests AS der
         CROSS APPLY sys.dm_exec_sql_text(der.sql_handle)
                                              AS dest
WHERE    objectid = object_id('test', 'p');
```

Listing 2.13: Returning the text of an executing stored procedure.

This will return (with a different `objectid`, most likely!):

```
dbid    objectid     number encrypted text
------  -----------  ------ ---------- ----
2       1077578877   1      0          CREATE PROCEDURE
                                       test
                                       AS
                                       SELECT *
                                       FROM    sys.objects
                                       WAITFOR DELAY
                                       '00:10:00'
```

Liberties were taken with the formatting of the text column, but you can see that the entire object's text is returned.

Isolating the executing statement within a SQL handle

As explained earlier, the `sql_handle` column presents us with the complete T-SQL batch submitted to the Query Engine via the request. This batch could comprise tens or even hundreds of individual statements. In order to isolate the statement within the batch that is currently executing, we use the `statement_start_offset` and `statement_end_offset` columns which, according to Books Online, are `INT` data types that store the *number of characters into the currently executing batch or stored procedure at which the currently executing statement starts and ends, respectively.*

If the value returned by `statement_start_offset` is 0, the active statement is at the start of the batch. If the value returned in the `statement_end_offset` column is -1, the end of the full batch is the ending character of the active statement. There are four possible combinations of outcomes for the combination of `statement_start_offset` and `statement_end_offset`.

- **statement_start_offset = 0 and statement_end_offset = - 1**
  The full query text returned by sys.dm_exec_sql_text is currently being executed.

- **statement_start_offset = 0 and statement_end_offset <> - 1**
  The active statement is the first statement in the full query text returned by sys.dm_exec_sql_text. The end of the active statement occurs n characters from the start of the full query where statement_end_offset = n.

- **statement_start_offset <> 0 and statement_end_offset = - 1**
  The active portion of the query text returned by sys.dm_exec_sql_text starts m characters from the start of the full query where statement_start_offset = m and ends at the end of the full query text.

- **statement_start_offset <> 0 and statement_end_offset <> - 1**
  The active portion of the query text returned by sys.dm_exec_sql_text starts m characters from the start of the full query where statement_start_offset = m. The end of the active statement occurs n characters from the start of the full query where statement_end_offset = n.

Be aware, though, that extracting the relevant portion of the text is not quite as simple as it sounds. The values in these offset columns are actually Unicode, with each character represented as two bytes (plus trailing and leading space characters if they exist), which causes complications when parsing the SQL text returned by sys.dm_exec_sql_text, which is a nvarchar(max) type, in that we have to divide the offset values by two.

So, in order to parse the string containing our SQL text, we use the SUBSTRING function, passing in for the first two parameters the SQL text, and the starting offset value (divided by two). What we pass in for the third parameter, where we specify the number of characters to return, depends on the situation. If the _end_offset is -1, then we just return the total number of bytes in the SQL text minus the start offset. Otherwise, we just return the end offset minus the start offset. In either case, we divide the result by two to account for the Unicode-text conversion.

```
SELECT    der.statement_start_offset ,
          der.statement_end_offset ,
          SUBSTRING(dest.text, der.statement_start_offset / 2,
                    ( CASE WHEN der.statement_end_offset = -1
                           THEN DATALENGTH(dest.text)
                           ELSE der.statement_end_offset
                      END - der.statement_start_offset ) / 2)
                                              AS statement_executing ,
          dest.text AS [full statement code]
FROM      sys.dm_exec_requests der
          INNER JOIN sys.dm_exec_sessions des
                    ON des.session_id = der.session_id
          CROSS APPLY sys.dm_exec_sql_text(der.sql_handle) dest
WHERE     des.is_user_process = 1
          AND der.session_id <> @@spid
ORDER BY der.session_id ;
```

Listing 2.14: Parsing the SQL text using statement_start_offset and statement_end_offset.

If you change the "<>" to "=" in the WHERE clause and run Listing 2.14, you'll simply get back the text of that query, with 0 for the start offset and -1 for the end offset. If you want to really see these offsets in action, open a tab in SSMS and run the query in Listing 2.15.

```
WAITFOR DELAY '00:01' ;
BEGIN TRANSACTION
-- WAITFOR DELAY '00:01' ;
INSERT   INTO AdventureWorks.Production.ProductCategory
         ( Name, ModifiedDate )
VALUES   ( 'Reflectors', GETDATE() )
ROLLBACK TRANSACTION

SELECT   Name ,
         ModifiedDate
FROM     AdventureWorks.Production.ProductCategory
WHERE    Name = 'Reflectors' ;
-- WAITFOR DELAY '00:01' ;
```

Listing 2.15: Investigating offsets.

While this code is waiting for 1 minute, open a second tab and execute our DMO query, as shown in Listing 2.14 (with <> @@spid), and you should see the following results:

	statement_start_offset	statement_end_offset	executing statement	full statement code
1	0	50	WAITFOR DELAY '00:01';	WAITFOR DELAY '00:01'; SELECT Name, ModifiedD...

The `statement_start_offset` shows the active statement for the batch is at the very beginning of the batch. The associated `statement_end_offset` tells us that the active statement is only 25 characters in length (remember, this is a Unicode value so each character consists of two bytes and includes trailing and leading space characters if they exist). This corresponds to the `WAITFOR DELAY '00:01';` statement at the beginning of the batch. Move the delay further into the batch and repeat the experiment, and you'll see the same `WAITFOR` statement returned each time, with offsets that reflect its position in the batch.

Now that we have a tool for parsing the active statement for a given request, let's move on to look at queries against `sys.dm_exec_requests` that give us insight into the state of active queries in our SQL instance.

Investigating work done by requests

The activity-based columns of `sys.dm_exec_requests` provide us with a means to query for requests that are consuming the triumvirate of resources with which we are so concerned as SQL Server Database Administrators: CPU, Memory, and I/O. Using `sys.dm_exec_requests` and `sys.dm_exec_sql_text`, we can isolate those statements consuming resources at a higher level than concurrent statements on the instance, at a given point in time. The join to `sys.dm_exec_query_plan` allows us to return the query plan (for each row returned, the query plan will be the plan for the entire batch or procedure to which the individual statement belongs).

By adapting the script in Listing 2.16, we can examine the activity of each currently active request in each active session in terms of CPU usage, number of pages allocated to the request in memory, amount of time spent waiting, current execution time, or number of physical reads.

Note that physical and logical reads are exposed separately in **sys.dm_exec_requests**. Physical reads, in other words those reads that require SQL Server to go to disk rather than cache to satisfy a read, are always more expensive and are therefore of a higher interest than those logical reads being satisfied from memory. Physical reads rely on the speed of your disk subsystem, which is often the slowest resource in the RDBMS stack.

```
SELECT  der.session_id ,
        DB_NAME(der.database_id) AS database_name ,
        deqp.query_plan ,
        SUBSTRING(dest.text, der.statement_start_offset / 2,
                    ( CASE WHEN der.statement_end_offset = -1
                        THEN DATALENGTH(dest.text)
                        ELSE der.statement_end_offset
                    END - der.statement_start_offset ) / 2)
                                        AS [statement executing] ,
        der.cpu_time
      --der.granted_query_memory
      --der.wait_time
      --der.total_elapsed_time
      --der.reads
FROM    sys.dm_exec_requests der
        INNER JOIN sys.dm_exec_sessions des
                    ON des.session_id = der.session_id
        CROSS APPLY sys.dm_exec_sql_text(der.sql_handle) dest
        CROSS APPLY sys.dm_exec_query_plan(der.plan_handle) deqp
WHERE   des.is_user_process = 1
        AND der.session_id <> @@spid
ORDER BY der.cpu_time DESC ;
-- ORDER BY der.granted_query_memory DESC ;
-- ORDER BY der.wait_time DESC;
-- ORDER BY der.total_elapsed_time DESC;
-- ORDER BY der.reads DESC;
```

session_id	database_name	query_plan
124	AdventureWorks	<ShowPlanXML xmlns="http://schemas.microsoft.com...
64	AdventureWorks	<ShowPlanXML xmlns="http://schemas.microsoft.com...
55	AdventureWorks	<ShowPlanXML xmlns="http://schemas.microsoft.com...
56	AdventureWorks	<ShowPlanXML xmlns="http://schemas.microsoft.com...
64	AdventureWorks	<ShowPlanXML xmlns="http://schemas.microsoft.com...
53	AdventureWorks	<ShowPlanXML xmlns="http://schemas.microsoft.com...
57	AdventureWorks	<ShowPlanXML xmlns="http://schemas.microsoft.com...

executing statement	cpu_time
If Exists (Select Top 1 * From PwHcProd01..TraSvc T...	155546
select form_id ,start_nrv ,end_nrv ,design_id ,tbl_name...	8297
SELECT TOP 101 t1.[TimeCreated] AS c0,t1.[LTCheck...	703
SELECT TOP 101 t1.[TimeCreated] AS c0,t1.[LTCheck...	531
SELECT TOP 101 t1.[TimeCreated] AS c0,t1.[LTCheck...	531
SELECT TOP 101 t1.[TimeCreated] AS c0,t1.[LTCheck...	407
SELECT TOP 101 t1.[TimeCreated] AS c0,t1.[LTCheck...	281

Listing 2.16: Requests by CPU consumption.

Dissecting user activity

We've explored the three DMVs that provide insight into user activity on a SQL Server instance, from the initial connections, to the sessions that they spawn, to the requests that are used to submit queries for transaction processing. Now it's time to put it all together to gain some deeper insight into point-in-time user activity on a SQL Server instance.

Who is running what, right now?

Listing 2.17 makes use of **sys.dm_exec_requests** and **sys.dm_exec_sql_text**, alongside our connections and sessions DMVs to provide a very useful "first look" at which sessions are running what on a given instance.

```
--   Who is running what at this instant
SELECT   dest.text AS [Command text] ,
         des.login_time ,
         des.[host_name] ,
         des.[program_name] ,
         der.session_id ,
         dec.client_net_address ,
         der.status ,
         der.command ,
         DB_NAME(der.database_id) AS DatabaseName
FROM     sys.dm_exec_requests der
         INNER JOIN sys.dm_exec_connections dec
                     ON der.session_id = dec.session_id
         INNER JOIN sys.dm_exec_sessions des
                     ON des.session_id = der.session_id
         CROSS APPLY sys.dm_exec_sql_text(sql_handle) AS dest
WHERE    des.is_user_process = 1
```

Listing 2.17: Who is running what?

A better version of sp_who2

Many of us DBAs are familiar with the **sp_who** and **sp_who2** system stored procedures for interrogating SQL Server activity. Listing 2.18 provides the syntax, and sample results, from an execution of **sp_who**.

```
EXEC sp_who;
```

	spid	ecid	status	loginame	hostname	blk	dbname	cmd	request_id
1	1	0	background	sa		0	NULL	RESOURCE MONITOR	0
2	2	0	background	sa		0	NULL	XE TIMER	0
3	3	0	background	sa		0	NULL	XE DISPATCHER	0
4	4	0	background	sa		0	NULL	LAZY WRITER	0

Listing 2.18: sp_who results.

Likewise Listing 2.19 shows the additional columns and level of detail afforded through sp_who2.

```
EXEC sp_who2;
```

	SPID	Status	Login	HostName	BlkBy	DBName	Command	CPUTime	DiskIO	LastBatch	ProgramName	SPID	REQUESTID
1	1	BACKGROUND	sa		.	NULL	RESOURCE MONITOR	0	0	06/05 09:38:21		1	0
2	2	BACKGROUND	sa		.	NULL	XE TIMER	0	0	06/05 09:38:21		2	0
3	3	BACKGROUND	sa		.	NULL	XE DISPATCHER	0	0	06/05 09:38:21		3	0
4	4	BACKGROUND	sa		.	NULL	LAZY WRITER	15	0	06/05 09:38:21		4	0

Listing 2.19: sp_who2 results.

Just as with **sys.dm_exec_sessions**, we see results for all sessions, user as well as system, on the SQL instance. Both **sp_who2** and **sp_who** use the old-style terminology and the information returned is not as detailed or as customizable as that returned from the DMOs.

The script provided in Listing 2.20, essentially provides a more detailed version of **sp_who2**. It returns all of the columns provided by **sp_who2**, and augments it with the executing portion of the T-SQL text associated with the request and the query plan in XML format. Unlike in **sp_who2**, this query breaks down the Disk I/O information into reads and writes. Finally, it also includes wait metrics and the **transaction_isolation_level**, to provide insight into how this session is interacting with other sessions currently running on the instance. As a whole, this information offers a very useful snapshot of activity, resource impact, and processing health on the SQL instance.

```
SELECT  des.session_id ,
        des.status ,
        des.login_name ,
        des.[HOST_NAME] ,
        der.blocking_session_id ,
        DB_NAME(der.database_id) AS database_name ,
        der.command ,
        des.cpu_time ,
        des.reads ,
        des.writes ,
        dec.last_write ,
        des.[program_name] ,
        der.wait_type ,
        der.wait_time ,
        der.last_wait_type ,
        der.wait_resource ,
        CASE des.transaction_isolation_level
          WHEN 0 THEN 'Unspecified'
          WHEN 1 THEN 'ReadUncommitted'
          WHEN 2 THEN 'ReadCommitted'
          WHEN 3 THEN 'Repeatable'
          WHEN 4 THEN 'Serializable'
          WHEN 5 THEN 'Snapshot'
        END AS transaction_isolation_level ,
        OBJECT_NAME(dest.objectid, der.database_id) AS OBJECT_NAME ,
        SUBSTRING(dest.text, der.statement_start_offset / 2,
                ( CASE WHEN der.statement_end_offset = -1
                       THEN DATALENGTH(dest.text)
                       ELSE der.statement_end_offset
                  END - der.statement_start_offset ) / 2)
                                        AS [executing statement] ,
        deqp.query_plan
FROM    sys.dm_exec_sessions des
        LEFT JOIN sys.dm_exec_requests der
                    ON des.session_id = der.session_id
        LEFT JOIN sys.dm_exec_connections dec
                    ON des.session_id = dec.session_id
        CROSS APPLY sys.dm_exec_sql_text(der.sql_handle) dest
        CROSS APPLY sys.dm_exec_query_plan(der.plan_handle) deqp
WHERE   des.session_id <> @@SPID
ORDER BY des.session_id
```

	session_id	status	login_name	host_name	blocking_session_id	database_name
1	100	sleeping	TEST\trevmoonford	SRVSQL01	0	dbPayrollMeister
2	637	running	TEST\trevmoonford	SRVSQL01	0	dbPayrollMeister

	command	cpu_time	reads	writes	last_write	program_name
1	SELECT	15	0	0	2009-07-14 22:23:52.647	PayrollMeister
2	SELECT	31	2	0	2009-07-14 22:17:36.533	PayrollMeister

	wait_type	wait_time	last_wait_type	wait_resource	transaction_isolation_level
1	NULL	0	SOS_SCHEDULER_YIELD		ReadCommitted
2	TRACEWRITE	625	TRACEWRITE		ReadCommitted

	object_name	executing statement	query_plan
1	NULL	SELECT TOP 1 dbo.Record.BasalRate, dbo.Re...	<ShowPlanXML xmlns="http://schemas.microsoft.com...
2	NULL	select * from OpenRowset(TrcData, @traceid, @reco...	<ShowPlanXML xmlns="http://schemas.microsoft.com...

Listing 2.20: A better sp_who2.

Others have taken this much further; in particular, SQL Server MVP Adam Machanic has created a script called Who Is Active, which is available here: HTTP://TINYURL.COM/ WHOISACTIVE.

Who Is Active returns, not only all columns provided by my script, but also detailed information on tempDB impact, context switches, memory consumption, thread metadata, and the query text rendered as XML. I strongly recommend taking the time to download this script.

Summary

Ultimately, if your SQL workload consists of poorly-designed queries, then they will cause needless extra I/O, CPU and memory overhead, and execution times will be slow. The situation will get worse and worse as the number of users grows, and their requests are forced to wait for access to the shared resources that your queries are monopolizing. Conversely, if you can minimize the number of individual SQL statements you need to get a particular job done, and then minimize the work done by each of those individual SQL statements, you are much more likely to have a fast, responsive SQL Server system which scales gracefully as the number of users grows.

First, however, you need to track down those queries that are causing the problems on your system. In some respects, the DMOs and scripts presented in this chapter represent our front-line response to issues that are occurring on our servers right now. For example, if we note that a particular instance is suffering a spike in CPU, I/O, or memory usage (for example, by using some of the scripts presented in *Chapter 7*), then we can use the scripts presented here to find out what requests are currently being executed on that instance, which of the queries being run might be causing the issue, and who owns the session that is running them.

With this information in hand, the DBA can respond appropriately, by dealing with the immediate problem, and then investigating further, to work out how to tune the offending statements so that the problem does not recur.

For longer term, more strategic performance tuning efforts, however, we need information beyond what is happening on the server at the current time. In *Chapter 3*, we'll take a broader look at our query workload, from the point of view of the plans that exist in the cache.

Chapter 3: Query Plan Metadata

The DMOs described in this chapter provide metadata and statistics regarding any query that has previously executed on your server, and the execution plan used to run it, provided that the plan for that query is in the plan cache. For example, if a stored procedure has been executed, and the plan for it is cached, then not only can we return and examine that plan, but we can also obtain statistics regarding execution of the stored procedure associated with the plan, such as total number of disk reads performed, total time spent executing, and so on.

We'll show how such statistics and query plan metadata can be used to answer questions like those below (the relevant DMO is indicated in brackets).

- What are the "top x" most expensive queries in the cache in terms of CPU / IO / memory? (`query_stats`)

- Which are the most "expensive" stored procedures? (`procedure_stats`)

- Are plans getting reused? (`cached_plans` and `plan_attributes`)

- How many ad hoc, single-use queries are taking up space in the plan cache? (`cached_plans`).

In each section, we'll provide T-SQL scripts to retrieve this data, and discuss how you can use it to get a feeling for certain aspects of your system's performance.

The focus in the previous chapter was "What is executing on my instance right now, and what is it doing?" The DMOs in this chapter can give you a broader perspective on your typical query workload, based on the plans that are stored in the cache. The really big win for the average DBA is the fact that you can access the statistics on what queries were run, what plans and system resources were used, and so on, *after the event*. Before DMOs, when a DBA was notified of a bad problem that occurred a little earlier, there were few tools to hand to help find out what happened, unless they happened to be running

Profiler traces to capture the event. Now, by querying these DMOs, we can retrospectively examine the damage that a rogue query did, and the impact on the server of running such queries will generally be far less than using a tool such as Profiler.

Why Cached Plan Analysis with DMOs?

As was discussed in *Chapter 1*, there are several strategies that one may use when seeking to resolve a SQL Server performance issue using the DMOs. However, regardless of the origin of an issue, whether it's related to CPU, I/O, memory, blocking, and so on, the final destination is most often a detailed examination of the queries that are causing the problem, and of possible ways to tune them.

The execution plans generated by the SQL Server Query optimizer and stored in memory in the plan cache are the DBA's premier window into the world of query optimization. If you are looking to improve your skills as a SQL Server programmer or DBA, then acquiring an understanding of **query plans** is an essential first step. There is a natural progression from being able to run a query, to understanding all the steps that SQL Server has to undertake in order to execute that query and serve up the results. In fact, I regard knowledge of query plans as a barometer by which to judge a programmer's ability to write optimal queries.

It is only with a deep knowledge of the operations that are being performed to execute a query, and the order in which these operations occur that you can really begin to look for opportunities to optimize the data access path for that query. Of course, the graphical execution plan is available by other, arguably simpler means, such as through SQL Server Management Studio (SSMS) or Profiler. However, with each of these tools, the actual, as opposed to the estimated, plan that was used to execute a given query can only be captured in real time, while the query is running. With the DMOs in this chapter, you can retrieve the actual plan for any query for which the plan is cached.

Furthermore, the metadata and statistics that these DMOs can provide alongside the plan are, as we will demonstrate, very useful in helping direct your query tuning efforts; in working out whether you need to reduce the computational complexity of the query to reduce CPU usage; add indexes, replace cursors with set-based constructs, tuning the search predicate to return less data, to reduce I/O; eliminate expensive sorts, reduce gratuitous use of temporary tables to reduce memory usage, and so on.

Again, you may be thinking that a similar set of statistics is available from the performance reports that can be accessed in Management Studio by right-clicking on the Server node and selecting Reports | Standard Reports.

SSMS reports

These reports are standard in SQL Server 2008 and are an add-in to SQL Server 2005, where they are referred to as Performance Dashboard Reports.

In fact, these reports use the DMVs under the covers. The problem is that they have significant limitations on how you can filter them and use the output. In this chapter, we will look at techniques to build your own queries against the DMOs that will allow you to view only the data you want to see. Once you've developed a core set of scripts it is very easy to refine them as required, to save the results to your own tables, so that you can compare current results with previous results, track performance over time, and so on.

Finally, but very importantly, remember that it's not only ensuring that the plans are good that is critical; it is ensuring that these plans are used, and **reused** time and again. As noted, SQL Server stores plans for previously executed queries in a shared memory area called the plan cache. Whenever a query is submitted for execution, SQL Server checks in the plan cache to see if there is an existing plan it can use to execute the query. Every time it cannot find a match, the submitted query must be parsed and optimized, and a plan generated.

Parsing and optimizing SQL statements is a CPU-intensive process, so it is not a "high concurrency" operation. Furthermore, each time it does this, SQL Server acquires latches on the plan cache to protect the relevant area of memory from other updates. The more this happens, the more it will restrict other processes from accessing the cache. Well-designed SQL needs to promote plan reuse ("parse once, use many times") as far as possible. If you have a lot of ad hoc, non-parameterized SQL in your workload, it will result in much higher CPU consumption and many more latches acquired, as a plan will be generated each time. At the same time, your cache will fill up with single-use plans that will probably never be used again.

It's even possible that, in such circumstances, useful plans could get flushed out of the cache. SQL Server flushes plans out of the cache when it needs space, based on an algorithm that considers the cost of recalculating the plan, how recently the plan was used, and other unpublicized factors. Generally speaking, the least interesting queries will be the ones removed from the cache first.

In any event, the DMOs and scripts in this chapter will help you uncover these sorts of problems, and help you ensure that the plans for your day-to-day query workload are in the cache, and are getting used.

An Overview of DMOs for Query Plan Metadata

In addition to the **sys.dm_exec_requests** DMV and **sys.dm_exec_sql_text** DMF, introduced in the previous chapter, we will extract our statistics and query plan metadata from the DMVs below, which belong to the "execution-related" category (this is why their names all begin with "**sys.dm_exec_**").

- **sys.dm_exec_query_stats** – returns aggregated performance statistics for a cached query plan. Returns one row per statement within the plan.

- **sys.dm_exec_procedure_stats** – returns aggregated performance statistics for cached stored procedures (SQL Server 2008 only). Returns one row per stored procedure.

- **sys.dm_exec_cached_plans** – provides detailed information about a cached plan, such as the number of times it has been used, its size, and so on. Returns a row for each cached plan.

- **sys.dm_exec_query_optimizer_info** – returns statistics regarding the operation of the query optimizer, to identify any potential optimization problems. For example, you can find out how many queries have been optimized since the last time the server was restarted.

In order to return the query plan for a given batch, as well as some interesting attributes of these plans, we can pass the identifier for that plan batch, the plan_handle, to one of the DMFs below.

- **sys.dm_exec_query_plan** – returns in XML format the query plan, identified by a plan_handle, for a SQL batch.

- **sys.dm_exec_text_query_plan** – returns in text format the query plan, identified by a plan_handle, for a SQL batch or, via the use of this DMF's offset columns, a specific statement within that batch.

- **sys.dm_exec_plan_attributes** – provides information about various *attributes* of a query plan, identified by a plan_handle, such as the number of queries currently using a given execution plan. It returns one row for each attribute.

To the query optimizer, a query and a query plan are not synonymous. When a batch is executed, it gets a plan. This plan comprises one or more individual queries, each of which will have a query plan of its own. The DMVs for query plans, such as cached_plans, return one row per distinct batch or object. The DMVs for queries, such as query_stats, return one row per independent query that is embedded in that plan. If, in our queries, we "join" from query_stats to the query_plan DMF, in order to return the plan, each row returned by query_stats will contain a link to the plan for the batch to which the row (i.e. individual query) belongs. If, instead, we join to `text_query_plan`, it's possible to extract from the batch the plan for only the individual query in question (but there are complications, as will soon be demonstrated).

As we progress through the chapter, we'll provide brief descriptions of some of the more useful (or confusing) columns that these DMOs provide, but we've tried to avoid rehashing Books Online as far as possible. A complete listing and reference for the DMOs covered in this chapter can be found at HTTP://MSDN.MICROSOFT.COM/EN-US/LIBRARY/ MS188068.ASPX.

Flushing the Cache?

Before we get started in earnest, it is important to realize that troubleshooting problem queries using the DMOs is not a perfect science. Firstly, we can only examine plans for queries that are in the cache; while the cache will usually hold plans for all the most active/costly queries, less costly/reused queries can fall out of the cache, and some queries with nominal plans are never cached in the first place; in short, some queries will be missed.

Secondly, plans may remain in the cache from when they are first compiled until the object is dropped or recompiled, or the cache is flushed. This means that some plans, especially frequently used ones, may remain in the cache for a long time. If your SQL Server instance has been up and running for long, it will contain lots of plans of different ages which will make it hard to analyze the statistics. For example, if you're looking for the plans for the most CPU-intensive procedures, the results will be heavily skewed towards those procedures that have been cached for a long period, compared to plans that have, for some reason, been recently recompiled.

One way around this might be to clear the cache, using `DBCC FREEPROCCACHE` for all databases on an instance, or using `DBCC FLUSHPROCINDB` for a single database, as shown in Listing 3.1.

```
--Determine the id of your database
DECLARE @intDBID INTEGER
SET @intDBID = ( SELECT dbid
                 FROM    master.dbo.sysdatabases
                 WHERE   name = 'mydatabasename'
               )

--Flush the procedure cache for your database
DBCC FLUSHPROCINDB (@intDBID)
```

Listing 3.1: Flushing the cache of plans belonging to a particular database.

The flushed plans will go back into the cache the next time they are executed, the result being that most of the stored procedures that are run frequently and are part of your normal workload will have a similar cache time. This will make the statistics much easier to interpret (until and unless they get recompiled again for some other reason).

Flushing the cache is a controversial suggestion; many DBAs avoid doing it on a production server. After all, clearing the cache means that new plans need to be determined and created, which has an associated cost. It's true that recompiling all of the query plans will cause some extra work for your processor(s), but many modern processors shrug this off with little effect beyond a brief (few seconds) spike of CPU activity.

Viewing the Text of Cached Queries and Query Plans

The root cause of many performance problems is the fact that the plan you get when query execution is optimized under a full production server load can be very different from the one you saw in Management Studio while building the query. For example, on your development server, you may have only a single CPU, several orders of magnitude fewer rows, different amounts of RAM, statistics that are completely up to date, fewer concurrent users, and so on.

Unfortunately, the excuse "it worked on my machine" is not acceptable with database applications, so it is very useful to be able to see the query plan that was actually used to optimize a query, when it was executed. This way you can find out why a query is performing as it is, and begin the process of optimization. This is also useful when troubleshooting poor performance caused by parameter sniffing, whereby the initial set of parameters chosen as a "guide" when first compiling the plan for a stored procedure turn out to be anomalous, and not representative of the parameters' values supplied during normal execution.

The process of retrieving the plan is very similar to that for retrieving the SQL text, which we discussed in *Chapter 2*. We simply extract the plan_handle from the sys.dm_exec_query_stats DMV (covered in detail later in this chapter). The plan_handle uniquely identifies the query plan for a given batch or stored procedure. We then pass it as a parameter to one of the following DMFs:

- **sys.dm_exec_query_plan**, which accepts the plan_handle as its only parameter and will return the plan for the identified batch or procedure, as XML. Note that Books Online states that it returns the plan in "text format." This is a little confusing since it refers to the type of column returned, not the format in which you will view the plan, which is XML.

- **sys.dm_exec_text_query_plan**, which accepts the plan_handle and adds two additional parameters, statement_start_offset and statement_end_offset, which mark the start and end points of individual SQL statements within the batch or procedure. This DMF returns the plan in text format (a nvarchar(max) typed object) and is available in SQL Server 2005 SP2 and later.

When returning the plan from the **sys.dm_exec_query_plan** DMF, SSMS will display a link to the plan, which you can click onto immediately to display the graphical plan. In any event, with either DMF, the output can be saved as a .SQLPLAN file that can be used to view the graphical plan in SSMS.

Note

One unfortunate limitation of these functions is that, in the absence of SSMS or another third-party tool that understands the .SQLPLAN format, they do not give you the type of easily readable output that you get when using the SHOWPLAN_TEXT setting in a query window.

As for the **sys.dm_exec_sql_text** function, described in *Chapter 2*, both of these functions return **dbid**, **objectid**, and **encrypted** columns. However, in place of the text column, in each case, the functions return a **query_plan** column, containing the current cached query plan.

The **sys.dm_exec_query_plan** function returns the plan as an XML typed value, which limits the size of the plan that can be returned, since the XML datatype does not support XML documents with more than 128 levels. The **sys.dm_exec_text_query_plan** object returns the plan as a **nvarchar(max)** typed object, thus removing these restrictions.

Returning the plan using sys.dm_exec_query_plan

Using the **sys.dm_exec_query_plan** DMF, we can return the plan for a given batch or procedure (which will contain "subplans" for each query comprising the batch). As an example, let's create a stored procedure, **ShowQueryText**, execute it, so the plan gets cached, and then extract the plan that was used to execute that stored procedure, as shown in Listing 3.2.

```
CREATE PROCEDURE ShowQueryText
AS
    SELECT TOP 10
            object_id ,
            name
    FROM    sys.objects ;
    --waitfor delay '00:00:00'
```

```
    SELECT  TOP 10
            object_id ,
            name
    FROM    sys.objects ;
    SELECT  TOP 10
            object_id ,
            name
    FROM    sys.procedures ;
GO
EXEC dbo.ShowQueryText ;
GO
SELECT  deqp.dbid ,
        deqp.objectid ,
        deqp.encrypted ,
        deqp.query_plan
FROM    sys.dm_exec_query_stats deqs
        CROSS APPLY sys.dm_exec_query_plan(deqs.plan_handle) AS deqp
WHERE   objectid = OBJECT_ID('ShowQueryText', 'p') ;
```

	dbid	objectid	encrypted	query_plan
1	9	1031674723	0	\<ShowPlanXML xmlns="http://schemas.microsoft.com...
2	9	1031674723	0	\<ShowPlanXML xmlns="http://schemas.microsoft.com...
3	9	1031674723	0	\<ShowPlanXML xmlns="http://schemas.microsoft.com...

Listing 3.2:   Retrieving the query plan for a cached stored procedure.

You will see that we get three rows returned by **query_stats**, and each row contains a link to a query plan; in each case this will be the same plan, i.e. the plan for the entire procedure.

Obtaining the **plan_handle**

As well as sys.dm_exec_query_stats, *the* plan_handle *can also be retrieved from* sys.dm_exec_requests, sys.dm_exec_query_memory_grants *and* sys. dm_exec_cached_plan.

In SQL Server 2005 Management Studio, you can click on the link to the query plan, thus opening it up as an XML document in SSMS, and then save it with a **.SQLPLAN** extension (by default it will be saved with an XML extension). You can open it up in SSMS and view the graphical plan. SQL Server 2008 Management Studio realizes the schema is a SQL plan, and so allows us to simply click the XML output to get a display that shows the graphical version of the plan, as shown in Figure 3.1 (cropped to save space).

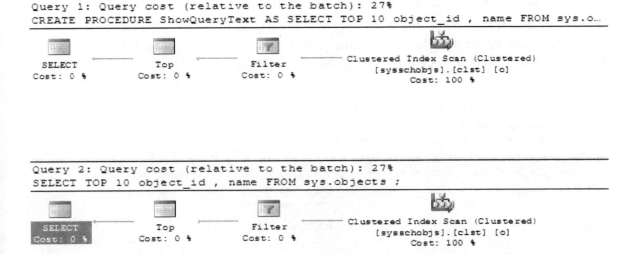

Figure 3.1: Viewing the query plan in Management Studio.

In this way, we can find out precisely how a stored procedure was executed at the time of being cached.

Dissecting the SQL text

In *Chapter 2*, we saw how to use the `sql_handle` from `sys.dm_exec_requests` to return the SQL text for the batch, from `sys.dm_exec_sql_text`, and then to dissect the text using the "statement offset" columns provided by the former, to get at the text of just the currently executing query.

We'll have to do the same thing when using `sys.dm_exec_query_stats`, in order to extract query statistics about individual statements within a cached batch/procedure. Let's take a look at the `sql_handle`, `plan_handle` and associated SQL text, returned for each query in our stored procedure, as shown in Listing 3.3.

```
SELECT    deqs.plan_handle ,
          deqs.sql_handle ,
          execText.text
FROM      sys.dm_exec_query_stats deqs
          CROSS APPLY sys.dm_exec_sql_text(deqs.plan_handle) AS execText
WHERE     execText.text LIKE 'CREATE PROCEDURE ShowQueryText%'
```

Listing 3.3:   Viewing the `sql_handle` and `plan_handle`.

As you can see, each row has the same `sql_handle`, same `plan_handle` and the same SQL text (referring to the whole procedure). I'm only showing two of the rows here:

```
plan_handle      sql_handle       text
-------------    -------------    -----------------
0x050002003...   0x03000200...    CREATE PROCEDURE
                                  ShowQueryText as…
0x050002003...   0x03000200...    CREATE PROCEDURE
                                  ShowQueryText as…
```

When you supply a `sql_handle` you are identifying the batch or procedure to which a query belongs; in just the same way, when you supply a `plan_handle` you are identifying the plan associated with a batch or procedure, and this batch or procedure may contain multiple queries. When you identify a plan for a batch, you identify the associated SQL text for the whole batch, and we'll need to extract the text for individual queries in that batch, in order to work with the `query_stats` DMV. Listing 3.4 shows how to do this.

```
SELECT   CHAR(13) + CHAR(10)
       + CASE WHEN deqs.statement_start_offset = 0
                 AND deqs.statement_end_offset = -1
             THEN '-- see objectText column--'
             ELSE '-- query --' + CHAR(13) + CHAR(10)
                 + SUBSTRING(execText.text, deqs.statement_start_offset / 2,
                                 ( ( CASE WHEN deqs.statement_end_offset = -1
                                          THEN DATALENGTH(execText.text)
                                          ELSE deqs.statement_end_offset
                                     END ) - deqs.statement_start_offset ) / 2)
         END AS queryText ,
         deqp.query_plan
FROM     sys.dm_exec_query_stats deqs
         CROSS APPLY sys.dm_exec_sql_text(deqs.plan_handle) AS execText
         CROSS APPLY sys.dm_exec_query_plan(deqs.plan_handle) deqp
WHERE    execText.text LIKE 'CREATE PROCEDURE ShowQueryText%'
```

Listing 3.4: Extracting the SQL text for individual queries in a batch.

We pass the `plan_handle` to the `sql_text` DMF (we could equally well pass the `sql_handle`), which returns the SQL text associated with the plan for that batch. We then extract the text for the individual queries in the same way as in *Chapter 2*, using the SUBSTRING function, and remembering to divide the offset values by 2 (the start offset, and then the difference between the end and start offsets in the SUBSTRING operation) before we use them, since they are stored in Unicode.

This query should return the three separate queries shown in Figure 3.2.

	queryText		query_plan
1	-- query -- SELECT TOP 10	objec...	<ShowPlanXML xmlns="http://schemas.microsoft.com...
2	-- query -- SELECT TOP 10	objec...	<ShowPlanXML xmlns="http://schemas.microsoft.com...
3	-- query -- SELECT TOP 10	objec...	<ShowPlanXML xmlns="http://schemas.microsoft.com...

Figure 3.2: Three queries returned by `sys.dm_exec_query_stats`.

Click on the plan links and you'll see that the plan returned for each row is still the plan for the whole batch.

Returning the plan using sys.dm_exec_text_query_plan

If we want, for each row, to show only the "subplan" for each individual query, it is a little trickier, and we have to use the `sys.dm_exec_query_plan` DMF, which returns the plan in text form and supports offset parameters, which we can use to dissect it. Unfortunately, the `sys.dm_exec_query_plan` DMF returns the plan in a form we can save and use, but not view in SSMS. Just for demo purposes here, we've cast the returned plan to an XML type, but this isn't a "safe" application.

```
SELECT  deqp.dbid ,
        deqp.objectid ,
        CAST(detqp.query_plan AS XML) AS singleStatementPlan ,
        deqp.query_plan AS batch_query_plan ,
        --this won't actually work in all cases because nominal plans aren't
        -- cached, so you won't see a plan for waitfor if you uncomment it
        ROW_NUMBER() OVER ( ORDER BY Statement_Start_offset )
                                            AS query_position ,
        CASE WHEN deqs.statement_start_offset = 0
                AND deqs.statement_end_offset = -1
            THEN '-- see objectText column--'
            ELSE '-- query --' + CHAR(13) + CHAR(10)
                + SUBSTRING(execText.text, deqs.statement_start_offset / 2,
                        ( ( CASE WHEN deqs.statement_end_offset = -1
```

```
                                  THEN DATALENGTH(execText.text)
                                  ELSE deqs.statement_end_offset
                        END ) - deqs.statement_start_offset ) / 2)
        END AS queryText
FROM    sys.dm_exec_query_stats deqs
        CROSS APPLY sys.dm_exec_text_query_plan(deqs.plan_handle,
                                       deqs.statement_start_offset,
                                       deqs.statement_end_offset)
                                                         AS detqp
        CROSS APPLY sys.dm_exec_query_plan(deqs.plan_handle) AS deqp
        CROSS APPLY sys.dm_exec_sql_text(deqs.plan_handle) AS execText
WHERE   deqp.objectid = OBJECT_ID('ShowQueryText', 'p') ;
```

Listing 3.5: Returning the plan using `sys.dm_exec_text_query_plan`.

This time, for each row returned, we get the individual plan for each query, as well as the batch plan, as shown in Figure 3.3.

	dbid	objectid	singleStatementPlan	batch_query_plan	query_position	queryText
1	9	1031674723	<ShowPlanXML xmlns="http://s...	<ShowPlanXML xmlns="...	1	-- query -- SELI
2	9	1031674723	<ShowPlanXML xmlns="http://s...	<ShowPlanXML xmlns="...	2	-- query -- SELI
3	9	1031674723	<ShowPlanXML xmlns="http://s...	<ShowPlanXML xmlns="...	3	-- query -- SELI

Figure 3.3: Seeing the individual query plans.

Cached Query Plan Statistics

In the previous section, we explained how to use the `sys.dm_exec_query_plan` function and `sys.dm_exec_query_stats` DMV to get the text of the plan for a given batch. In this section, we'll start retrieving some meatier information about the query plans that have been used to execute queries on the server.

The ability to retrieve the text of a query or query plan becomes more interesting when combined with data stored in the `sys.dm_exec_cached_plans` DMV. It returns basic metadata regarding each plan, such as its size and the type of object to which it's attached, but also, and most interestingly, a `usecounts` column that lets us investigate plan reuse.

The sys.dm_exec_cached_plans DMV

The `sys.dm_exec_cached_plans` DMV "supersedes" the `syscacheobjects` object, available in versions of SQL Server prior to 2005. In many ways, `syscacheobjects` is easier to work with as it includes the text of the query and several attributes about the cached plan, but it is more limited, in that it doesn't quite give access to the rich array of information that is available through `sys.dm_exec_cached_plans`, especially when used in concert with `sys.dm_exec_query_plan`, `sys.dm_exec_sql_text` and `sys.dm_exec_plan_attributes`.

The data that the `sys.dm_exec_cached_plans` view will return is a snapshot of values, based on the current contents of the plan cache. The columns in this view are all pretty useful for seeing how plans are being cached, and are listed below.

- **bucketid** – the id of the hash bucket where the plan is held. You can see the maximum number of buckets available in the `sys.dm_os_memory_cache_hash_tables` view. Ideally, cached items (such as plans, and anything else that SQL Server puts into cache) will be spread evenly amongst the hash buckets.

- **refcounts** – number of cache objects that reference this cached plan.

- **usecounts** – number of times the plan has been used since its creation. This counter is incremented every time the query is executed, and a match to the plan is made.

- **size_in_bytes** – size of the plan.

- **memory_object_address** – internal address of the cached object. Can be used to reference sys.dm_os_memory_objects and sys.dm_os_memory_cache_ entries to see the objects in the SQL Server cache.

- **cacheobjtype** – type of object in the cache. The domain is:

  - Compiled Plan

  - Parse Tree

  - Extended Proc

  - CLR Compiled Func

  - CLR Compiled Proc.

- **objtype** – the type of object. The domain is:

  - Proc (stored procedure, function)

  - Prepared (prepared statement)

  - Adhoc (query)

  - Repl Proc (replication filter procedure)

  - Trigger

  - View

  - Default

  - UsrTab (user table)

  - SysTab (system table)

  - CHECK

  - Rule.

- **plan_handle** – can be used with query plan functions, including **sys.dm_exec_query_plan** and **sys.dm_exec_sql_text**, to get the plan of the query or the text of the query, respectively.

- **pool_id** – the resource governor pool to which the plan is tied. You can use **sys.resource_governor_resource_pools** to decipher the value, if you are utilizing resource governor. Note that this column is in SQL Server 2008 only and is part of the Enterprise-only resource governor feature.

A few of these columns merit a bit more discussion. The **cachobtype** column describes the type of plan that is cached, which can be a normal SQL plan (compiled plan), a parse tree or the stored plan for an extended procedure or CLR object. A parse tree is a bare-bones plan for an object such as a view. It specifies the objects referenced by the view, but does not specify a full execution plan. Views are compiled into the query at run time; they do not have plans of their own.

The **objtype** column, in turn, specifies the type of object, determining whether it is typical T-SQL or a compiled object such as a stored procedure or prepared statement. Note that a prepared statement (an ad hoc statement from the client, where they have used the API to prepare a plan ahead of time) has a different plan than an ad hoc query.

Zero cost and stale plans

Remember, again, that not all queries that have been executed on your server will have saved a plan. Zero cost plans like "SELECT 'hi'" would not, for sure. Also, as plans become stale, they could be removed from the cache, particularly if the server is under memory pressure.

So, for example, you can retrieve the plans for any compiled object, using the query shown in Listing 3.6.

```
SELECT  refcounts ,
        usecounts ,
        size_in_bytes ,
        cacheobjtype ,
        objtype
FROM    sys.dm_exec_cached_plans
WHERE   objtype IN ( 'proc', 'prepared' ) ;
```

Listing 3.6:   Retrieving the plans for compiled objects.

You are likely to find that there are compiled plans for both procedures and prepared statements, as well as some extended and CLR objects, if you use them.

Investigating plan reuse

Good plan reuse is one sign of a heathy system. Compiling a query plan can be a CPU-intensive operation, especially with complex queries, so reuse is a very good thing. The greater the value in the usecount column for each of your plans, the greater the number of times query plans are reused, and the smaller the number of times a new query plan has to be recreated. Conversely, a usecount of 1 for a large number of plans indicates that your cache space is being taken up with plans that were compiled and used once to execute an ad hoc query, then never used again. By querying sys.dm_exec_ cached_plans and aggregating on the usecount column we can, as we will show, get a good overview of the extent to which plans are being reused in your system.

The more you can use stored procedures or, at the very least, prepared SQL, the more likely you are to get plan reuse. The more reusable plans you have, the less work the optimizer needs to do.

One of the most critical factors in determining reuse is the text of the query. If the text of a query submitted for execution matches the text of a query in the cache, then the plan for that cached query may be reused.

> ### *Criteria in determing plan reuse*
>
> *The text of the query is not the only criterion in determining plan reuse. The attributes of the plan are also figured in, which we will cover in a later section, entitled Query Plan Attributes.*

Of course, if you use stored procedures as the primary interface to your SQL Server data, you have a much cleaner way of ensuring reuse.

A database setting that can be helpful to plan reuse is forced parameterization (set using `ALTER DATABASE <databaseName> SET PARAMETERIZATION FORCED`). Normally, the query optimizer is very conservative when deciding what queries can be parameterized, but this setting makes the optimizer be more liberal in choosing parameters. For more reading on this subject, look for *Forced Parameterization* in Books Online.

Finally, bear in mind that you need to be careful when interpreting the results of data based on plan reuse. After a restart, cache flush, procedure recreation, and so on, plan use counts will be low without this being indicative of a problem. Alternatively, you may have been doing some special processing that inflates the counts and makes things look better than normal. As is true with most of the DMVs, the data you get from the `cached_plans` DMV is not information until it has context. Context comes from tracking the data over long periods of time and comparing like time periods of server activity.

As dicussed earlier, you might want, particularly for testing purposes, to consider clearing the cache at a fixed time (e.g. 12 a.m.) each day, to give the results more context.

The plan reuse "distribution curve"

A simple query, such as that shown in Listing 3.7, will show you how many plans are cached.

```
SELECT   COUNT(*)
FROM     sys.dm_exec_cached_plans ;
```

Listing 3.7: Total number of cached plans.

More useful though, is to get a feel for the "distribution" of plan reuse on your system. To do this, we can group on the usecounts column, and use the CASE expression to roll up bands of usecounts as shown in Listing 3.8.

```
SELECT   MAX(CASE WHEN usecounts BETWEEN 10 AND 100 THEN '10-100'
                  WHEN usecounts BETWEEN 101 AND 1000 THEN '101-1000'
                  WHEN usecounts BETWEEN 1001 AND 5000 THEN '1001-5000'
                  WHEN usecounts BETWEEN 5001 AND 10000 THEN '5001-10000'
                  ELSE CAST(usecounts AS VARCHAR(100))
             END) AS usecounts ,
         COUNT(*) AS countInstance
FROM     sys.dm_exec_cached_plans
GROUP BY CASE WHEN usecounts BETWEEN 10 AND 100 THEN 50
              WHEN usecounts BETWEEN 101 AND 1000 THEN 500
              WHEN usecounts BETWEEN 1001 AND 5000 THEN 2500
              WHEN usecounts BETWEEN 5001 AND 10000 THEN 7500
              ELSE usecounts
         END
ORDER BY CASE WHEN usecounts BETWEEN 10 AND 100 THEN 50
              WHEN usecounts BETWEEN 101 AND 1000 THEN 500
              WHEN usecounts BETWEEN 1001 AND 5000 THEN 2500
              WHEN usecounts BETWEEN 5001 AND 10000 THEN 7500
              ELSE usecounts
         END DESC ;
```

Listing 3.8: An overview of plan reuse.

For a server that had been up for two days, we got the following results:

```
usecounts    countInstance
-----------  -------------
169279       1
100911       1
18379        1
17817        1
16608        1
10004        1
5001-10000   19
1001-5000    87
101-1000     127
10-100       359
9            9
8            55
7            12
6            51
5            18
4            628
3            73
2            277
1            1988
```

So, for example, we have five plans that have been reused over 10,000 times, 359 plans that have been reused between 10 and 100 times, 1,988 plans that have only been used once, and so on. Clearly, this is only an overview, and just to give you an overall feel for plan reuse. It's a query I like to run semi-regularly to see if there's any noticable change in the "distribution" to more (or less) reuse.

While it is clear from the listing that we are probably getting decent reuse (particularly on a few, often-executed queries), what we cannot tell at this point is how many queries are being executed on the server (although we can find that out) or how many get flushed from the cache. What you will be able to tell is the most important queries that get reused, and a place to look for improvements.

The next step is to examine those plans at the extreme ends of the spectrum. If we can improve the efficiency of a plan that that is being reused many times, it could be highly beneficial. Likewise, we need to find out more information about the plans that are never reused, why this might be, and if there is anything we can do about it.

Examining frequently used plans

Using sys.dm_exec_cached_plans in conjunction with sys.dm_exec_query_ plan and sys.dm_exec_sql_text, we can construct a query to return the text of the plan, plus the text of the query that is associated with the plan and has the highest use counts. So if, using Profiler or one of the operating system DMOs discussed in *Chapter 7*, we identify a query that is offensive for some performance reason (CPU pressure, duration, memory utilization, etc.), and then find that it is attached to a plan with a very high usecount, then we know we've found a good place to start our tuning efforts for the day.

The script in Listing 3.9 returns, for the most reused plans, the query plan itself, the type of object or query with which the plan is associated and the SQL text for that query or object.

```
SELECT TOP 2 WITH TIES
        decp.usecounts ,
        decp.cacheobjtype ,
        decp.objtype ,
        deqp.query_plan ,
        dest.text
FROM    sys.dm_exec_cached_plans decp
        CROSS APPLY sys.dm_exec_query_plan(decp.plan_handle) AS deqp
        CROSS APPLY sys.dm_exec_sql_text(decp.plan_handle) AS dest
ORDER BY usecounts DESC ;
```

	usecounts	cacheobjtype	objtype	query_plan
1	6	Compiled Plan	Adhoc	<ShowPlanXML xmlns="http://schemas.microsoft.com...
2	6	Compiled Plan	Adhoc	<ShowPlanXML xmlns="http://schemas.microsoft.com...

text

SELECT ISNULL(SUSER_SNAME(), SUSER_NAME())

select @@microsoftversion

Listing 3.9: Investigating the most used plans.

The real beauty of being able to do this from SQL, rather than some prebuilt report, is that you have the full power of the query engine in your hands. For example, if we want to look only at plans for stored procedures, we can simply filter on `objtype = 'proc'`.

Of course, this is only one piece of the puzzle and, later in the chapter, when we start to look at how we can see the individual queries from a batch or compiled object that make up the entire plan, it will become more useful to the tuning efforts. We can examine our frequently-reused plans for queries that contain certain text, as we did in Listing 3.3. Alternatively, we can filter on the `objectid`, to examine plan reuse for a single procedure, as shown in Listing 3.10.

```
SELECT   usecounts ,
         cacheobjtype ,
         objtype ,
         OBJECT_NAME(dest.objectid)
FROM     sys.dm_exec_cached_plans decp
         CROSS APPLY sys.dm_exec_sql_text(decp.plan_handle) AS dest
WHERE    dest.objectid = OBJECT_ID('<procedureName>')
         AND dest.dbid = DB_ID()
ORDER BY usecounts DESC ;
```

Listing 3.10: Examining plan reuse for a single procedure.

In SQL Server 2008, we can use the **sys.dm_exec_procedure_stats** DMV to look exclusively at cached plans for stored procedures. We'll examine this DMV a little later.

Examining ad hoc single-use plans

The script in Listing 3.11 uses the sys.dm_exec_cached_plans DMV and sys.dm_ exec_sql_text DMF to retrieve the text for each single-use plan that is bloating the plan cache.

```
-- Find single-use, ad hoc queries that are bloating the plan cache
SELECT TOP ( 100 )
        [text] ,
        cp.size_in_bytes
FROM    sys.dm_exec_cached_plans AS cp
        CROSS APPLY sys.dm_exec_sql_text(plan_handle)
WHERE   cp.cacheobjtype = 'Compiled Plan'
        AND cp.objtype = 'Adhoc'
        AND cp.usecounts = 1
ORDER BY cp.size_in_bytes DESC ;
```

Listing 3.11: Examining single-use plans in the cache.

This query will identify ad hoc queries with a use count of 1, ordered by the size of the plan. It provides the text and size of single-use ad hoc queries that waste space in the plan cache. This usually happens when T-SQL commands are built by concatenating a variable at the end of a "boilerplate" T-SQL statement. Listing 3.12 shows a simplified example.

```
-- Query 1
SELECT  FirstName ,
        LastName
FROM    dbo.Employee
WHERE   EmpID = 5

-- Query 2
SELECT  FirstName ,
        LastName
FROM    dbo.Employee
WHERE   EmpID = 187
```

Listing 3.12: Non-parameterized ad hoc SQL.

Even though these two queries are essentially identical, they might each have a separate plan in the cache, just because the literal value is different in each case. Actually these two queries are so simple (with no joins) that SQL Server would probably parameterize them, even using just the default simple parameterization (as opposed to forced parameterization). However, in more complex cases, plan reuse would probably not be possible. While we can do our best to make sure queries are written in a way that enables plan reuse, users and utilities often execute batches that will simply have little reuse.

For SQL Server 2008, if you determine that you have a mostly ad hoc workload with minimal reuse, check out the "optimize for ad hoc workloads" system option. This setting changes SQL Server behavior and does not store a plan on first usage, only the query text. If it matches a second time, the plan is stored. Note that "ad hoc," in this sense, does vary from some people's understanding of the term. Here, it simply refers to the use of random queries that don't promote reuse.

Query Plan Attributes

In the previous sections, we've covered how we get the text of a query plan and then examine plan reuse on your system, using the `cached_plans` DMV. In addition, a DBA will sometimes want to find out "state" information about a particular plan, along with further details about how that plan is currently being used.

The database engine takes into account several factors when considering a plan for reuse. One of these factors, as we discussed previously, is the text of the query.

However, other attributes are important, too, the values for which are stored in the **sys. dm_exec_plan_attributes** function, described by Books Online as follows:

> *Returns one row per plan attribute for the plan specified by the plan handle. You can use this table-valued function to get details about a particular plan, such as the cache key values or the number of current simultaneous executions of the plan.*

Like sys.dm_exec_query_plan, sys.dm_exec_plan_attributes takes a plan_handle as a parameter and returns the following columns:

- **attribute** – name of the attribute

- **value** – the current value assigned to the attribute

- **is_cache_key** – indicates if the attribute is part of how SQL Server resolves the plan; A value of 1 indicates that it is, and 0 that it is not.

This DMV returns one row per plan attribute, and available attributes include:

- **set_options** – the options values (the ones that can be found using @@options, such as SET NOCOUNT) that were in use when the plan was built

- **date_format** – the date format of the connection that created the plan

- **inuse_exec_context** – the number of currently executing batches that are using the plan.

If the value of is_cache_key is 1 for a given attribute, that attribute forms part of the "key" that is used when SQL Server searches the cache for a suitable plan. During the process of checking the cache for a match, the text of a submitted query is compared to the text of other queries that have been executed and for which a plan is stored. Even if the text of the queries matches exactly, the submitted query's attributes would also need to match exactly those for the cached plan, for every attribute with a value of 1 for the is_cache_key column in sys.dm_exec_plan_attributes.

Consider, for example, the code in Listing 3.13, which uses a `plan_handle` extracted from **sys.dm_exec_cached_plans**, on my test server, and supplies it as a parameter to **sys.dm_exec_plan_attributes**. Note the use of TOP 1 ... ORDER BY usecounts DESC in the derived table to get the largest reused plan.

```
SELECT   CAST(depa.attribute AS VARCHAR(30)) AS attribute ,
         CAST(depa.value AS VARCHAR(30)) AS value ,
         depa.is_cache_key
FROM     ( SELECT TOP 1
                       *
           FROM       sys.dm_exec_cached_plans
           ORDER BY   usecounts DESC
         ) decp
         OUTER APPLY sys.dm_exec_plan_attributes(decp.plan_handle) depa
WHERE    is_cache_key = 1
ORDER BY usecounts DESC ;
```

Listing 3.13: Examining plan attributes.

This returns the following results:

```
attribute                        value        is_cache_key
-------------------------------  ---------    ------------
set_options                      187                     1
objectid                         733550834               1
dbid                             4                       1
dbid_execute                     0                       1
user_id                          -2                      1
language_id                      0                       1
date_format                      1                       1
date_first                       7                       1
status                           8                       1
required_cursor_options          0                       1
acceptable_cursor_options        0                       1
```

So, in order for a cached plan to be used to execute the query in Listing 3.13, all of the returned attribute values would have to match. For example, both the submitted query and the cached plan would need to have `set_options = 187`, `objectid = 733550834`, `dbid = 4`, and so on. If there was a mismatch of any kind, a new plan would be generated. So, say you were testing the query in Management Studio in the context of a database different from the one used when an application first issued the query. The attributes of the existing plan for the application-issued query and those for your SSMS-issued query might match in terms of the SQL text and maybe even the `objectid` (somewhat less likely), but the `dbid` would be different, so the plan would not get reused and a new one would be created. In such cases, the SQL text for the query, as identified by the `sql_handle`, would now be associated with more than one plan, i.e. there would be more than one `plan_handle` associated with a given `sql_handle`.

This sounds rather horrible, but it's important to realize that each of these attributes, including security attributes, is important for determining how the query will be executed. Furthermore, one shouldn't really expect the same plan to be used, even if the SQL text and some of the attributes match. One database may have zero rows in table X, whereas the other one may have 1.5 billion; same exact query text, vastly different plans.

Checking the attributes of a plan is not necessarily a very common thing to need to do as, most of the time, your client will have a very standard set of settings. However, on that rare occasion that you see no plan reuse, but you can clearly see multiple queries with the same query text, the `sys.dm_exec_plan_attributes` DMV will help you seek out the reasons.

Gathering Query Execution Statistics

Up to this point in the chapter, we've shown how to get the text of a cached plan, and how to return detailed information about those plans. One plan is stored for a batch or an object and we used `sys.dm_exec_cached_plans` to get plan information.

Each plan has 1-to-N queries and in this section we're going to explore how to get detailed information about the individual queries in the batch or object. To get these query statistics, be it for a standalone query or a query within a larger stored procedure or prepared statement, we use the `sys.dm_exec_query_stats` DMV.

The `sys.dm_exec_query_stats` DMV will return one row per query that is executed within a batch or stored procedure, and provides columns such as `total_worker_time` (CPU), `total_physical_reads`, `total_logical_reads`, which can give you a very useful overview of the system resources that your queries are eating up.

Pre-SQL Server 2005, the only way to get this sort of information was through Profiler. However, Profiler only lets you collect the information *as the queries occur*, not after the event. Now, the next time you hear about a problem second-hand, while walking down the hallway, which is too often how users report problems, you'll be able to interrogate the `sys.dm_exec_query_stats` DMV and find out what happened. This is an exciting step forward for most DBAs, especially given that resorting to Profiler after the event often entailed capturing traces over long periods of time, in order to reobserve the problem, and this could be really costly in terms of server resources and programmer sanity, since doing the matching of query text after the fact is very difficult.

Overview of sys.dm_exec_query_stats

The `sys.dm_exec_query_stats` DMV contains quite a few columns that are incremented counters, and provide information about how many times a query has been executed and the resources that were used. It is described in Books Online as follows:

> *Returns aggregate performance statistics for cached query plans. The view contains one row per query statement within the cached plan, and the lifetime of the rows is tied to the plan itself. When a plan is removed from the cache, the corresponding rows are eliminated from this view.*

As a whole, it provides a wealth of information regarding resource-hungry queries on your system for which a plan is cached. The columns that can be returned are as follows:

- `sql_handle` – identifies the batch or procedure to which a query belongs; it is used by `sys.dm_exec_sql_text` to get the text of the batch

- `statement_start_offset` – the starting point of the query within the batch or object to which the query belongs

- `statement_end_offset` – the end point of the query that is currently executing, within the batch or object to which the query belongs

- `plan_generation_num` – indicates the version of the query plan that has been created after a recompile; used for comparisons because the actual plan may change (or even partially change for a statement-level recompile), even though the SQL stays the same

- `plan_handle` – identifies the cached query plan for a batch or stored procedure that has been executed; used by `sys.dm_exec_query_plan` or `sys.dm_exec_text_query_plan` to get the plan of an executed query in XML format

- `creation_time` – time the plan was created

- `last_execution_time` – last time the execution plan was used to execute a query

- `execution_count` – number of times the plan has been used to execute a query

- `total_worker_time`, `last_worker_time`, `min_worker_time`, `max_worker_time` – total, last, min and max amount of time spent in CPU utilization to execute the query, based on this plan

- `total_physical_reads`, `last_physical_reads`, `min_physical_reads`, `max_physical_reads` – total, last, min and max number of reads to the physical hard disk system

- `total_logical_writes`, `last_logical_writes`, `min_logical_writes`, `max_logical_writes` – total, last, min and max number of writes to the buffer cache to be written by lazy writer

- `total_logical_reads, last_logical_reads, min_logical_reads, max_logical_reads` – total, last, min and max number of reads from the SQL Server cache buffer that never had to go to the physical hard disk system to satisfy the current request; this data was read in previously and was still in cache

- `total_clr_time, last_clr_time, min_clr_time, max_clr_time` – total, last, min and max amount of time spent in the CLR processor for the query that utilized this plan

- `total_elapsed_time, last_elapsed_time, min_elapsed_time, max_elapsed_time` – in ms, the total, last, min and max amounts of time it took to execute the entire query.

Note: Time columns are in microseconds.

Putting sys.dm_exec_query_stats to work

Once you are able to extract individual statements from a batch, as demonstrated in the earlier section, *Dissecting the SQL Text,* you can use **sys.dm_exec_query_stats** to access the query statistics for individual SQL statements that are executing on your system. The sky is the limit with regard to how you might use this information to find where you have performance issues.

Generally speaking, at the point where you would turn to **sys.dm_exec_query_stats**, you would already have an idea of whether your system is IO bound, CPU bound, or having CLR performance issues, and so on, likely from using other DMVs or a tool such as the performance monitor (PerfMon). So, your goal at this stage would be to get a ranked list of the queries that are having the biggest effect on the issue that you've identified.

Before we look at the scripts, it is important to remember when using this DMV that there is usually, but not necessarily, a one-to-one relationship between a `sql_handle` and a `plan_handle`. One `sql_handle` can sometimes be associated with more than one `plan_handle`. This can be caused by statement-level recompilation (see HTTP://TECHNET.MICROSOFT.COM/EN-US/LIBRARY/EE343986(SQL.100).ASPX for more details), or by the exact same SQL text being executed with different attribute values, as discussed earlier.

Let's say that you've identified that your sytem is CPU bound. Using the `total_worker_time` column, you can find out which queries your server is spending the most time executing. However, it isn't enough just to know that the server is spending a lot of time executing a particular query. In fact, without context, this piece of information is more or less meaningless. It might be that the query is run a million times, and no other query is executed more than a thousand times. So, to add the required context, we include the `execution_count`, along with a calculation of the average CPU time, as shown in Listing 3.14.

```
SELECT TOP 3
        total_worker_time ,
        execution_count ,
        total_worker_time / execution_count AS [Avg CPU Time] ,
        CASE WHEN deqs.statement_start_offset = 0
                AND deqs.statement_end_offset = -1
            THEN '-- see objectText column--'
            ELSE '-- query --' + CHAR(13) + CHAR(10)
                + SUBSTRING(execText.text, deqs.statement_start_offset / 2,
                        ( ( CASE WHEN deqs.statement_end_offset = -1
                                THEN DATALENGTH(execText.text)
                                ELSE deqs.statement_end_offset
                            END ) - deqs.statement_start_offset ) / 2)
        END AS queryText
FROM    sys.dm_exec_query_stats deqs
        CROSS APPLY sys.dm_exec_sql_text(deqs.plan_handle) AS execText
ORDER BY deqs.total_worker_time DESC ;
```

	total_worker_time	execution_count	Avg CPU Time	queryText	ObjectText
1	3070595407	527	5826556	-- see objectText column--	SELECT * FROM "Extract033642_...
2	1212108233	18431	65764	-- query -- SELECT C.Typ...	CREATE PROCEDURE [dbo].[Fin...
3	289050796	1	289050796	-- query -- insert into #Workin...	--set ANSI_NULLS ON --set QUO...

Listing 3.14: Finding the CPU-intensive queries.

The results, representing a set of queries from a busy server, were extensive, but we've only shown the first three queries here (we don't get paid by the page, unfortunately). From here, we can start to get a feeling for what queries are hurting the CPU the most since the last system reboot. However, bear in mind the earlier discussion in the *Flushing the Cache?* section, with regard to the different lengths of time plans will have been in the cache, and how this can skew the results.

At this stage, it's somewhat difficult to gauge which of these queries is the most pertinent to the performance issue, but these statistics make an excellent starting point for our investigations. The first query executed 527 times and is taking the most time, while the second one has been executed almost four times as frequently, but is taking one-third of the CPU time. The third query only ran once, but took a huge amount of CPU time. This is troublesome since it is impossible to know whether this was a one-off event, or if this query just hasn't run that often since the server was restarted or DBCC FREEPROCCACHE was executed to clear the query cache. An interesting column to check, especially with regard to a plan with a single execution like this one, is last_execution_time, which will tell you exactly when the plan was last used. Along with the query text, this can help you to judge whether or not this execution was planned, and is part of your normal query workload, or is just an unfortunate ad hoc query execution.

The next step would be to plug the plan_handle for each query (which I didn't include in the results due to space constraints) into the sys.dm_exec_query_plan (see the section entitled *Viewing the Text of Cached Queries and Query Plans*) and investigate how each query is being executed, and whether the query can be optimized.

There is a lot more useful data that can be extracted from the **sys.dm_exec_query_stats** DMV using variations of the previously described techniques, based on "isolating" individual queries through the **_offset** values, filtering on specific objects, and so on. For example, you could write similar queries focusing on the following DMV columns:

- **excessive logical writes** – data written to cache (which gets written to the physical hard disk via the lazy writer)
  `total_logical_writes, last_logical_writes, min_logical_writes, max_logical_writes`

- **excessive logical reads** – queries that required the most data to be read from cache (possibly causing memory pressure)
  `total_logical_reads, last_logical_reads, min_logical_reads, max_logical_reads`

- **excessive physical reads** – queries that forced the most physical hard disk access (generally caused by the need for more cache memory than was available, equating to heavy memory pressure since data could not be read from the cache)
  `total_physical_reads, last_physical_reads, min_physical_reads, max_physical_reads`

- **long-running queries**
  `total_elapsed_time, last_elapsed_time, min_elapsed_time, max_elapsed_time`

- **expensive CLR code**
  `total_clr_time, last_clr_time, min_clr_time, max_clr_time.`

As discussed in the introduction to this chapter, it's true that you can get similar information from the management reports in SSMS. The real win with the DMOs is the degree of control and granularity you can achieve through the **WHERE** clause. For example, we could easily modify the query in Listing 3.13 as follows, to return statistics only for batches that reference the **account** table, simply by adding the appropriate **WHERE** clause.

```
WHERE  execText.text like '%account%'
```

Of course, we will probably have to be cleverer with the LIKE criteria if we have tables (not to mention columns) named account and accountContact, but this is just a SQL task. We could also use the entire definition of queryText and just look for the individual queries. This technique will come in handy many times when optimizing data access to a given object because, unlike most tools that come prebuilt, we can create queries that only look at a very small subsection of queries, eliminating noise that is perhaps not interesting to us during the current tuning process.

Finally, there are times when we want to see the results at a complete query/batch level, rather than for the individual parts of the query, which may have their own plans. This is complicated by the fact that, as discussed, one sql_handle may be associated with more than one plan_handle. Therefore, in order to see the total stats for all queries in the same batch, we need to group on the sql_handle and sum the values, as shown in Listing 3.15.

```
SELECT TOP 100
        SUM(total_logical_reads) AS total_logical_reads ,
        COUNT(*) AS num_queries , --number of individual queries in batch
        --not all usages need be equivalent, in the case of looping
        --or branching code
        MAX(execution_count) AS execution_count ,
        MAX(execText.text) AS queryText
FROM    sys.dm_exec_query_stats deqs
        CROSS APPLY sys.dm_exec_sql_text(deqs.sql_handle) AS execText
GROUP BY deqs.sql_handle
HAVING  AVG(total_logical_reads / execution_count) <> SUM(total_logical_reads)
        / SUM(execution_count)
ORDER BY 1 DESC
```

Listing 3.15: Grouping by sql_handle to see query stats at the batch level.

Investigating Expensive Cached Stored Procedures

New to SQL Server 2008 is the **sys.dm_exec_procedure_stats** DMV that focuses only on stored procedures and will not require you to aggregate on **sql_handle** to get an overall view of your object's performance characteristics. Books Online describes it as:

> *Returns aggregate performance statistics for cached stored procedures. The view contains one row per stored procedure, and the lifetime of the row is as long as the stored procedure remains cached. When a stored procedure is removed from the cache, the corresponding row is eliminated from this view. At that time, a Performance Statistics SQL trace event is raised similar to* **sys.dm_exec_query_stats**.

It is similar in nature to **sys.dm_exec_query_stats**, but with a few differences in the columns available. It only links to the plan of the procedure or object, not the individual statements in the procedure. This DMV allows you to discover a lot of very interesting and important performance information about your cached stored procedures.

```
-- Top Cached SPs By Total Logical Reads (SQL 2008 only).
-- Logical reads relate to memory pressure
SELECT TOP ( 25 )
        p.name AS [SP Name] ,
        deps.total_logical_reads AS [TotalLogicalReads] ,
        deps.total_logical_reads / deps.execution_count AS [AvgLogicalReads] ,
        deps.execution_count ,
        ISNULL(deps.execution_count / DATEDIFF(Second, deps.cached_time,
                                    GETDATE()), 0) AS [Calls/Second] ,
        deps.total_elapsed_time ,
        deps.total_elapsed_time / deps.execution_count AS [avg_elapsed_time] ,
        deps.cached_time
FROM    sys.procedures AS p
        INNER JOIN sys.dm_exec_procedure_stats
                        AS deps ON p.[object_id] = deps.[object_id]
WHERE   deps.database_id = DB_ID()
ORDER BY deps.total_logical_reads DESC ;
```

Listing 3.16: Investigating logical reads performed by cached stored procedures.

Depending on what columns we include, and which column we order by, we can discover which cached stored procedures are the most expensive from several different perspectives. In this case, we are interested in finding out which stored procedures are generating the most total logical reads (which relates to memory pressure). This query is especially useful if there are signs of memory pressure, such as a persistently low page life expectancy and/or persistent values above zero for memory grants pending. This query is filtered by the current database, but we can change it to be instance-wide by removing the WHERE clause.

Simply by selecting the `total_physical_reads` column, instead of `total_logical_reads` in this query, we can perform the same analysis from the perspective of physical reads, which relates to read, disk I/O pressure. Lots of stored procedures with high total physical reads or high average physical reads, could indicate severe memory pressure, causing SQL Server to go to the disk I/O subsystem for data. It could also indicate lots of missing indexes or "bad" queries (with no WHERE clauses, for example) that are causing lots of clustered index or table scans on large tables.

Be aware, though, that there are a couple of caveats with these queries. The big one is that you need to pay close attention to the `cached_time` column as you compare rows in the result set. If you have stored procedures that have been cached for different periods of time, this will skew the results. One easy, but perhaps controversial, solution to this problem is to periodically clear your procedure cache, by running DBCC FREEPROCCACHE with a SQL Agent job, as previously discussed.

The second caveat is that only cached stored procedures will show up in these queries. If you are using WITH RECOMPILE or OPTION(RECOMPILE), which is usually not a good idea anyway, then those plans won't be cached.

Getting Aggregate Query Optimization Statistics for All Optimizations

In this section, we will look at how we can get statistics on all optimizations that have been performed by the optimizer, regardless of whether or not a plan has been stored. This data is available from the `sys.dm_exec_query_optimizer_info` DMV and it will allow us to get a feel for how queries have been optimized, and how many of them have been optimized, since the last time the server was restarted.

The data available from this DMV is often not obtainable by looking at actual plan usage, and it can be very useful in gaining an overall understanding of the performance of a server. For example, trivial plans are not stored in cache, so we can't get any information on them from the cached plan views but `_query_optimizer_info` can tell us the number of times a trivial plan was obtained.

This view also provides a lot of other information that can only be found here (or attained in real time, using Profiler), such as the types of statements that are being optimized, the number of hints used, and so on.

The `sys.dm_exec_query_optimizer_info` DMV provides information on optimizer activity in the form of a set of counters. Every time a type of optimization occurs, the counter will be incremented and, in some cases, a current value will be included in an average. The counters are only incremented when a new query plan is created, so when query plans are matched and reused, there is no need for a compilation, and there would be no change to these counters. The three columns returned by this DMV are as follows:

- **counter** – the type of operation that the optimizer has done

- **occurrence** – number of times the operation the counter represents has occurred

- **value** – may or may not have some value, but is typically an average of the values that were recorded when the counter was written to.

The view will return one row for each of the possible counter types. The domain of counter values includes `optimizations`, which is the total count of optimizations since system start; `elapsed time` which is the average elapsed time to complete the optimization of an individual statement, in seconds (averaged over total count of optimizations) and a lot of other interesting values that can tell you the number of insert, delete, or update statements that have been optimized, queries optimized with subqueries, and many others.

For example, on a freshly restarted server, let's take a look at three of the counters, as shown in Listing 3.17.

```
SELECT  counter ,
        occurrence ,
        value
FROM    sys.dm_exec_query_optimizer_info
WHERE   counter IN ( 'optimizations', 'elapsed time', 'final cost' ) ;
```

Listing 3.17: Examine optimizer counters.

This returns something along the lines of:

```
counter              occurrence     value
-------------------  -------------  -------------
optimizations        5                         1
elapsed time         5                    0.0074
final cost           5               0.0225006594
```

From this data we can see that:

- there have been a total of five statements optimized, and for which a plan has been created (the value column for optimizations is documented as having no meaning in Books Online)

- the average average elapsed time spent optimizing each of the five statements was 0.0074 seconds

- the average cost of producing an optimized plan in each case was ~ 0.023.

Using these counters and some of the others, we can determine how often statements are being compiled. Of course, the usual caveats apply in that, since the values start accumulating as of the start of the server, there may be more or less information to be gathered from the data. I certainly won't make the claim that you can necessarily discern anything from these values without any other data. It can help to track the accumulating counter type values over time.

Assuming there is only one user on the system, if we re-execute the query in Listing 3.17 the values will probaly remain the same, as we just executed the same exact statement and a plan already exists. However, try making the query upper case, as shown in Listing 3.18.

```
SELECT   COUNTER ,
         OCCURRENCE ,
         VALUE
FROM     SYS.DM_EXEC_QUERY_OPTIMIZER_INFO
WHERE    COUNTER IN ( 'optimizations', 'elapsed time', 'final cost' ) ;
```

Listing 3.18: Trivial changes to query text can affect plan reuse.

Now the query text does not match that of the previous query so, when we execute it, a new plan will have to be created and we should see the **occurrence** column incremented in value; there may also be some difference in the average times.

```
counter               occurrence      value

-------------------   ------------    -------
optimizations         9                     1
elapsed time          9               0.03867
final cost            9               0.10053
```

Note that the number of optimizations didn't increment by just 1. When a server is starting up there are many things going on. I also started up Agent when I restarted the server and there were compilations for those queries as well.

Summary

With the information in this chapter, you can really start to get a picture of a system's query health, even if you have not had long-term access to the server. The scripts presented are especially useful when you need to start to drill down into a performance bottleneck, having established a high-level idea of what is the biggest one.

One of the greatest advantages of examining cached queries and plans is that the DBA can take a longer-term view of performance diagnosis, beyond simply responding to what is happening right now on the server. By running these scripts regularly, the DBA can proactively tune queries that may be hogging resources, but not yet to the extent that it is being noticed by an end-user (thereby raising it to the level of national emergency).

We've seen how to extract the query plan and SQL text from `sys.dm_exec_sql_text` and `sys.dm_exec_query_plan` functions, and how to investigate plan reuse, using `sys.dm_exec_cached_plans` and `sys.dm_exec_plan_attributes`. However, the centerpieces of our diagnostic efforts, in this chapter, were the `sys.dm_exec_query_stats` and `sys.dm_exec_procedure_stats` views, from which we obtained extremely valuable information regarding the time and resources used by our most expensive queries and stored procedures. Bear in mind that the plans don't stay in the cache forever, so it isn't a perfect science, but larger-cost plans do tend to stick around.

Lastly, we looked at the `sys.dm_exec_query_optimizer_info` DMV that lets you get an understanding of the overall performance of the optimizer, which includes all optimizations, including ones that create trivial plans that are never stored in the cache.

Chapter 4: Transactions

In *Chapter 2*, we used the Dynamic Management Objects to observe connectivity into our SQL Server instances, and identify potentially troublesome user sessions currently executing on these instances. We did this by examining the work being performed by SQL Server as a result of the SQL being executed by the requests belonging to each session. In *Chapter 3*, we extended our analysis of query execution to the **execution plans** that SQL Server generates, stores and, hopefully, reuses during this process. This allowed a broader analysis of our query workload, from the point of view of what was in the plan cache, rather than just examining those requests being executed at a given time.

In this chapter, we step to the next level down in terms of granularity, with an investigation of the transaction-related DMOs, all of which are prefixed `sys.dm_tran_`, and the information they provide. Ultimately, every statement executed against SQL Server is transactional, and SQL Server implements various transaction isolation levels, to ensure the ACID (Atomicity, Consistency, Isolation, and Durability) properties of these transactions. In practical terms, this means that it uses locks and latches to mediate transactional access to shared database resources and prevent "interference" between the transactions. When a transaction encounters a locked resource it must, of course, wait for the resource to become free before proceeding. If such blocking occurs frequently or is protracted, it greatly restricts the number of concurrent users that can access the system.

One of the major goals of this chapter is to describe the DMOs and scripts which will allow a DBA to locate the transactions that are causing locking and blocking issues on their SQL Server instances, and the sessions to which they belong. Having located the offending transactions, the DBA can then take steps to alleviate the blocking, either by tuning the SQL or, if this is not possible, by careful scheduling of the more resource-hungry and/or longer-running business reports, so that they occur separately from the main Online Transaction Processing (OLTP) load.

We'll also examine how to use the transaction-related DMOs, for example, to investigate long-running transactions that may be preventing transaction log truncation, and transactions that are causing large amounts of data to be written to the transaction log, making it grow rapidly in size.

Finally, we'll examine the set of DMOs dedicated to investigating issues relating to use of the snapshot isolation level, which aims to improve concurrency by using row versioning rather than issuing locks inside a database. These row versions, which maintain a transactional history for a particular database, are held in a version store within the `tempdb` database, so snapshot isolation comes at a price in terms of `tempdb` consumption.

What is a transaction, anyway?

Microsoft Books Online (HTTP://MSDN.MICROSOFT.COM/EN-US/LIBRARY/AA213068(SQL.80). ASPX) is as good a place as any to start for a definition of the term, transaction:

> *A transaction is a sequence of operations performed as a single logical unit of work. A logical unit of work must exhibit four properties, called the ACID properties, to qualify as a transaction.*

For a transaction to pass the ACID Test, all of its data modifications must complete or be rolled back (*Atomic*); the end result must be that all data and supporting structures such as indexes must be consistent with the rules that apply to them (*Consistent*).

A transaction cannot be impacted by any other transactions occurring concurrently (*Isolated*); the results of the transaction being permanently recorded in the RDBMS (*Durability*).

As noted in the introduction to this chapter, every statement executed against SQL Server is transactional. If we issue a single SQL statement, an implicit transaction is run under

the covers, which auto-starts and auto-completes. If we use explicit **BEGIN TRAN /**
COMMIT TRAN commands, then we can group together, in an explicit transaction, a set of
statements that must fail or succeed together. This is easily demonstrated by the series of
queries shown in Listing 4.1 and the resulting output.

```
SELECT   DTAT.transaction_id
FROM     sys.dm_tran_active_transactions DTAT
WHERE    DTAT.name <> 'worktable' ;

SELECT   DTAT.transaction_id
FROM     sys.dm_tran_active_transactions DTAT
WHERE    DTAT.name <> 'worktable' ;

BEGIN TRAN
SELECT   DTAT.transaction_id
FROM     sys.dm_tran_active_transactions DTAT
WHERE    DTAT.name <> 'worktable' ;

SELECT   DTAT.transaction_id
FROM     sys.dm_tran_active_transactions DTAT
WHERE    DTAT.name <> 'worktable' ;
COMMIT TRAN
```

```
transaction_id
--------------------
18949550
...
18949551
...
18949552
...
18949552
```

Listing 4.1:   All statements within SQL Server are transactional.

According to the results of these queries, any statements executed outside of an explicit
transaction will execute as separate transactions, and each will result in a row with a
unique **transaction_id** in our result sets. All statements executed within an explicit
transaction will be reported with a single **transaction_id**.

SQL Server will attempt to ensure that each unit of work, be it a single-statement implicit transaction, or any number of individual SQL statements within an explicit transaction, conforms to the ACID test characteristics.

What we hope to demonstrate in this chapter is how to observe these units of work via the DMOs. Since the lifespan of these transactions is measured in milliseconds, when everything is going right the focus will be on those transactions that are having difficulty completing in a timely fashion, whether due to contention for resources, poor tuning, or other issues.

Investigating Locking and Blocking

Locking is an integral aspect of any RDBMS. Locks control how transactions are allowed to interact, impact, and impede one another when running simultaneously against common objects. Unless you restrict data access to one user at a time, clearly not a viable option, locks are necessary to the smooth functioning of any RDBMS.

Locks are to be neither feared nor shunned but they can, nevertheless, cause problems for the reckless or unwary. When using SQL Server's default isolation level, READ COMMITTED, **shared read locks** are acquired during data reads. These locks prevent another transaction from modifying that data while the query is in progress, but do not block other readers. Furthermore, "dirty reads" are forbidden, so SQL Server acquires **exclusive locks** during updates, to prevent a transaction from reading data that has been modified by another transaction, but not committed. Of course, this means that if one transaction (A) encounters data that is being modified by another transaction (B), then transaction A is blocked; it needs access to a resource that is locked by B and cannot proceed until B either commits or rolls back.

As noted, this is normal behavior but, in conditions of highly concurrent user access, the potential for blocking will increase. The situation will be exacerbated, for example, by transactions that are longer than they need to be or are poorly written, causing locks to be held for longer than necessary. As locking and blocking increase, so does the overhead on the RDBMS and the end result is a significant reduction in concurrency.

READ UNCOMMITTED – *Don't do it*

If you want concurrency at all costs, then READ UNCOMMITTED *isolation level will shun locks as far as possible. This mode allows dirty reads, so use it at the expense of your data consistency and integrity.*

In READ COMMITTED mode, shared read locks are released as soon as a query completes, so data modification transactions can proceed at that point, even if the transaction to which the query belongs is still open. Therefore, non-repeatable reads are possible; if the same data is read twice in the same transaction, the answer may be different. If this is not acceptable, the isolation level can be made more restrictive. The REPEATABLE READ level will ensure that all the rows that were read cannot be modified or deleted until the transaction which reads them completes. However, even this level does not prevent new rows (called phantom rows) being inserted that satisfy the query criteria, meaning that reads are not, in the true sense, repeatable. To prevent this, you could switch to SERIALIZABLE, the most restrictive isolation level of all, which basically ensures that a transaction is completely isolated from the effects of any other transaction in the database.

However, as the isolation level becomes more restrictive, so the use of locks becomes more prevalent and the likelihood of blocking, and even deadlocking, where transaction A is waiting for a resource that is held by B and vice versa, increases dramatically. Note also, that it is not only competing modifications that can cause a deadlock. It is just as possible for a modification to deadlock with a reporting query.

Snapshot isolation level

SQL Server 2005 introduced this new isolation level, with the goal of allowing consistent reads without causing the blocking or deadlocking that is associated with REPEATABLE READ *or* SERIALIZ-ABLE. *We'll save discussion of this new level till later, in the section entitled "Snapshot Isolation and the* tempdb *Version Store."*

In short, DBAs need a way of investigating blocking on their SQL Server instances.

DMOs, Activity Monitor and sp_who2

Pre-SQL Server 2005, the only way a DBA could analyze blocking behavior in a SQL Server instance was to query the sysprocesses system table or to use sp_who and sp_who2. With SQL 2005, the situation has improved dramatically, and this information is now available through several new routes:

- using the sys.dm_tran_locks DMV
- the "blocked process report" in SQL Server Profiler
- using Activity Monitor in SSMS.

Activity Monitor is basically a graphical representation of sysprocesses and it can provide basic information regarding sessions that are blocked and blocking. For example, if we establish some blocking on a table in AdventureWorks, then open Activity Monitor (*Ctrl+Alt+A*), we can quickly establish that session 54 is blocked by session 52, as shown in Figure 4.1.

Session ID	User Process	Login	Database	Task State	Comm.	Applic.	Wait Time (ms)	Wait Type	Wait Resou	Bl By	He Bl
51	1	sa	master			Microsoft...	0				
52	1	sa	AdventureW...			Microsoft...	0				1
54	1	sa	AdventureW...	SUSPENDED	SELECT	Microsoft...	26172	LCK_M_S	keylock ...	52	
55	1	sa	tempdb	RUNNING	SELECT	Microsoft...	0	OLEDB			

Figure 4.1: Investigating blocking with Activity Monitor.

However, the information provided is pretty limited and, as we hope to demonstrate, the sys.dm_tran_locks DMV provides a wealth of extra information regarding the lock being held; you can query the available data in such a way that everything you need to resolve the problem is presented in a single result set.

An overview of the sys.dm_tran_locks DMV

The sys.dm_tran_locks DMV provides insight into the current state of locking in a SQL Server instance, across all databases. It returns a row for every currently active request to the lock manager for a lock that has been granted or is waiting to be granted. The columns provided offer information regarding both the resource on which the lock is being held (or has been requested), and the owner of the request. Like the previously discussed views, sys.dm_tran_locks provides only a snapshot of the state of the server at the point in time the query is executed.

The resource-related columns identify the resource being locked, its type, and the database on which the locking is occurring.

- **resource_type** – target resource object for the lock, such as **Table (OBJECT locks)**, **Page (PAGE locks)**, **Row (RID locks)**, or Key (KEY locks). Discussed in more detail shortly.

123

- **resource_database_id** – ID of the database on which the locked resource resides. This column can be used to join to the **dbid** column in **sys.sysdatabases**, as well as to several other system views and DMVs.

- **resource_associated_entity_id** – depending upon the resource_type, this value is either:

  - the object_id of the target object, if resource_type = OBJECT

  - the object_id of the parent object (courtesy of **sys.partitions**), if the resource_type is a KEY, PAGE, or RID.

  - Returning the name of the object is possible via the OBJECT_ID() system function, by passing in both the object_id and the database_id (respectively).

The remaining columns offer a means to determine the nature, status, and owner of the lock request, and to relate this locking information to that available from other DMVs, regarding the sessions or transactions with which the locks are associated.

- **request_mode** – type of lock that is being held, or has been requested, such as Shared (**S**), Update (**U**), Exclusive (**X**), Intent Exclusive (**IX**), and so on. Discussed in more detail shortly.

- **request_status** – status of the lock:

- GRANT –indicates the lock has been taken

  - CONVERT – the request is in the process of being fulfilled

  - WAIT – the resource is not locked, but is trying to lock the resource.

- **request_owner_type** – type of owner of the transaction:

  - TRANSACTION

  - CURSOR

  - SESSION

- `SHARED_TRANSACTION_WORKSPACE`

- `EXCLUSIVE_TRANSACTION_WORKSPACE`.

- **`request_session_id`** – the `session_id` of the requestor. Exposing this column allows the DBA to join back to the information provided in any of the `sys.dm_exec_*` DMVs as well as `sys.sysprocesses` (via a join to its `spid` column).

- **`request_owner_id`** – this column is only valid when the `request_owner_type` is `TRANSACTION`. In that case, the value is the `transaction_id` for the associated transaction.

One final column that is very useful is the **`lock_owner_address`**, which is a binary address used internally to track the lock request. It is not interesting to the DBA in its own right, but in the fact that it can be used to join to the `resource_address` column in the `sys.dm_os_waiting_tasks` DMV, to relate locking information to tasks that are waiting for a resource to become available before proceeding (i.e. which are blocked). We'll discuss this in much more detail in the section entitled *Investigating Blocking*.

***

Other `sys.dm_tran_locks` *columns*

This DMV provides other columns that I don't often use as a DBA, and so have omitted. For a full column listing, please refer to: HTTP://TECHNET.MICROSOFT.COM/EN-US/LIBRARY/MS190345.ASPX.

***

In order to interpret properly the data exposed by this DMV, we'll need to review in a little more detail some core locking concepts, namely **lock types** (exposed through the `resource_type` column) and **lock modes** (exposed through the `request_mode` column).

Lock types

SQL Server can lock a number of different types of resource, the most obvious being **tables** (OBJECT locks), **pages** (PAGE locks), **rows** (RID locks), and **keys** (KEY locks), in order of increasing granularity. Locks are granted and released on these objects as needed, in order to satisfy the requirements of the isolation levels in use by the various sessions. In the locking hierarchy, row and key locks are the lowest level, most granular forms of lock. The more granular the lock, the higher the degree of concurrent access that can be supported. However, with that comes a higher memory overhead, from having to manage a large number of individual locks.

SQL Server automatically chooses locks of the highest possible granularity, suitable for the given workload. However, if too many individual locks are being held on an index or heap, or if forced to do so due to memory pressure, SQL Server may use lock escalation to reduce the total number of locks being held. For example, a large number of individual row locks may be escalated to a single table lock, or a number of page locks may be escalated to a table lock (escalation is always to a table lock). While this will result in lower overhead on SQL Server, the cost will be lower concurrency. If processes are running on your servers that are causing lock escalation, it's worth investigating whether the escalation is justified, or if SQL tuning can be performed to prevent it. The index_lock_promotion_count column of the sys.dm_db_index_operational_stats DMV, covered in *Chapter 5*, can let you know if lock escalation is occurring frequently on a given index or heap.

Lock escalation

A full discussion of this topic is beyond the scope of this book, but good explanations are offered on MSDN (HTTP://TECHNET.MICROSOFT.COM/EN-US/MAGAZINE/2008.04.BLOCKING.ASPX) and by Sunil Agarwal, Program Manager for the Storage Engine Group (HTTP://BLOGS.MSDN.COM/B/SQLSERVER-STORAGEENGINE/ARCHIVE/2006/05/17/LOCK-ESCALATION.ASPX).

In addition to tables, pages, rows and keys, the following listing provides information on the other common types of resources that are targets for locks. These will crop up from time to time in your queries against `sys.dm_tran_locks`.

- **Key ranges** – only occur under the `SERIALIZABLE` isolation level where protection against phantom reads requires locking of a range of values to ensure that no one can insert records into a range that is scanned.

- **Extents** – locked when tables and indexes grow, and extents are added as a result.

- **Databases** – processes will be issued a shared (S) lock against a database if it locks a resource within a database. This occurs in any database on a SQL instance with the exception of master and `tempdb`, which allows the SQL engine to perform a check for locks prior to dropping a database or taking it offline, for instance. You will see a `DATABASE` lock for each request. I filter out `DATABASE` locks in my locking / blocking queries and consider them noise results.

- **Allocation units** – locked when they are in the process of being de-allocated.

- **Metadata** – occur when a transaction is attempting to change the definition for a given object. For example, altering the recovery model on a database would register an exclusive lock on the Metadata object type for the affected database.

The resource targeted by a given lock is exposed by the `resource_type` column in the `sys.dm_tran_locks` DMV. A full listing of target resources for locks can be found on Microsoft TechNet at HTTP://TECHNET.MICROSOFT.COM/EN-US/LIBRARY/MS189849.ASPX.

Lock modes

SQL Server employs five different lock modes, in order to control how concurrent transactions interact. These modes are exposed in the `request_mode` column of the `sys.dm_tran_locks` DMV.

- **Shared (S)** – shared locks are issued for read-only operations, such as `SELECT` statements. They prevent other transactions from updating the same data while the query is processing. Multiple shared locks can be issued for the same resource, hence the term "shared."

- **Update (U)** – update locks prevent data being modified by another transaction in the time between finding the data that needs to be updated, and actually modifying it. A U lock is obtained while the data is located, and then this is converted to an exclusive lock to perform the update. Only a single update lock can be issued for a given resource, and it must be converted to an exclusive lock before a data modification can occur.

- **Exclusive (X)** – exclusive locks are used for data modification requests (`INSERT`, `UPDATE`, and `DELETE`) to ensure that multiple updates do not occur against the same resource. Only a single exclusive lock can be placed on a resource at any given point in time. This prevents any other transaction from reading or modifying the X-locked data.

- **Intent (IX, IU, IS)** – intent locks, as their name suggest, indicate an intention to lock a resource lower in the locking hierarchy. So, for example, immediately before obtaining an S lock on a row in a table, SQL Server will briefly obtain an **Intent Shared (IS)** lock on the table (or page), which will prevent another transaction from obtaining an exclusive lock on the table. Other types of intent lock are **Intent Exclusive (IX)** and **Intent Update (IU)**. All intent locks can be acquired only on pages and tables. If an X lock is obtained on a key column, then both the page and the table associated with that key would be assigned an **IX** lock.

- **Conversion** – these locks are the result of conversion from one locking mode to another. There are three types of conversion lock:

  - **(SIX)** – **Shared with Intent Exclusive** – a transaction currently holds a shared (S) lock on a resource, then subsequently needs to obtain an exclusive (X) lock on a component of the resource that is S locked

- **(SIU) – Shared with Intent Update** – similar to an SIX lock, an SIU lock occurs when a transaction process is currently locking a resource with a shared (S) lock, but requires a subsequent update (U) lock

- **(UIX) – Update with Intent Exclusive** – as you would expect from the name, this occurs when a resource is currently locked with an update (U) lock, but a subsequent exclusive (X) lock is required as a part of the same transaction.

- **Schema** – schema locks are issued when an operation affecting the schema of the database is running:

  - **(Sch-S) Schema Stability** locks are issued when compiling a query on a database

  - **(Sch-M) Schema Modification** locks are granted when the underlying database schema is being modified by Data Definition Language queries (DDL).

Investigating locking

A single request to query or modify some data may cause multiple locks to be granted against several resources in the database. For example, consider the UPDATE statement below against the `Production.ProductCategory` table in the `AdventureWorks` database, shown in Listing 4.2.

```
BEGIN TRANSACTION
UPDATE [Production].[ProductCategory]
SET [Name] = 'Parts'
WHERE [Name] = 'Components';
--ROLLBACK TRANSACTION
```

Listing 4.2: An uncommitted update of the `Production` table in `AdventureWorks`.

A query against the `sys.dm_tran_locks` DMV, shown in Listing 4.3, will reveal the locks acquired in the `AdventureWorks` database, as a result of our uncommitted UPDATE.

```
SELECT   [resource_type] ,
         DB_NAME([resource_database_id]) AS [Database Name] ,
         CASE WHEN DTL.resource_type IN ( 'DATABASE', 'FILE', 'METADATA' )
              THEN DTL.resource_type
              WHEN DTL.resource_type = 'OBJECT'
              THEN OBJECT_NAME(DTL.resource_associated_entity_id,
                              DTL.[resource_database_id])
              WHEN DTL.resource_type IN ( 'KEY', 'PAGE', 'RID' )
              THEN ( SELECT  OBJECT_NAME([object_id])
                     FROM    sys.partitions
                     WHERE   sys.partitions.hobt_id =
                                        DTL.resource_associated_entity_id
                   )
              ELSE 'Unidentified'
         END AS requested_object_name ,
         [request_mode] ,
         [resource_description]
FROM     sys.dm_tran_locks DTL
WHERE    DTL.[resource_type] <> 'DATABASE' ;
```

Listing 4.3:   Locking due to single UPDATE statement against a user table in SQL Server.

The query is actually very straightforward, but made to look a little more intimidating by the CASE statement, where we return a value for the object name (or parent object name, when dealing with PAGE and KEY locks, in this case) for the locked resource. The way in which we need to do this depends on the type of lock being held. In the case of DATABASE, FILE, or METADATA locks, the query simply returns the value for the lock type. For OBJECT locks, the parent object is directly associated with the object_id. For PAGE, RID, or KEY locks, we need to look up the object_id associated to the object_id in the sys.partitions catalog view, by joining the hobt_id in that view to the resource_associated_entity_id in sys.dm_tran_locks. Each session on SQL Server also creates a DATABASE shared lock, which I've filtered out in the WHERE clause.

The output of the query is shown in Figure 4.2.

	resource_type	Database Name	requested_object_name	request_mode	resource_description
1	OBJECT	AdventureWorks	ProductCategory	IX	
2	PAGE	AdventureWorks	ProductCategory	IX	1:759
3	PAGE	AdventureWorks	ProductCategory	IX	1:1510
4	KEY	AdventureWorks	ProductCategory	X	(020068e8b274)
5	KEY	AdventureWorks	ProductCategory	X	(f801bc83f97e)
6	KEY	AdventureWorks	ProductCategory	X	(3501d000851f)

Figure 4.2: Locking results for the `AdventureWorks` database.

You'll note that locks are issued against multiple objects and at different granularities to allow for the update.

- An intent-exclusive lock is placed on the `ProductCategory` table denoting the intent to take exclusive locks lower in the hierarchy.

- Two pages (one in each of two indexes) are also granted intent-exclusive locks. The n:x notation in the `resource_description` column signifies the nth partition and the xth page in that partition, for a given `PAGE` lock.

- Three exclusive `KEY` locks are granted against the individual index keys. The values listed in `resource_description` are hashes of the key value.

When everyone plays by the rules this architecture works fairly well. However, situations arise when transactions don't release locks in a timely manner, due to I/O bottlenecks on the server, or when locks are held longer than they should be due to poorly coded T-SQL.

Reducing lock times

In this book, we must focus on the DMOs, so a full discussion of strategies for minimizing the length of time that locks are held is out of scope. SQL Server MVP Brad McGehee offers his take on reducing lock times in this post on SQLServerPerformance.com: HTTP://WWW.SQL-SERVER-PERFORMANCE.COM/TIPS/ REDUCING_LOCKS_P1.ASPX.

If, from a second tab in SSMS, we now run a second query, shown in Listing 4.4 (having neither committed nor rolled back the query in Listing 4.2), we'll introduce some blocking in the **AdventureWorks** database.

```
SELECT   *
FROM     [Production].[ProductCategory] ;
```

Listing 4.4: A simple query against the `ProductCategory` table, which will be blocked.

We'll present a more detailed script for detecting blocking in the next section, but the one in Listing 4.5 demonstrates the basic pattern for joining to the execution-related DMOs to find out which sessions are involved in blocking, which login "owns" these sessions, and what SQL statements they are executing.

```
SELECT   DTL.[request_session_id] AS [session_id] ,
         DB_NAME(DTL.[resource_database_id]) AS [Database] ,
         DTL.resource_type ,
         CASE WHEN DTL.resource_type IN ( 'DATABASE', 'FILE', 'METADATA' )
              THEN DTL.resource_type
              WHEN DTL.resource_type = 'OBJECT'
              THEN OBJECT_NAME(DTL.resource_associated_entity_id,
                             DTL.[resource_database_id])
              WHEN DTL.resource_type IN ( 'KEY', 'PAGE', 'RID' )
              THEN ( SELECT   OBJECT_NAME([object_id])
                     FROM     sys.partitions
                     WHERE    sys.partitions.hobt_id =
                                             DTL.resource_associated_entity_id
                   )
              ELSE 'Unidentified'
         END AS [Parent Object] ,
         DTL.request_mode AS [Lock Type] ,
         DTL.request_status AS [Request Status] ,
         DER.[blocking_session_id] ,
         DES.[login_name] ,
         CASE DTL.request_lifetime
           WHEN 0 THEN DEST_R.TEXT
           ELSE DEST_C.TEXT
         END AS [Statement]
FROM     sys.dm_tran_locks DTL
```

```
            LEFT JOIN sys.[dm_exec_requests] DER
                    ON DTL.[request_session_id] = DER.[session_id]
        INNER JOIN sys.dm_exec_sessions DES
                    ON DTL.request_session_id = DES.[session_id]
        INNER JOIN sys.dm_exec_connections DEC
                    ON DTL.[request_session_id] = DEC.[most_recent_session_id]
        OUTER APPLY sys.dm_exec_sql_text(DEC.[most_recent_sql_handle])
                                                    AS DEST_C
        OUTER APPLY sys.dm_exec_sql_text(DER.sql_handle) AS DEST_R
WHERE    DTL.[resource_database_id] = DB_ID()
         AND DTL.[resource_type] NOT IN ( 'DATABASE', 'METADATA' )
ORDER BY DTL.[request_session_id] ;
```

Listing 4.5: Which sessions are causing blocking and what statement are they running?

The result set returned is shown in Figure 4.3.

	session_id	Database	resource_type	Parent Object	Lock Type	Request Status	blocking_session_id
1	53	AdventureWorks	PAGE	ProductCategory	IS	GRANT	58
2	53	AdventureWorks	OBJECT	ProductCategory	IS	GRANT	58
3	53	AdventureWorks	KEY	ProductCategory	S	WAIT	58
4	58	AdventureWorks	KEY	ProductCategory	X	GRANT	NULL
5	58	AdventureWorks	KEY	ProductCategory	X	GRANT	NULL
6	58	AdventureWorks	OBJECT	ProductCategory	IX	GRANT	NULL
7	58	AdventureWorks	PAGE	ProductCategory	IX	GRANT	NULL
8	58	AdventureWorks	PAGE	ProductCategory	IX	GRANT	NULL
9	58	AdventureWorks	KEY	ProductCategory	X	GRANT	NULL

login_name	Statement
FordTrevor	SELECT * FROM [Production].[ProductCategory];
FordTrevor	SELECT * FROM [Production].[ProductCategory];
FordTrevor	SELECT * FROM [Production].[ProductCategory];
FordAusten	BEGIN TRANSACTION UPDATE [Production].[ProductCategory] SET [Name] = 'Parts' WHERE [Name] = 'Components';
FordAusten	BEGIN TRANSACTION UPDATE [Production].[ProductCategory] SET [Name] = 'Parts' WHERE [Name] = 'Components';
FordAusten	BEGIN TRANSACTION UPDATE [Production].[ProductCategory] SET [Name] = 'Parts' WHERE [Name] = 'Components';
FordAusten	BEGIN TRANSACTION UPDATE [Production].[ProductCategory] SET [Name] = 'Parts' WHERE [Name] = 'Components';
FordAusten	BEGIN TRANSACTION UPDATE [Production].[ProductCategory] SET [Name] = 'Parts' WHERE [Name] = 'Components';
FordAusten	BEGIN TRANSACTION UPDATE [Production].[ProductCategory] SET [Name] = 'Parts' WHERE [Name] = 'Components';

Figure 4.3: Locking and blocking results in AdventureWorks, based upon two sample transactions.

The **LEFT JOIN** in Listing 4.5 is necessary because the request no longer exists for the initial (blocking) **UPDATE** statement; although it is neither committed nor rolled back, execution is complete. Therefore, an **INNER JOIN** would omit those rows in the **sys.dm_tran_locks** view that refer to the updating query. This is also part of the reason why we need two **OUTER APPLY** joins to **sys.dm_exec_sql_text**: one using **sql_handle** from **sys.dm_exec_requests** and one using **sys.dm_exec_connections.most_recent_sql_handle**. Since the request no longer exists for the blocking update, **sys.dm_exec_connections** needs to supply the **sql_handle**.

Conversely, **sys.dm_exec_connections** (and **sys.dm_exec_sessions**) is only updated with cumulative values for such columns as **cpu_time**, **memory_usage**, and **sql_handle** *after* associated requests complete execution. The blocked query is still executing and so we can't rely on **SDEC.most_recent_sql_handle** for the command text of the live request. The acid test for deciding how to call **sys.dm_exec_sql_text** is the **request_lifetime** column in **sys.dm_tran_locks**. If **request_lifetime** is zero, it signifies that the request is still active and **sys.dm_exec_requests.sql_handle** should be used. Otherwise, the value needs to come from **sys.dm_exec_connections.most_recent_sql_handle**.

Blocking analysis using sys.dm_tran_locks and sys.dm_os_waiting_tasks

A certain amount of blocking activity is normal and to be expected in SQL Server. In the course of daily operation, SQL Server will intentionally prevent one process from accessing an object if another process has a lock on it, in order to preserve data integrity and present a consistent view of the data. The DBA always hopes that the lifespan of a request, i.e. the time between the first transaction starting to execute and the final commit for the last transaction associated with the request, is fleeting; more akin to the digital equivalent of the fruit fly than the tortoise. In such cases, blocking will generally be of the order of milliseconds and users will be unaffected by it.

In systems with many concurrent transactions, some degree of blocking is probably unavoidable, but the situation can be greatly exacerbated by transactions that are longer or more complex than is strictly dictated by the business requirements, or transactions that need to use more restrictive transaction isolation levels (such as REPEATABLE READ or SERIALIZABLE). In my experience as a DBA, the most common causes of these issues are listed below.

- **Poorly written transactions** – these include transactions that contain an unnecessarily high number of statements, and transactions that process an unnecessarily large amount of data due to lack of a WHERE clause, or predicates that are not as restrictive as they could be. The best query is one that makes as few passes through the data as possible, returns as few rows as is necessary, and only returns the columns required to satisfy the user's needs.

- **Poorly designed databases** – absent indexing, lack of foreign keys, incorrect or inadequate clustering keys, and poorly chosen data types may all lead to decreased concurrency and excessive blocking.

- **Poorly maintained databases** – fragmented indexes and outdated statistics can lead to suboptimal query execution, which causes locks to be held longer than is necessary, and results in table or index scans when a seek should, and could, be used.

- **Poorly designed applications** – in terms of crimes against databases committed by application code, I've seen it all: applications that request a batch of records from the database and iterate through the recordset row by row; applications that make almost exclusive use of SELECT *... queries; applications that submit ad hoc SQL code and make no use of stored procedures or other optimized processes. In many cases, particularly when hosting the database for third-party applications, the DBA cannot alter the code and has little influence over getting it fixed

All of this leads to transactions that take longer than necessary to complete, hold locks for longer than necessary, and so cause significant blocking of other transactions.

When investigating blocking issues as a DBA, what we really need is a clear, single page of data that shows the transactions involved in blocking, including the actual SQL statements within those transactions, the sessions to which these transactions belong, and the users who own these sessions.

In order to achieve this, we can start our investigation at the **sys.dm_os_ waiting_tasks** DMV. This DMV returns one row for each task that is waiting for a resource to become available before proceeding (i.e. is blocked). Armed with a **session_ id** for any tasks that are currently waiting, we can use the **resource_address** column in this DMV to join back to the **lock_owner_address** column in the **sys.dm_tran_ locks** DMV, and so relate the waiting tasks information to information on the locks that are being held. Initially, it might seem more logical to join on **session_id** rather than **resource_address**, but remember that the goal is to determine what *resource* contention is occurring; what resource is locked and therefore causing waits for other sessions that need to acquire locks on the object in contention.

From here, we can join to other session/transaction-related views in order to arrive, ultimately, at a big picture overview of locks that may be causing blocking problems, the sessions and statements that caused those locks to be acquired and those that are blocked as a result. The resulting script, shown in Listing 4.6, will present both the blocking and blocked requests on the same row, and so provide a very easy way to spot, analyze, and diagnose blocking issues.

```
USE [AdventureWorks] ;
GO
SELECT  DTL.[resource_type] AS [resource type] ,
        CASE WHEN DTL.[resource_type] IN ( 'DATABASE', 'FILE', 'METADATA' )
            THEN DTL.[resource_type]
            WHEN DTL.[resource_type] = 'OBJECT'
            THEN OBJECT_NAME(DTL.resource_associated_entity_id)
            WHEN DTL.[resource_type] IN ( 'KEY', 'PAGE', 'RID' )
            THEN ( SELECT  OBJECT_NAME([object_id])
                FROM    sys.partitions
                WHERE   sys.partitions.[hobt_id] =
                        DTL.[resource_associated_entity_id]
            )
```

```
               ELSE 'Unidentified'
           END AS [Parent Object] ,
           DTL.[request_mode] AS [Lock Type] ,
           DTL.[request_status] AS [Request Status] ,
           DOWT.[wait_duration_ms] AS [wait duration ms] ,
           DOWT.[wait_type] AS [wait type] ,
           DOWT.[session_id] AS [blocked session id] ,
           DES_blocked.[login_name] AS [blocked_user] ,
           SUBSTRING(dest_blocked.text, der.statement_start_offset / 2,
                   ( CASE WHEN der.statement_end_offset = -1
                        THEN DATALENGTH(dest_blocked.text)
                        ELSE der.statement_end_offset
                   END - der.statement_start_offset ) / 2
                                          AS [blocked_command] ,
           DOWT.[blocking_session_id] AS [blocking session id] ,
           DES_blocking.[login_name] AS [blocking user] ,
           DEST_blocking.[text] AS [blocking command] ,
           DOWT.resource_description AS [blocking resource detail]
FROM       sys.dm_tran_locks DTL
           INNER JOIN sys.dm_os_waiting_tasks DOWT
                   ON DTL.lock_owner_address = DOWT.resource_address
           INNER JOIN sys.[dm_exec_requests] DER
                   ON DOWT.[session_id] = DER.[session_id]
           INNER JOIN sys.dm_exec_sessions DES_blocked
                   ON DOWT.[session_id] = DES_Blocked.[session_id]
           INNER JOIN sys.dm_exec_sessions DES_blocking
                   ON DOWT.[blocking_session_id] = DES_Blocking.[session_id]
           INNER JOIN sys.dm_exec_connections DEC
                   ON DTL.[request_session_id] = DEC.[most_recent_session_id]
           CROSS APPLY sys.dm_exec_sql_text(DEC.[most_recent_sql_handle])
                                                   AS DEST_Blocking
           CROSS APPLY sys.dm_exec_sql_text(DER.sql_handle) AS DEST_Blocked
WHERE      DTL.[resource_database_id] = DB_ID()
```

Listing 4.6: Investigating locking and blocking based on waiting tasks.

To see it in action, we'll set up some activity on the Production.Culture table of the AdventureWorks database. It's a narrow table with three columns and two indexes, one clustered index on the primary key and one unique non-clustered index on the Name column. Additionally, there is a DEFAULT constraint on the ModifiedDate column that sets the value to the results of the getdate() function.

Open a tab in SSMS and execute the query shown in Listing 4.7. This is our blocking session.

```
BEGIN TRANSACTION
UPDATE   Production.Culture
SET      Name = 'English-British'
WHERE    Name = 'English' ;
--ROLLBACK TRANSACTION
```

Listing 4.7:   An uncommitted UPDATE transaction on the Production.Culture table.

In a separate session, execute the code in Listing 4.8, to read data from the same table.

```
SELECT   ModifiedDate
FROM     Production.Culture
WHERE    Name = 'English' ;
```

Listing 4.8:   A blocked query against the Production.Culture table.

Finally, in a third session, INSERT a new value into the same table and then read the table.

```
INSERT   INTO Production.Culture
         ( CultureID, Name )
VALUES   ( 'jp', 'Japanese' ) ;

SELECT   *
FROM     Production.Culture ;
```

Listing 4.9:   An INSERT against the Production.Culture table.

Having executed all three queries, run the DMO script in Listing 4.6. What we expect to see is that the UPDATE query blocks both subsequent SELECT queries from the other sessions, but not the INSERT, as confirmed by the results shown in Figure 4.4.

	resource type	Parent Object	Lock Type	Request Status	wait duration ms	wait type
1	KEY	Culture	S	WAIT	81059	LCK_M_S
2	KEY	Culture	S	WAIT	104271	LCK_M_S

	blocked session id	blocked_user	blocked command
1	53	FordAmy	SELECT * FROM Production.[Culture] PC;
2	54	FordAusten	SELECT [ModifiedDate] FROM [Production].[Cultur...

	blocking session id	blocking user
1	55	FordTrevor
2	55	FordTrevor

blocking command	blocking resource detail
INSERT INTO Production.[Culture] ([CultureID], [Name...	keylock hobtid=72057594044088320 dbid=7 id=lock86b8a00 mode=X
(@1 varchar(8000))SELECT [ModifiedDate] FROM [Pr...	keylock hobtid=72057594048937984 dbid=7 id=lock86b8ec0 mode=X

Figure 4.4: Blocking in AdventureWorks.

This script is one of my favorites; it provides exactly what I need to know. The first half of the results displays information regarding who and what is being blocked, while the second half of the results provides metrics regarding who and what is doing the blocking.

The final column, resource_description (aliased in the results as *blocking resource detail*) provides a value that concatenates the lock type, object type and id, database id, lock id, lock type, and parent/associated object id for the lock. Quite a bit of information for a single column wouldn't you say? This is a result of the denormalized nature of the information that this column stores. The problem is in parsing the values in it; any universal process to do so is undocumented at this time, and we can only hope that at some point (SQL 11 perhaps) Microsoft makes it easier to parse the information, or normalizes the information by adding columns to sys.dm_os_waiting_tasks.

The value of the script really becomes evident when one encounters a multi-session blocking situation. Figure 4.5 shows how it can reveal a real-life blocking chain (one I encountered just today on one of my servers). I've omitted all security and identifier columns for my environment, but the remaining data is real.

	resource type	Parent Object	Lock Type	Request Status	wait duration ms	wait type	blocked session id	blocking session id
1	KEY	FldCfg	U	WAIT	34270500	LCK_M_U	63 →	65
2	KEY	FldCfg	U	WAIT	34270500	LCK_M_U	63 →	65
3	KEY	FldCfg	U	WAIT	83719	LCK_M_U	78	63
4	KEY	FldCfg	U	WAIT	1208422	LCK_M_U	70	78
5	KEY	FldCfg	U	WAIT	1208422	LCK_M_U	111	70
6	KEY	FldCfg	U	WAIT	1208407	LCK_M_U	87	70
7	KEY	FldCfg	U	WAIT	1003735	LCK_M_U	89	87
8	KEY	FldCfg	U	WAIT	1000235	LCK_M_U	120	89
9	KEY	FldCfg	U	WAIT	963891	LCK_M_U	93	89
10	KEY	FldCfg	U	WAIT	950391	LCK_M_U	124	89
11	KEY	FldCfg	U	WAIT	781000	LCK_M_U	128	89
12	KEY	FldCfg	U	WAIT	283188	LCK_M_U	52	89
13	KEY	FldCfg	U	WAIT	226735	LCK_M_U	88	89
14	KEY	FldCfg	U	WAIT	181844	LCK_M_U	115	89
15	KEY	FldCfg	U	WAIT	160985	LCK_M_U	122	89
16	KEY	FldCfg	U	WAIT	156157	LCK_M_U	123	89
17	KEY	FldCfg	U	WAIT	146219	LCK_M_U	127	89
18	KEY	FldCfg	U	WAIT	115719	LCK_M_U	86	89
19	KEY	AudRaw	S	WAIT	33372454	LCK_M_S	69 →	65

Figure 4.5: A real-life blocking chain.

Session 65 was blocking Session 63 which, in turn, blocked Session 78, which blocked 70, which blocked both 111 and 87. Session 87 blocked Session 89 which, in turn, blocked about ten other sessions. My DMO script revealed that Session 65 was the root cause of the blocking, and the command text returned for this session revealed that I could safely kill that session. Having done so, and by the time I switched query windows in SSMS to re-execute the DMO query, the results were clean. All blocking had been resolved.

Analyzing Transactional Activity

There are three DMVs that allow us to monitor active transactions on our SQL Server instances and, in particular, long-running transactions, as well as those transaction that are causing the transaction log to grow rapidly:

- **sys.dm_tran_session_transactions** – is primarily an intermediate view that allows us to join the `sys.dm_exec` DMVs (identified primarily on the `session_id` column) with the other `sys.dm_tran_*` DMVs

- **sys.dm_tran_active_transactions** – stores transactional information relating to status, type, and state of each transaction currently initiated but not yet completed, on the SQL instance; it also provides information on distributed transactions, though some of the DTC-centric columns have been deprecated in SQL Server 2008

- **sys.dm_tran_database_transactions** – stores much of the same information in regard to transaction state, status, and type; but also provides extremely granular transaction log metrics and record count and size metadata.

Over the coming sections we'll very briefly review some of the more interesting columns in these DMVs, and then provide some sample troubleshooting scripts. Please refer to the relevant section of Books Online (HTTP://MSDN.MICROSOFT.COM/EN-US/LIBRARY/MS178621. ASPX) for a full column description of each DMV.

Transactional DMOs vs. DBCC OPENTRAN

Prior to SQL Server 2005, most DBAs used the DBCC OPENTRAN command to return information regarding currently open transactions on their SQL Server instances. I continue to use DBCC OPENTRAN for the purpose for which it was designed: to provide information about the oldest transaction still active in a specific database. This tool is a one-trick pony, however. The scripts we're going to use based upon the DMVs provide a wealth of extra information. For more information on the syntax and use of DBCC

OPENTRAN please visit Microsoft Books Online: HTTP://MSDN.MICROSOFT.COM/EN-US/LIBRARY/MS182792.ASPX.

sys.dm_tran_session_transactions

As stated, this view is used primarily for joining the **sys.dm_exec_*** DMVs introduced in *Chapter 2* to the **sys.dm_tran_*** DMVs we're discussing here.

- **session_id** – identifies which session the transaction belongs to. The **session_id** may be the most important column for this particular DMV as it allows us to join transactional metadata with, for example, the execution-related DMOs covered in *Chapter 2*, as well as the **sys.sysprocesses** system compatibility view (as **spid**).

- **transaction_id** – just as **session_id** allows us to join back to the various **sys.dm_exec_** DMVs, so **transaction_id** allows the join to the myriad of **sys.dm_tran_** DMVs we discuss in this chapter. This provides the link between sessions and transactions, from a logical perspective, allowing the DBA to make associations between user sessions and requests and the transactions they run, in terms of their activity, characteristics, and locking behavior.

The only other column that we'll mention here is **is_user_transaction**, which denotes whether the transaction is a user-initiated transaction (1) or a system transaction (0). This is particularly valuable when we wish to isolate only user transactions. Other columns allow us to exclude or isolate distributed, enlisted, or bound transactions, as required by our circumstances.

Listing 4.10 illustrates a very simple query against this DMV, just to illustrate the sort of result set returned for current transactions on the active session.

```
BEGIN TRANSACTION
SELECT  DTST.[session_id] ,
        DTST.[transaction_id] ,
        DTST.[is_user_transaction]
FROM    sys.[dm_tran_session_transactions] AS DTST
WHERE   DTST.[session_id] = @@SPID
ORDER BY DTST.[transaction_id]
COMMIT
```

```
session_id  transaction_id       is_user_transaction
----------- -------------------- --------------------
56          1550381              1

(1 row(s) affected)
```

Listing 4.10: Basic query against `sys.dm_tran_session_transactions` for transactions on the current session.

sys.dm_tran_active_transactions

The `sys.dm_tran_active_transactions` DMV returns a list of all transactions that are active at the time the query is executed. This view operates at the scope of the entire SQL instance, meaning that results are returned for all databases on the instance. Since this view provides a point-in-time snapshot of currently active transactions, the results will change each time the query is executed, depending upon the state of the individual transactions.

Identification columns returned by this view are `transaction_id`, which uniquely identifies a transaction across the entire SQL Server instance, and `name`, which is the name of the transaction. I consider it a good habit, if not a best practice, to name transactions, as the following code snippet demonstrates:

```
BEGIN TRANSACTION Trans_Name
--Some SQL Code goes here
COMMIT TRANSACTION Trans_Name
```

143

In this example, `Trans_Name` will be returned as the value for the `name` column for this record in **sys.dm_tran_active_transactions**, assuming the transaction is still active when you issue a query against this DMV. If the transaction is not explicitly named, this column will be populated by values such as **SELECT, INSERT, UPDATE, DELETE** in the case of those Data Modification Language (DML) transactions. You'll also see **Worktable** as a value when returning results from **tempdb** for the hashing and temp/intermediate transactional processing that occurs there. Finally, you will see the value of **DTCXACT** for unnamed distributed transactions.

This DMV also returns the time that the transaction was started (`transaction_begin_time`), as well as columns that identify the type (`transaction_type`) and state (`transaction_state`, or `dtc_state` for distributed transactions). These type and state columns return integer values, the meanings of which are deciphered in the sample query shown in Listing 4.11.

```
SELECT    DTAT.transaction_id ,
          DTAT.[name] ,
          DTAT.transaction_begin_time ,
          CASE DTAT.transaction_type
            WHEN 1 THEN 'Read/write'
            WHEN 2 THEN 'Read-only'
            WHEN 3 THEN 'System'
            WHEN 4 THEN 'Distributed'
          END AS transaction_type ,
          CASE DTAT.transaction_state
            WHEN 0 THEN 'Not fully initialized'
            WHEN 1 THEN 'Initialized, not started'
            WHEN 2 THEN 'Active'
            WHEN 3 THEN 'Ended' -- only applies to read-only transactions
            WHEN 4 THEN 'Commit initiated'-- distributed transactions only
            WHEN 5 THEN 'Prepared, awaiting resolution'
            WHEN 6 THEN 'Committed'
            WHEN 7 THEN 'Rolling back'
            WHEN 8 THEN 'Rolled back'
          END AS transaction_state ,
          CASE DTAT.dtc_state
            WHEN 1 THEN 'Active'
            WHEN 2 THEN 'Prepared'
```

```
            WHEN 3 THEN 'Committed'
            WHEN 4 THEN 'Aborted'
            WHEN 5 THEN 'Recovered'
        END AS dtc_state
FROM      sys.dm_tran_active_transactions DTAT
        INNER JOIN sys.dm_tran_session_transactions DTST
                        ON DTAT.transaction_id = DTST.transaction_id
WHERE     [DTST].[is_user_transaction] = 1
ORDER BY DTAT.transaction_begin_time
```

Listing 4.11: Querying sys.dm_db_tran_active_transactions.

Notice that we are able to isolate user transactions via a join back to sys.dm_tran_session_transactions, filtering on the is_user_transaction column. The results of this query are shown in Figure 4.6.

	transaction_id	name	transaction_begin_time	transaction_type	transaction_state	dtc_state
1	6288623412	implicit_transaction	2010-06-24 12:20:20.247	Read/write	Active	NULL
2	6302973892	UPDATE	2010-06-24 13:59:30.250	Read/write	Active	NULL
3	6302973893	implicit_transaction	2010-06-24 13:59:30.250	Read/write	Active	NULL

Figure 4.6: Currently active user transactions.

Had we not filtered out transactions associated with system sessions, we'd also have seen results for hash work being performed in tempdb, similar to the record shown in Figure 4.7.

	transaction_id	name	transaction_begin_time	transaction_type	transaction_state	dtc_state
1	5156	worktable	2010-05-23 15:01:30.673	Read-only	Active	NULL

Figure 4.7: Worktable transaction records in sys.dm_db_tran_active_transactions.

Queries against sys.dm_tran_active_transactions will often return a great number of results that look like this, since these worktables are created and destroyed all the time on our SQL instances as a result of sorting and hashing intermediate results sets before returning them to an end-user.

An alternative way to eliminate the worktables would be to add a predicate to the name column, as the code snippet in Listing 4.12 demonstrates.

```
...
FROM sys.dm_tran_active_transactions DTAT
WHERE DTAT.name <> 'worktable'
ORDER BY DTAT.transaction_begin_time
```

Listing 4.12: Eliminating worktables from the results returned by `active_transactions`.

While information regarding the transaction start time, type and the current state of the transaction may be valuable, it is rare to query this DMV in isolation, as it provides an incomplete picture of transactional activity. We cannot tell, for example, the databases on which these transactions are running, the sessions or users that are running them, or the statements that comprise each transaction. To retrieve this information, we'll need to join DMVs via the `transaction_id` column, as will be demonstrated shortly.

sys.dm_tran_database_transactions

The `sys.dm_tran_database_transactions` DMV is server-scoped (the name is deceptive) and provides detailed information about the transactions occurring on your SQL Server instance. Like the `sys.dm_db_tran_active_transactions` view, it provides point-in-time snapshot data, so the results may vary each time the view is queried. A cursory glance at the available columns may lead one to assume that the data returned will be similar to that provided by the `sys.dm_tran_active_transactions` view. In fact, however, `sys.dm_tran_database_transactions` provides a much more granular level of detail about each transaction and gives "physical presence" to a transaction, in that it returns information about how it is using the transaction log file.

Alongside a `transaction_id` column, the DMV exposes a `database_id` column, which identifies the database to which the transaction is associated. Occasionally, for example, when isolating issues associated with just those databases using a particular isolation level or recovery model, it is useful to use this column to join to the `sys. database` system catalog view in order to return such columns as the `snapshot_ isolation_state`, `recovery_model`, and so on. The `database_id` column can also be used as the sole parameter of the `DB_NAME()` function, in order to return the name of the database.

Like the `active_transactions` DMV, the `database_transactions` DMV also exposes columns describing the type (`database_transaction_type`) and state (`database_transaction_state`) of a transaction. The integer values returned must be "decoded" in our queries, as demonstrated for the state column by the code snippet in Listing 4.13.

```
CASE SDTDT.database_transaction_state
    WHEN 1 THEN 'Not initialized'
    WHEN 3 THEN 'initialized, but not producing log records'
    WHEN 4 THEN 'Producing log records'
    WHEN 5 THEN 'Prepared'
    WHEN 10 THEN 'Committed'
    WHEN 11 THEN 'Rolled back'
    WHEN 12 THEN 'Commit in process'
```

Listing 4.13: Decoding the integer values returned by `database_transaction_state`.

Below is a list of some of the other important columns available through `sys.dm_tran_ database_transactions` that allow us to investigate long-running transactions, as well as use and abuse of the transaction log.

database_transaction_begin_time – time at which the transaction began producing log records. Note that this may not be the same as the time when the transaction was initiated, as there may be a delay between a transaction being initiated and it starting processing, if required resources are locked or if there is a wait for server resources such as CPU.

- **`database_transaction_log_record_count`** – number of log records for the transaction at the time the query executed. Note that, if the value of `database_transaction_state` is 5 or less, the transaction will still be producing log records, so the value of `database_transaction_log_record_count` will not be equal to the total number of records that will be generated by the transaction.

- **`database_transaction_log_bytes_used`** – amount of bytes this transaction currently contributes to the total used in the transaction log for the database.

- **`database_transaction_log_bytes_reserved`** – bytes reserved in the log for this transaction.

- **`database_transaction_begin_lsn`**, **`database_transaction_last_lsn`** – Log Sequence Number (LSN) of the first and last records in the log for this transaction.

- **`database_transaction_most_recent_savepoint_lsn`** – if savepoints are used, this is the most recent one that can be rolled back to. Savepoints are not discussed further in this book, but see Microsoft Books Online: HTTP://MSDN.MICROSOFT.COM/EN-US/LIBRARY/MS181299.ASPX.

- **`database_transaction_commit_lsn`** – the LSN that recorded the commit for the transaction.

- **`database_transaction_last_rollback_lsn`** – if a rollback has occurred, this is the most recent LSN that the transaction was rolled back to. If there was no rollback, the value will be the last LSN recorded in the log.

- **`database_transaction_next_undo_lsn`** – during the undo portion of a recovery, this will be the LSN to be rolled back (undone).

Assessing transaction log impact

The sys.dm_tran_database_transactions DMV is the only one that provides insight into the effects of user activity on the database transaction logs. Using this DMV, and joining across to other transaction-related and execution-related DMVs, as described previously, we can develop a query, shown in Listing 4.14, which will identify all active transactions and their physical effect on the databases' transaction logs. This is especially useful when seeking out transactions that may be causing explosive transaction log growth.

```
SELECT DTST.[session_id],
  DES.[login_name] AS [Login Name],
  DB_NAME (DTDT.database_id) AS [Database],
  DTDT.[database_transaction_begin_time] AS [Begin Time],
  -- DATEDIFF(ms,DTDT.[database_transaction_begin_time], GETDATE()) AS [Duration
ms],
  CASE DTAT.transaction_type
    WHEN 1 THEN 'Read/write'
    WHEN 2 THEN 'Read-only'
    WHEN 3 THEN 'System'
    WHEN 4 THEN 'Distributed'
  END AS [Transaction Type],
  CASE DTAT.transaction_state
    WHEN 0 THEN 'Not fully initialized'
    WHEN 1 THEN 'Initialized, not started'
    WHEN 2 THEN 'Active'
    WHEN 3 THEN 'Ended'
    WHEN 4 THEN 'Commit initiated'
    WHEN 5 THEN 'Prepared, awaiting resolution'
    WHEN 6 THEN 'Committed'
    WHEN 7 THEN 'Rolling back'
    WHEN 8 THEN 'Rolled back'
  END AS [Transaction State],
  DTDT.[database_transaction_log_record_count] AS [Log Records],
  DTDT.[database_transaction_log_bytes_used] AS [Log Bytes Used],
  DTDT.[database_transaction_log_bytes_reserved] AS [Log Bytes RSVPd],
  DEST.[text] AS [Last Transaction Text],
  DEQP.[query_plan] AS [Last Query Plan]
FROM sys.dm_tran_database_transactions DTDT
```

```
INNER JOIN sys.dm_tran_session_transactions DTST
  ON DTST.[transaction_id] = DTDT.[transaction_id]
INNER JOIN sys.[dm_tran_active_transactions] DTAT
  ON DTST.[transaction_id] = DTAT.[transaction_id]
INNER JOIN sys.[dm_exec_sessions] DES
  ON DES.[session_id] = DTST.[session_id]
INNER JOIN sys.dm_exec_connections DEC
  ON DEC.[session_id] = DTST.[session_id]
LEFT JOIN sys.dm_exec_requests DER
  ON DER.[session_id] = DTST.[session_id]
CROSS APPLY sys.dm_exec_sql_text (DEC.[most_recent_sql_handle]) AS DEST
OUTER APPLY sys.dm_exec_query_plan (DER.[plan_handle]) AS DEQP
ORDER BY DTDT.[database_transaction_log_bytes_used] DESC;
-- ORDER BY [Duration ms] DESC;
```

Listing 4.14: Transaction log impact of active transactions.

Note the use of OUTER APPLY to join to `sys.dm_exec_query_plan`. The OUTER APPLY functions as a hybrid of OUTER JOIN and CROSS APPLY in that it will return NULL if no value is returned by the function. This prevents the entire row from being excluded from the result set in cases where a plan does not exist for the request (the request may no longer exist in `sys.dm_exec_requests` by the time Listing 4.14 is run). Sample output from this listing is shown in Figure 4.8.

	Login Name	Database	Begin Time	Transaction Type	Transaction State
1	DOMAIN\tomsawyer	Cygnus_x1	2010-06-29 20:22:58.163	Read/write	Active

	Log Records	Log Bytes Used	Log Bytes RSVPd	Last Transaction Text
1	12831	1768316	1853432	(@P1 int)delete from dbo.demo_table where fk_madrigal = @P1

	Last Query Plan
1	<ShowPlanXML xmlns="http://schemas.microsoft.com/sqlserver/2004/07/showplan" Version="1.0'

Figure 4.8: Transactions writing heavily to the transaction log.

Simply by un-commenting the calculation of the transaction duration in Listing 4.14, and swapping the ORDER BY clause, we can investigate the activity of long-running transactions that may be bloating the transaction log file, or preventing it from being truncated.

Snapshot Isolation and the tempdb Version Store

The snapshot isolation level was introduced in SQL Server 2005 and eliminates blocking and deadlocking by using row versioning in the tempdb database to maintain concurrency, rather than establishing locks on database objects. As such, the goal of snapshot isolation is increased performance through greater concurrency. Snapshot isolation is a huge topic and we can do little more than provide a brief overview here. Please see Microsoft Books Online or MSDN for further details on isolation levels, concurrency, and locking models.

Each time a row is modified in a database running under snapshot isolation, a version of the row from prior to the modification is stored within tempdb in a **version store**. In other words, this version store is populated with versions of data rows as they existed before the initialization of an explicit transaction. The version store is shared by all databases that are running under snapshot isolation on the SQL Server instance.

Read transactions targeting the affected rows will use the row version(s) from the tempdb, while the writing transaction will modify the actual table data. Update locks are issued for writes, and when a read transaction encounters such a lock, it is diverted to the version store.

This row-versioning mechanism ensures that write transactions do not block reads. It is no longer necessary to take exclusive locks on data being modified, to prevent dirty reads, because the reads are made against versions of the rows that were in a committed state from prior to the transaction or statement initialization. It also means that readers do not block writers, since read transactions will no longer take shared read locks.

Any DML queries will continue to block other DML queries as is necessary to maintain data integrity.

SNAPSHOT and READ_COMMITTED_SNAPSHOT modes

Snapshot isolation introduces two new modes of operation:

- **SNAPSHOT** mode isolates read transactions from modifications that committed after the transaction began

- **READ_COMMITTED_SNAPSHOT** mode isolates read transactions from modifications which committed after the current statement began.

SNAPSHOT mode is initiated at the database level using Listing 4.15.

```
ALTER DATABASE Test SET ALLOW_SNAPSHOT_ISOLATION ON;
```

Listing 4.15: Enabling snapshot isolation at the database level.

Note that this command only instructs the database to begin using a version store within tempdb. It does not affect the behavior of any sessions running against the database. Any session using the default **READ COMMITTED** level will continue to operate as normal, unless to use the version store and take advantage of snapshot isolation, by issuing the command in Listing 4.16, from within the session.

```
SET TRANSACTION ISOLATION LEVEL SNAPSHOT;
```

Listing 4.16: Enabling SNAPSHOT isolation mode for a given session.

The requirement to set the **SNAPSHOT** isolation level on each session is unrealistic; much of the code used to access a database is compiled and inaccessible to the Database Administrator. If this was the only method for changing the default **READ COMMITTED** isolation level behavior for SQL Server sessions, it would be nearly useless in a production environment. Fortunately, we can alter the default **READ COMMITTED** behavior globally for a given database, using the **READ_COMMITTED_SNAPSHOT** mode.

The **READ_COMMITTED_SNAPSHOT** mode is enabled at the database level using Listing 4.16. Be warned, though – you must have exclusive access to the database when setting **READ_COMMITTED_SNAPSHOT**. Any active sessions against the database will block this command from running.

```
ALTER DATABASE Test SET READ_COMMITTED_SNAPSHOT ON;
```

Listing 4.17: Enabling READ_COMMITTED_SNAPSHOT mode for a database.

Unlike **SNAPSHOT** mode, enabling **READ_COMMITTED_SNAPSHOT** affects the default session behavior for all sessions against the database. At this point, any sessions that are running under the default **READ COMMITTED** mode will actually be running under **READ_COMMITTED_SNAPSHOT**. The transactions in these sessions will no longer take shared read locks when reading data, and will instead use the version store to obtain a consistent point-in-time view of that data at the time the current statement in the transaction began.

Listing 4.18 will let you know which databases on your instance are running under **SNAPSHOT** or **READ_COMMITTED_SNAPSHOT** isolation.

```
SELECT   SD.[name] ,
         SD.snapshot_isolation_state_desc ,
         SD.is_read_committed_snapshot_on
FROM     sys.databases SD
WHERE    SD.snapshot_isolation_state_desc = 'ON'
```

Listing 4.18: Which databases are using snapshot isolation?

Sample output is shown in Figure 4.9.

	name	snapshot_isolation_state_desc	is_read_committed_snapshot_on
1	master	ON	0
2	msdb	ON	0
3	AdventureWorksDW2008	ON	0
4	AdventureWorks	ON	1
5	AdventureWorksDW	ON	0

Figure 4.9:   Master and msdb databases always run under snapshot isolation.

Note that this query will return a minimum of two rows, since both **master** and **msdb** run under **SNAPSHOT** isolation. Concurrency is extremely important in these two system databases because so many crucial actions require rapid reads against them, in order to keep SQL Server and SQL Server Agent running. For example, SQL Server accesses the master database every time it needs to perform a restore, check rights and validate a login's password, or maintain mirroring or log shipping. If it were forced to wait for shared read locks to be released before proceeding, SQL Server would grind to a halt!

Investigating snapshot isolation

While the use of snapshot isolation can be beneficial in terms of improving the concurrency, its use does, of course, lead to increased storage requirements, and higher traffic in **tempdb**. It is important to be able to investigate the effects on **tempdb** and to monitor the objects that are causing the most version-generating activity, and the impact of snapshot isolation on the SQL instance as a whole.

The proactive DBA will wish to know which objects are producing the most records in the version store within `tempdb` for databases running under snapshot isolation, as well as version store space associated with online index rebuilds and possibly trigger usage.

SQL Server provides five DMVs for the investigation of snapshot activity on an instance, three of which provide a point-in-time view of current snapshot activity, and two of which provide cumulative data regarding use of the version store.

DMVs for current snapshot activity

The three DMVs that provide a snapshot of a specific point in time in the instance's history are:

- **sys.dm_tran_active_snapshot_database_transactions**
- **sys.dm_tran_currrent_snapshot**
- **sys.dm_tran_transactions_snapshot**

In each case, in order to review the results of these DMVs, you must either be a member of the sysadmins server role or have been granted **VIEW SERVER STATE** permission.

sys.dm_tran_active_snapshot_database_transactions

In Books Online this DMV is described as follows:

> *In a SQL Server instance, this dynamic management view returns a virtual table for all active transactions that generate or potentially access row versions.*

In other words, it returns records for all active transactions that either create or read row versions from the version store in `tempdb`. It is an instance-level view, and so will return rows for transactions using snapshot isolation for all databases on a given instance.

However, version store usage is not limited to just sessions running under snapshot isolation, but also occurs as a result of triggers, online indexing, or the use of MARS (Multiple Active Results Sets – see Books Online for details). Triggers were the first SQL Server construct to make use of row versioning. DML triggers make use of temporary, non-materialized tables that mimic the structure of the tables upon which they are based. There is both an `inserted` and a `deleted` table. The `inserted` table stores versions of the rows affected by an `INSERT` or `UPDATE` query; specifically, the new rows added to the underlying (trigger) table. The `deleted` table stores a copy of the records deleted from the underlying table via a `DELETE` statement. Both tables are hit in the case of an `UPDATE` statement, as an `UPDATE` is nothing more than a `DELETE` followed by an `INSERT`. The rows are first moved from the underlying table to the deleted "virtual table." Then the new rows are added to the `inserted` "virtual table" after being added to the underlying table. In the case of online indexing, available as a benefit of licensing Enterprise Edition SQL Server 2005 and 2008, row versioning is used to maintain concurrency during the online indexing process. All these transactions will be noted in a query against `sys.dm_tran_active_snapshot_database_transactions`.

In terms of identifier columns, this DMV provides a **transaction_id** column, which identifies the transaction at the instance level and can be used to join to other transaction-related DMOs. It also provides a **session_id** column, which identifies the session with which the transaction is associated and can be used to join to execution-related DMOs, as well as to `spid` in `sys.sysprocesses`. Other relevant columns include:

- **transaction_sequence_num** – for transactions that access or modify the version store; this is a sequence number given to the transaction the first time it reads or writes to the version store; Transaction Sequence Numbers (XSNs) increment serially for each transaction

- **commit_sequence_num** – indicates the order that the transaction was committed; will be **NULL** if the transaction is still active

- **is_snapshot**

  - I if this is a **SNAPSHOT** isolation level transaction

  - o if it is in here for a different reason, such as a **READ_COMMITTED_SNAPSHOT** transaction.

- **first_snapshot_sequence_num** – the lowest active **transaction_sequence_num** value of any of the transactions that were active when the current **SNAPSHOT** transaction was started (any subsequent XSNs would need to be preserved for this transaction's use; column displays o for non-**SNAPSHOT** transactions

- **elapsed_time_seconds** – elapsed time since this transaction acquired XSN.

sys.dm_tran_current_snapshot

This single-column DMV returns the **transaction_sequence_num** of all the active transactions in the version store relevant to the current transaction at the time the current **SNAPSHOT** transaction started. No results are returned if the current transaction is not a **SNAPSHOT** transaction.

In and of itself, this DMV does not provide much information for the DBA. I find it pertinent only for running an **IF EXISTS** query to determine if there is valid row versioning occurring when I am about to execute a query against a snapshot-enabled database.

sys.dm_tran_transactions_snapshot

The final non-aggregate DMV pertaining to snapshot isolation is **sys.dm_tran_transactions_snapshot**. The results are a superset of those that are returned for **sys.dm_tran_current_snapshot**. It returns the active snapshots for all sessions, not just the current one. It returns the `transaction_sequence_num`, as described previously, plus two others:

- **snapshot_id** – used for T-SQL transactions started in the READ COMMITTED isolation level when the READ_COMMITTED_SNAPSHOT option is enabled for a database; whereas SNAPSHOT isolation works at the transaction level, READ_COMMITTED_SNAPSHOT works at the statement level, as will be demonstrated shortly

- **snapshot_sequence_num** – lists any `transaction_sequence_num` values that were active when this transaction first started.

The results provide you with a chaining scheme within the version store and determine what row versions (via `transaction_sequence_num`) are being used as the basis of active transactions relying upon the version store.

So, for example, in Figure 4.10 we have two active snapshot transactions, 77 and 80. When XSN 77 was started, there were two transactions active that were using the version store and the results of which could affect what was returned by XSN 77; when XSN 80 started, there were four.

	transaction_sequence_num	snapshot_id	snapshot_sequence_num
1	77	0	75
2	77	0	76
3	80	0	75
4	80	0	76
5	80	0	77
6	80	0	78

Figure 4.10: Relating XSNs to the snapshot sequence numbers that were active at the time the given XSN was created.

Current snapshot activity

To provide a quick demonstration of how snapshot isolation works, and how to track current activity using the DMOs, let's create a small test database called DMV, containing an inexact copy of the Production.Culture table from the AdventureWorks database, with only three rows.

```
CREATE TABLE [dbo].[Culture]
    (
        [CultureID] [nchar](6) NOT NULL ,
        [Name] NVARCHAR(50) NOT NULL ,
        [ModifiedDate] [datetime] NOT NULL ,
        CONSTRAINT [PK_Culture_CultureID] PRIMARY KEY CLUSTERED
            ( [CultureID] ASC )
            WITH ( PAD_INDEX = OFF, STATISTICS_NORECOMPUTE = OFF,
                    IGNORE_DUP_KEY = OFF, ALLOW_ROW_LOCKS = ON,
                    ALLOW_PAGE_LOCKS = ON ) ON [PRIMARY]
    )
ON  [PRIMARY]
GO
```

Listing 4.19: Creating the sample table.

The first step is to enable snapshot isolation for the DMV database, as shown in Listing 4.20.

```
-- Specify that snapshot isolation is enabled
-- does not affect the default behavior.
ALTER DATABASE DMV  SET ALLOW_SNAPSHOT_ISOLATION ON ;
GO

-- READ_COMMITTED_SNAPSHOT becomes the default isolation level.
ALTER DATABASE DMV  SET READ_COMMITTED_SNAPSHOT ON ;
GO
```

Listing 4.20: Enabling snapshot isolation in the DMV database.

Open a tab in SSMS that queries the `Culture` table, starts a transaction that updates a row in the table, and keeps the transaction open.

```
USE DMV ;
GO

SELECT  CultureID ,
        Name
FROM    dbo.Culture ;

BEGIN TRANSACTION
UPDATE  dbo.[Culture]
SET     [Name] = 'English-British'
WHERE   [Name] = 'English' ;

-- COMMIT ;
-- ROLLBACK;
```

Listing 4.21: Tab 1, query then update the `Culture` table.

Open a second tab in SSMS and start a transaction that inserts one more row into the table, and keep the transaction open.

```
USE DMV ;
GO

BEGIN TRANSACTION ;
INSERT  INTO dbo.[Culture] ([CultureID], [Name], [ModifiedDate])
VALUES  ('jp', 'Japanese', '2010-08-01') ;

-- COMMIT ;
```

Listing 4.22: Tab 2, an open transaction that inserts a row into the `Culture` table.

A transaction running with an isolation level such as **REPEATABLE READ** will be blocked if some of the data it needs to read is locked. However, under **SNAPSHOT** isolation mode, the transaction is not blocked; open a third tab and execute the query shown in Listing 4.23. It will return from the version store the data as it existed at the time the transaction began.

```
IF @@TRANCOUNT = 0
    BEGIN ;
        SET TRANSACTION ISOLATION LEVEL SNAPSHOT ;
        PRINT 'Beginning transaction' ;
        BEGIN TRANSACTION ;
    END ;
SELECT  CultureID ,
        Name
FROM    dbo.Culture ;

--commit;
```

	CultureID	Name
1	ar	arabic
2	en	English
3	es	spanish

Listing 4.23: Tab 3, a query using SNAPSHOT isolation.

The same query under READ_COMMITTED_SNAPSHOT also completes, and the output is exactly the same. To see this, open a fourth tab and run the script shown in Listing 4.24.

```
IF @@TRANCOUNT = 0
    BEGIN ;
-- since we have already set READ_COMMITTED_SNAPSHOT to ON
-- this is  READ_COMMITTED_SNAPSHOT
        SET TRANSACTION ISOLATION LEVEL READ COMMITTED ;
        PRINT 'Beginning transaction' ;
        BEGIN TRANSACTION ;
    END ;
SELECT  CultureID ,
        Name
```

```
FROM     dbo.Culture ;

-- COMMIT;
```

Listing 4.24: Tab 4, a query using READ_COMMITTED_SNAPSHOT isolation.

So far, the queries return exactly the same results under either **SNAPSHOT** or **READ_ COMMITTED_SNAPSHOT** mode. At this point, let's investigate current snapshot activity using our DMOs. The first simple query we can run is simply to get a count of currently active snapshots, from the **sys.dm_tran_transactions_snapshot** DMV, as shown in Listing 4.25.

```
SELECT   COUNT([transaction_sequence_num]) AS [snapshot transaction count]
FROM     sys.dm_tran_transactions_snapshot ;
```

Listing 4.25: A count of currently active snapshot transactions.

This returns a snapshot transaction count of two, since our **SNAPSHOT** query in Listing 4.5 relies on the ultimate result of our two open transactions in Listings 4.21 (Tab 1) and 4.22 (Tab 2). Next, let's interrogate the **active_snapshot_database_transactions** DMV, as shown in Listing 4.26.

```
SELECT   DTASDT.transaction_id ,
         DTASDT.session_id ,
         DTASDT.transaction_sequence_num ,
         DTASDT.first_snapshot_sequence_num ,
         DTASDT.commit_sequence_num ,
         DTASDT.is_snapshot ,
         DTASDT.elapsed_time_seconds ,
         DEST.text AS [command text]
FROM     sys.dm_tran_active_snapshot_database_transactions DTASDT
         INNER JOIN sys.dm_exec_connections DEC
                    ON DTASDT.session_id = DEC.most_recent_session_id
         INNER JOIN sys.dm_tran_database_transactions DTDT
                    ON DTASDT.transaction_id = DTDT.transaction_id
```

```
        CROSS APPLY sys.dm_exec_sql_text(DEC.most_recent_sql_handle) AS DEST
WHERE   DTDT.database_id = DB_ID()
```

Listing 4.26: Interrogating the `active_snapshot_database_transactions` DMV.

Notice that we join on `session_id` to retrieve the text of the executing SQL for each active transaction and that, in the **WHERE** clause, we limit the results to the current database. The results should look as shown in Figure 4.11 (for space reasons I've omitted the `elapsed_time_seconds` and the `commit_sequence_number` columns (the value for the latter was **NULL** in each case).

Results | Messages

	usecounts	cacheobjtype	objtype	query_plan
1	6	Compiled Plan	Adhoc	<ShowPlanXML xmlns="http://schemas.microsoft.com...
2	6	Compiled Plan	Adhoc	<ShowPlanXML xmlns="http://schemas.microsoft.com...

text
SELECT ISNULL(SUSER_SNAME(), SUSER_NAME())
select @@microsoftversion

Figure 4.11: Transactions that are using the version store.

We have four transactions assigned a `transaction_sequence_number`, since we have four transactions using the version store. Only one of these, our query in Tab 3 (`session_id = 55`), is running in **SNAPSHOT** mode; the rest are using **READ_COMMITTED_SNAPSHOT**. Notice that the **SNAPSHOT** session has a `first_snapshot_sequence_num` of 183, referring to the first snapshot transaction (`session_id` = 52) on which this session relies, the second one being `session_id` = 54.

We can complicate matters further by opening yet another new session and rerunning our **SNAPSHOT** query from Listing 4.23. If we then get a new count of currently active snapshots (rerun Listing 4.25) we'll see that the count has increased from 2 to 6.

In order to get a clearer picture of what's going on, we can run the query shown in Listing 4.27 to correlate the activity of the various transactions that are using the version store.

```
SELECT   DTTS.[transaction_sequence_num] ,
         trx_current.[session_id] AS current_session_id ,
         DES_current.[login_name] AS [current session login] ,
         DEST_current.text AS [current session command] ,
         DTTS.[snapshot_sequence_num] ,
         trx_existing.[session_id] AS existing_session_id ,
         DES_existing.[login_name] AS [existing session login] ,
         DEST_existing.text AS [existing session command]
FROM     sys.dm_tran_transactions_snapshot DTTS
         INNER JOIN sys.[dm_tran_active_snapshot_database_transactions]
                                                        trx_current
                    ON DTTS.[transaction_sequence_num] =
                            trx_current.[transaction_sequence_num]
         INNER JOIN sys.[dm_exec_connections] DEC_current
                    ON trx_current.[session_id] =
                                DEC_current.[most_recent_session_id]
         INNER JOIN sys.[dm_exec_sessions] DES_current
                    ON DEC_current.[most_recent_session_id] =
                                DES_current.[session_id]
         INNER JOIN sys.[dm_tran_active_snapshot_database_transactions]
                                                        trx_existing
                    ON DTTS.[snapshot_sequence_num] =
                            trx_existing.[transaction_sequence_num]
         INNER JOIN sys.[dm_exec_connections] DEC_existing
                    ON trx_existing.[session_id] =
                                DEC_existing.[most_recent_session_id]
         INNER JOIN sys.[dm_exec_sessions] DES_existing
                    ON DEC_existing.[most_recent_session_id] =
                                DES_existing.[session_id]
         CROSS APPLY sys.[dm_exec_sql_text]
                    (DEC_current.[most_recent_sql_handle]) DEST_current
         CROSS APPLY sys.[dm_exec_sql_text]
                    (DEC_existing.[most_recent_sql_handle]) DEST_existing
ORDER BY DTTS.[transaction_sequence_num] ,
         DTTS.[snapshot_sequence_num] ;
```

Listing 4.27: Correlating the activity of the various transactions that are using the version store.

By making parallel joins through the DMV stack to `sys.dm_exec_connections`, `sys.dm_exec_sessions`, and `sys.dm_exec_sql_text`, for both the `transaction_sequence_number` and `snapshot_sequence_number` obtained from the `sys.dm_tran_transactions_snapshot` DMV, we're able to give some immediate meaning to the sequence numbers provided. Six rows are returned in the results, as shown in Figure 4.12. For space reasons I've omitted the two login columns from the output, as well as the "current session command" which, in each case, returned the text of our **SNAPSHOT** query from Listing 4.21.

	transaction_sequence_num	current_session_id	snapshot_sequence_num
1	185	55	183
2	185	55	184
3	189	58	183
4	189	58	184
5	189	58	185
6	189	58	186

existing_session_id	existing session command
52	SELECT CultureID , Name FROM dbo.Cultur...
54	BEGIN TRANSACTION ; INSERT INTO dbo.[Cultur...
52	SELECT CultureID , Name FROM dbo.Cultur...
54	BEGIN TRANSACTION ; INSERT INTO dbo.[Cultur...
55	IF @@TRANCOUNT = 0 BEGIN ; SET TRA...
56	IF @@TRANCOUNT = 0 BEGIN ; -- since we hav...

Figure 4.12: Active transactions that may affect the results returned by a given XSN.

Notice that session 58 (our second **SNAPSHOT** query), assigned a XSN of 189, returns 4 rows, since the results that XSN 189 ultimately returns rely on the results of four currently active transactions, with snapshot sequence numbers of 183, 184, 185, and 186. If any of these transactions make modifications to the underlying data, transaction XSN 189 will rely upon the version store for its data, not the database directly. The other two rows relate to the requirements of our original **SNAPSHOT** query.

In short, this script is very useful in allowing the DBA to identify transactions that will rely upon the version store if other transactions, competing for the same resources/rows, make modifications to those rows. High count of versions in the version store may point to a row/resource that is in high demand, i.e. a lot of other transactions are also hitting the same row/resource and the version store needs to spawn frequent versions of it to maintain concurrency under snapshot isolation. You may find yourself needing to adjust the size of your `tempdb` in order to accommodate this situation.

Finally, in order to observe the difference in behavior between the two **SNAPSHOT** and **READ_COMMITTED_SNAPSHOT** queries, return to Tab 1 (Listing 4.19) and Tab 2 (Listing 4.20) and commit the modifications. Go to Tab 3 (Listing 4.21), which is running in **SNAPSHOT** mode, highlight only the **SELECT** query and rerun it. Since the initial *transaction* in this session started before the addition of the fourth row was committed, only the three rows committed before the transaction began are returned.

Now go to Tab 4 (Listing 4.22), which is running in **SNAPSHOT_READ_COMMITTED** mode, and rerun the query. Since the **INSERT** and **UPDATE** transactions were committed before the *statement* was run, all four rows will be returned, as shown in Figure 4.13.

	CultureID	Name
1	ar	arabic
2	en	English-British
3	es	spanish
4	jp	Japanese

Figure 4.13: Demonstrating the difference in behavior between **SNAPSHOT** and READ_COMMITTED_SNAPSHOT.

As a final clean up, commit or roll back all outstanding transactions.

Version store usage

SQL Server provides two DMVs that store data with regard to version store usage on a given instance, as follows (definitions taken from Books Online).

- **sys.dm_tran_version_store** – returns a virtual table that displays all version records in the version store. sys.dm_tran_version_store is inefficient to run because it queries the entire version store, and the version store can be very large. Each versioned record is stored as binary data together with some tracking or status information. Similar to records in database tables, version store records are stored in 8,192-byte pages. If a record exceeds 8,192 bytes, the record will be split across two different records. Because the versioned record is stored as binary, there are no problems with different collations from different databases. Use sys.dm_tran_version_store to find the previous versions of the rows in binary representation as they exist in the version store.

- **sys.dm_tran_top_version_generators** – returns a virtual table for the objects that are producing the most versions in the version store. sys.dm_tran_top_version_generators returns the top 256 aggregated record lengths that are grouped by the database_id and rowset_id. sys.dm_tran_top_version_generators retrieves data by querying the dm_tran_version_store virtual table. sys.dm_tran_top_version_generators is an inefficient view to run because this view queries the version store, and the version store can be very large. We recommend that you use this function to find the largest consumers of the version store.

Both are aimed at allowing us to investigate the highest consumers of space within the version store. Heed the warning in each case that, if the version store is large, queries against these DMVs can be expensive, and may have performance implications (a classic case of the "watcher" effect).

Using sys.dm_tran_version_store

The `sys.dm_tran_version_store` DMV provides details of the version records stored in the version store in `tempdb`. This information is cumulative from the moment when snapshot isolation was enabled, and remains until the last transaction relying upon the row's versions is committed or rolled back.

The records returned indicate where queries that need the same data from the database will go to fetch the previous version of the row, in cases where the row is being modified under the snapshot isolation level. As is the case with the other DMVs we've reviewed, the results of this DMV reflect the current point in time when the view was queried. Books Online (HTTP://MSDN.MICROSOFT.COM/EN-US/LIBRARY/MS186328.ASPX) has a complete list of columns associated with this DMV. Only the columns used in this book will be covered below.

- **transaction_sequence_num** – the sequence number for the transaction within the version store.

- **version_sequence_num** – sequence of version records added to the version store under the same `transaction_sequence_num`. The `version_sequence_number` value will be unique for a given `transaction_sequence_num` value.

- **database_id** – the database that the version records come from. Surrogate key of the database (relates to `sys.databases`).

- **status** – the versioned record inside the store may be stored across one or two pages. The value of this column indicates whether the version spans more than one page. 0 indicates the version is stored on a single page; 1 signifies the version spans two pages. I must say this is one of those unfortunate metrics that is misleading beyond belief: 0 equals one page. 1 equals two pages.

- **record_length_first_part_in_bytes** – length of the first part of the version record.

- **record_image_first_part** – first `varbinary(8000)` part of the versioned row.

- **record_length_second_part_in_bytes** – length of the second part of the version record.

- **record_image_second_part** – second **varbinary(8000)** part of the versioned row.

Listing 4.28 returns raw data from this view regarding the current state of our version store.

```
SELECT   DB_NAME(DTVS.database_id) AS [Database Name] ,
         DTVS.[transaction_sequence_num] ,
         DTVS.[version_sequence_num] ,
         CASE DTVS.[status]
            WHEN 0 THEN '1'
            WHEN 1 THEN '2'
         END AS [pages] ,
         DTVS.[record_length_first_part_in_bytes]
         + DTVS.[record_length_second_part_in_bytes] AS [record length (bytes)]
FROM     sys.dm_tran_version_store DTVS
ORDER BY DB_NAME(DTVS.database_id) ,
         DTVS.transaction_sequence_num ,
         DTVS.version_sequence_num
```

Listing 4.28: Returning raw data from **sys.dm_tran_version_store**.

Sample results are shown in Figure 4.14.

	Database Name	transaction_sequence_num	version_sequence_num	pages	record length (bytes)
1	AdventureWorks	1200	1	1	69
2	AdventureWorks	1200	2	1	55
3	AdventureWorks	1206	1	1	59
4	AdventureWorks	1206	2	1	45

Figure 4.14: Version store usage for the **AdventureWorks** database.

In Listing 4.29, we identify overall storage requirements inside the version store, by database, by aggregating on the `database_id`.

```
SELECT   DB_NAME(DTVS.[database_id]) ,
         SUM(DTVS.[record_length_first_part_in_bytes]
             + DTVS.[record_length_second_part_in_bytes]) AS [total store bytes
consumed]
FROM     sys.dm_tran_version_store DTVS
GROUP BY DB_NAME(DTVS.[database_id]) ;
```

Listing 4.29: Storage requirements for the version store in the **AdventureWorks** database.

Sample results are shown in Figure 4.15.

Figure 4.15:   Total storage space used in the version store, by **AdventureWorks**.

Currently, we're only using 228 bytes within `tempdb` for the version store, because this is a test system with only a few sample transactions running. When I ran this query against one of my production servers that is using snapshot isolation, I saw figures closer to 200 MB. This figure must be taken into consideration when you size `tempdb` for a given instance. Obviously that figure is not too alarming in this day and age of cheap storage, but when you start dealing with version stores in the 10s and 100s of GB it will at least begin to register on the DBA's radar – or so I would hope!

However, a more informative breakdown of version store usage, in terms of the highest-consuming version store record within `tempdb`, is given in Listing 4.28.

```
WITH      version_store ( [rowset_id], [bytes consumed] )
          AS ( SELECT TOP 1
                         [rowset_id] ,
                         SUM([record_length_first_part_in_bytes]
                             + [record_length_second_part_in_bytes])
                                                  AS [bytes consumed]
               FROM      sys.dm_tran_version_store
               GROUP BY [rowset_id]
               ORDER BY SUM([record_length_first_part_in_bytes]
                            + [record_length_second_part_in_bytes])
              )
     SELECT  VS.[rowset_id] ,
             VS.[bytes consumed] ,
             DB_NAME(DTVS.[database_id]) AS [database name] ,
             DTASDT.[session_id] AS session_id ,
             DES.[login_name] AS [session login] ,
             DEST.text AS [session command]
     FROM    version_store VS
             INNER JOIN sys.[dm_tran_version_store] DTVS
                        ON VS.rowset_id = DTVS.[rowset_id]
             INNER JOIN sys.[dm_tran_active_snapshot_database_transactions]
                                                         DTASDT
                        ON DTVS.[transaction_sequence_num] =
                                         DTASDT.[transaction_sequence_num]
             INNER JOIN sys.dm_exec_connections DEC
                        ON DTASDT.[session_id] = DEC.[most_recent_session_id]
             INNER JOIN sys.[dm_exec_sessions] DES
                        ON DEC.[most_recent_session_id] = DES.[session_id]
             CROSS APPLY sys.[dm_exec_sql_text](DEC.[most_recent_sql_handle])
                                                         DEST ;
```

Listing 4.30: Finding the highest-consuming version store record within tempdb.

Sample results are shown in Figure 4.16.

	rowset_id	bytes consumed	database name	session_id	session login
1	72057594048937984	45	AdventureWorks	56	FordAusten

existing session command
UPDATE Production.[Culture] SET [Name] = 'English-British' WHERE [Name] = 'English' ; ...

Figure 4.16: The top generator of version store records.

sys.dm_tran_top_version_generators

The **sys.dm_tran_top_version_generators** DMV simply returns aggregated records from the **sys.dm_tran_version_store** DMV. If you examine the graphical execution plan, shown in Figure 4.17, for the call to **sys.dm_tran_top_version_generators**, you can see that it is making a call to **sys.dm_tran_version_store** and then performing the aggregation processes within the query engine.

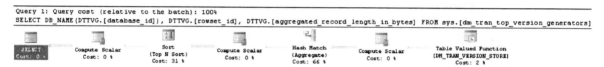

Figure 4.17: Execution plan for a query against the **sys.dm_tran_top_version_generators** DMV.

This DMV groups results from **sys.dm_tran_version_store** on the **database_id** and **rowset_id** columns. Notable columns for this view include:

- **database_id** – the database of the item in the version store

- **rowset_id** – the identifier of the rowset in the version store

- **aggregated_record_length_in_bytes** – total length of all rows for the rowset.

Listing 4.31 returns raw data from this DMV.

```
SELECT   DB_NAME(DTTVG.[database_id]) ,
         DTTVG.[rowset_id] ,
         DTTVG.[aggregated_record_length_in_bytes]
FROM     sys.[dm_tran_top_version_generators] DTTVG
ORDER BY DTTVG.[aggregated_record_length_in_bytes] DESC ;
```

Listing 4.31: Returning raw data from **sys.dm_tran_top_version_generators**.

Sample results are shown in Figure 4.18.

	(No column name)	rowset_id	aggregated_record_length_in_bytes
1	AdventureWorks	72057594044088320	59
2	AdventureWorks	72057594048937984	45

Figure 4.18: Results from `sys.dm_tran_top_version_generators`.

Whereas the raw query results against this DMV will provide you with the space consumed within the version store, they do little else to flesh out the statement or object that is associated with the value. Sure, they provide you with a `rowset_id`, the unique identifier for the record in the version store. Unfortunately, the only other Dynamic Management Object that provides that information is `sys.dm_tran_version_store`, which is what is used "under the covers" to provide this information within *this* DMV. In my not-so-humble opinion, this renders the entire DMV useless (in its current instantiation). Perhaps in future revisions of SQL Server this DMV may be fleshed out better by the development team to hold some practical value for the DBA. Until then, I recommend aggregating `sys.dm_tran_version_store` directly and augmenting it with the descriptive columns that fit your individual needs, as demonstrated previously in Listing 4.30.

Summary

The `sys.dm_tran`-prefixed Dynamic Management Objects have a broad scope in SQL Server. They not only span the range of DMOs associated with activity at the transactional level of the query engine, but also expose locking and blocking between user sessions, as well as exposing the effects and existence of snapshot isolation in your SQL Server database and the instance in general.

Via queries against `sys.dm_tran_locks`, joining to various `sys.dm_exec`-prefixed DMOs as well as `sys.dm_os_waiting_tasks`, we were able to diagnose locking and blocking occurring within our SQL databases.

Using `sys.dm_tran_session_transactions` we were able to correlate session-based results from `sys.dm_exec_connections`, `sys.dm_exec_sessions`, and `sys.dm_exec_requests` with data from the `sys.dm_tran`-prefixed DMOs. Using `sys.dm_tran_active_transactions` and `sys.dm_tran_database_transactions`, we collected metrics on the duration and status of our users' transactions, and observed the physical effects of those transactions on the database transaction log files on disk.

Finally, we covered the DMVs associated with the new snapshot isolation level, which makes use of a version store in `tempdb` rather than obtaining locks. We examined scripts that allowed us to monitor the overhead in `tempdb` associated with the implementation of snapshot isolation on our SQL Server instances.

Chapter 5: Indexing Strategy and Maintenance

Well-designed SQL code, as discussed in *Chapter 3*, will "touch" the data in the base tables as few times as possible, will return only the set data that is strictly needed to satisfy the request, and will then use efficient, set-based logic to manipulate this data into the required result set. However, regardless of how intelligently you design your SQL, you will still read more data than is necessary, and perform poorly, unless you also make intelligent use of indexes. Even if you diligently return only the required 20 rows, from 3 columns, in a 100,000 row table, if there is no suitable non-clustered index from which the query engine can retrieve all of the required data, then it may end up scanning most of those 100,000 rows in the table (or clustered index) just to retrieve the 20 you need.

Defining an effective indexing strategy is the only way to ensure that the most significant and frequent queries in your workload are able to read *only* the required data, and in a logical, ordered fashion, thus returning that data quickly and efficiently, with minimal I/O. Generally speaking, the ultimate goal of your indexing strategy is to "cover" as many of your significant queries as possible, with as few narrow indexes as possible.

Finding the correct balance between too many and too few indexes, and having the "proper" set of indexes in place, is extremely important for any DBA who wants to get the best performance from SQL Server. However, it is a delicate art and one that requires sound knowledge of your database design, how the data within the tables is distributed, and how that data is typically queried.

It is for these reasons that the indexing-related set of DMOs is probably the most widely used of any category. The indexing DMOs, all of which have names starting with `sys.dm_db_`, can help the DBA answer such questions as the following (some of the relevant DMOs are indicated in brackets).

- Are there any indexes that are no longer in use, or have never been used? (`index_usage_stats`)

- For indexes that are in use, what is the usage pattern? (`index_operational_stats`)

- Which indexes are missing? (`missing_index_details`, `missing_index_group_stats`)

In this chapter we'll describe, by example, how to answer these questions using the DMOs. We'll also consider the burning question of index maintenance. As data is added, removed and modified, so the ordering of data in the index is disturbed, gaps appear, and so on. This process is known as fragmentation, and it greatly reduces the efficiency with which the index can be read, thus negating its intended benefit. We'll discuss how to use the **sys.dm_db_index_physical_stats** DMF to investigate the degree of fragmentation in your indexes. Many SQL Server Professionals "roll their own" dynamic index maintenance scripts, based on the DMOs covered in this chapter.

Before we get start on all this, though, we need to briefly review some of the indexing system catalog views that we'll need alongside our DMOs, to pull together all of the required diagnostic data.

The Indexing System Catalog Views

Occasionally, we will need to retrieve details of the indexes and objects that we are investigating, such as an index name or the data type of a column in the index, which are simply not available from the DMOs. On these occasions, we'll need to join to the system catalog views to retrieve this data.

The main indexing catalog view that we'll use in this chapter is **sys.indexes**, which provides metadata at the index level, such as index identifiers (e.g. index name) and configuration settings (e.g. fill factor). Consider, for example, the query shown in Listing

5.1, which returns some statistics from the **dm_db_index_usage_stats** DMV, and joins to **sys.indexes** to get the index names.

```
SELECT   DB_NAME(ddius.[database_id]) AS database_name ,
         OBJECT_NAME(ddius.[object_id], DB_ID('AdventureWorks'))
                                               AS [object_name] ,
         asi.[name] AS index_name ,
         ddius.user_seeks + ddius.user_scans + ddius.user_lookups AS user_reads
FROM     sys.dm_db_index_usage_stats ddius
         INNER JOIN AdventureWorks.sys.indexes asi
                ON ddius.[object_id] = asi.[object_id]
                AND ddius.index_id = asi.index_id ;
```

Listing 5.1:   Querying index use in the AdventureWorks database.

The results are shown in Figure 5.1.

	database_name	object_name	index_name	user_reads
1	AdventureWorks	Contact	PK_Contact_ContactID	211
2	AdventureWorks	Product	PK_Product_ProductID	1610

Figure 5.1:   Results for indexes in the AdventureWorks database.

Firstly, you may notice the use of the **OBJECT_NAME** function to return the table/view that owns the indexes retrieved from **sys.dm_db_index_usage_stats**. Note that **database_id** is not an identified column in these system catalog views. This is because these views reside in each database on the SQL Server instance, not within one of the system databases (globally) across the instance. Therefore, we'll make use of a little-known feature of the **OBJECT_NAME** function which, in SQL 2005 and later editions, accepts the **database_id** in the second parameter slot. In Listing 5.1, we could have simply used:

```
OBJECT_NAME(ddius.[object_id], ddius.[database_id]) AS [object_name]
```

However, I wanted to show that we can pass the value of `database_id` even if we do not know it, by embedding the `DB_ID` function.

When we make joins from the DMOs at the instance level to the system catalog views that reside in each database, in order to extract index details, we need to ensure that we uniquely identify the index in question at the instance level. In fact, this isn't possible directly. In Listing 5.1, we join on the combination of `object_id` and `index_id`, which guarantees uniqueness at the database level (`index_id` alone is only unique at the table level).

However, not even the combination of `object_id` and `index_id` can guarantee uniqueness at the instance level, as Listing 5.2 demonstrates.

```
SELECT   DB_NAME(ddius.[database_id]) AS [database_name] ,
         ddius.[database_id] ,
         ddius.[object_id] ,
         ddius.[index_id]
FROM     sys.[dm_db_index_usage_stats] ddius
         INNER JOIN AdventureWorks.sys.[indexes] asi
             ON ddius.[object_id] = asi.[object_id]
                AND ddius.[index_id] = asi.[index_id]
```

Listing 5.2:   The combination of `object_id` and `index_id` cannot guarantee uniqueness at the instance level.

The first few rows of the resultset are shown in Figure 5.2, and it's clear that, for example, the key of `object_id = 4` and `index_id = 1` exists in both the `master` and the `AdventureWorks` databases.

	database_name	database_id	object_id	index_id
1	AdventureWorks	6	4	1
2	DMV	7	5	1
3	AdventureWorks	6	5	1
4	DMV	7	4	1
5	DMV	7	7	1
6	AdventureWorks	6	7	1
7	master	1	7	1
8	master	1	5	1
9	master	1	4	1
10	DMV	7	13	1

Figure 5.2: Both the `master` and `AdventureWorks` databases have an object identified by `object_id = 4` and `index_id = 1`.

This is why we had to filter the results by database in the **WHERE** clause in Listing 5.1. That allows us to run this query under the context of any database and still receive the same results. Alternatively, we could have used **WHERE ddius.[database_id] = DB_ID()**. However, we would then have had to run the query under the context of the `Northwind` database in order to return the same results.

Occasionally, we may need to join to other indexing catalog views, such as **sys.columns**, to find out details about specific columns in the index, such as their length, data type, and so on. When we do so, we need to join via the intermediate view, **sys.index_columns**, as shown in Figure 5.3.

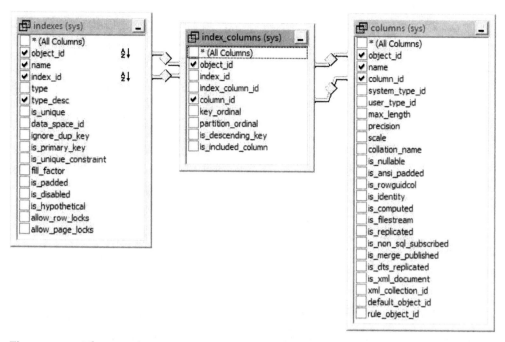

Figure 5.3: The `sys.index_columns` view resolves the many-to-many relationship between `sys.indexes` and `sys.columns`.

The many available columns, shown in Figure 5.3, are well documented and won't be covered further here. Other system views, not explicitly index related, which we'll need to join to throughout this chapter are:

- **sys.objects** – system catalog view for all objects in a database; we will frequently rely on joins to this view to pull in information associated with an `object_id` obtained from the DMOs

- **sys.partitions** – system catalog view that provides information about the partitions in tables and views (when partitioning is utilized in a database)

- **sys.sysuser** – system catalog view for information associated with users in a database; we will rely on joins to this view to provide more descriptive information regarding a `user_id`.

Using the Indexing DMOs

Amongst many other things, the query optimizer in Microsoft SQL Server caches metadata pertaining to the use of existing indexes. This information is deleted when the SQL Server service is restarted, so we recommend you store it in a persisted table in order to maintain a rich, deep set of data for performance tuning. Otherwise, the queries we are going to create in the remainder of the chapter will force you to make decisions on the long-term structure of your instance using data that may be only days or hours old; we would never advocate making such decisions with such weak data. We will proceed on the basis that you have sufficient days of data available when running these queries and making the decisions that you intend to, once these queries are returning data for your attention.

Index Strategy

Indexes do indeed increase efficiency and performance in query resolution, but the wrong index can be just as bad as the right index is good. If an index is not used, it still incurs the overhead on any write operation: entries are written to it as necessary when records are inserted into the underlying table or view; entries are modified or deleted when the underlying, persisted records are altered or deleted. This activity results in fragmentation that, over time, must be reactively corrected by index rebuilds or reorganizations. All these actions consume vital system resources that detract from the user transactions occurring simultaneously when these events are encountered. That's why it is important to walk the thin line that lies between too few indexes and too many. At the same time, you also need to factor into the mix that the indexes you do create are the right ones for the encountered load.

Unfortunately, every DBA has been in many situations where indexing is either entirely absent or entirely chaotic. Personally, I've come across the following on many occasions:

- every column is indexed individually

- the same column participates in three or more composite keys, and is also indexed individually

- no primary key is defined, but just about all columns have non-clustered indexes defined on them.

In short, it's one heap of a mess. However, I have to confess that the manner in which some DBAs have traditionally gone about sorting out such issues is often equally chaotic, and ruled more by "gut feel" than science. For example, when discovering a situation as just described, how many DBAs out there have proceeded as follows?

- Placed a clustered index on the primary key for the table and moved on without much thought.

- Simply removed all the extra indexes your gut told you were unnecessary.

- Confronted the developer:
  <DBA> "You placed indexes on every column in the table. Can you tell me why you designed the table in this fashion?"
  <Developer> "Indexes make the queries run faster. The more indexes, the better. I'm thinking about placing two indexes on each column if that is OK with you!"

In SQL Server 2005, via the indexing DMOs covered in this section, we DBAs fortunately now have proper insight into the indexes that are used and those that are being ignored. This removes the "gut feel" factor from the process of cleaning up incorrect, unused, and downright ignorant indexes.

However, before we start examining the scripts that we can use to uncover this information, it's worth stating up front that blindly following the advice offered by these DMOs is not the right way to go, either. As noted earlier, defining an effective indexing strategy is a delicate art and one that requires sound knowledge of your database design, how the data within the tables is distributed, and how that data is typically queried. It is beyond the scope of this book to provide a full tutorial on how to determine an effective set of indexes, but having covered some of the things we don't like to see, it's worth taking just a brief look at some of the things we do like.

Clustered indexes and PKs

More or less every table in SQL Server should have a clustered index to allow efficient searching of the data in that table. You can either cluster on a key that naturally reflects the way the data will be queried, or you can cluster on a narrow, ever-increasing integer key (to minimize subsequent fragmentation) and use non-clustered indexes for query efficiency. Most of the advice out there points to the latter approach but, regardless, most tables should have a clustered index and every table should have primary key (which may or may not be the clustered index).

Covering indexes

A covering index is one that contains all of the columns and data required by a query. This means that any columns used in join or search conditions are included in the index, along with any columns that are simply selected. The latter should be included as `INCLUDE` columns rather than as part of the actual index. If an index covers a query, it means the data can be returned entirely from the index, without the need to perform a dreaded table scan, or "key lookup," to get any non-covered data from the clustered index. This results in fewer reads, and is *usually* the quickest, most efficient way to return the data. The "usually" qualification is there because, even if an index exists that you think a query should be using, there is no guarantee that the optimizer will choose to use it.

High selectivity

If you've chosen a low selectivity column for the index key (i.e. where each key value matches many rows), then the optimizer may decide to simply perform a table scan to return a piece of data. Table scans have a bad reputation, but this is because they often mean reading a huge number of rows; in small tables, scanning all the rows is sometimes quicker than reading the data from the leaf levels of an index.

You're looking for selective columns to form your index key and, certainly, the leading (first) column should be selective. However, this does not mean each index should start with the PK column; it must be a column that is likely to get searched on. A good discussion of index selectivity and column ordering can be found at HTTP:// SQLSERVERPEDIA.COM/WIKI/INDEX_SELECTIVITY_AND_COLUMN_ORDER.

Neither too many nor too few

The drive to cover queries does not mean you should simply create an index for every query in your workload. If a table contains many rows and is subject to frequent modifications, the presence of numerous indexes will significantly slow down these modifications, as the data must be maintained in both the index and the underlying table.

Examine the workload characteristics for a given table as this will affect how many indexes you might want to have per table. If a table is pretty static, you can manage with more indexes, but on tables subject to frequent updates, you'll want as few as you can get away with.

Narrow indexes (within reason)

Neither does the drive to cover queries mean that you should create huge, 16-column indexes in an attempt to "cover everything at once;" if your index key values are wide, you'll fit few on a page, your index will take up a lot of space, and scanning it will be inefficient. Searching on narrow index keys is much quicker.

Again, though, it is a balancing act; having a huge number of single column indexes is a bad idea, too. Your goal is to make your indexes as narrow as possible while being usable by as many queries as possible. For example, if users search on employees' last names, an index on the `LastName` column is probably a good idea. If users also sometimes qualify the search with first names, then create a single index on (`LastName`, `Firstname`) as this will satisfy both queries.

Investigating index usage (index_usage_stats)

In this section, we'll use the DMV `sys.dm_db_index_usage_stats`, along with various system catalog views, as described earlier, to obtain statistics on how our indexes have been used to resolve queries. This DMV provides, in particular, the following columns for each index:

- **database_id** – ID of the database

- **object_id** – identifies the table or view to which the index belongs, unique only at the database level

- **index_id** – index ID, unique only to the scope of the `object_id`; an `index_id` of 0 signifies a heap (no clustered index on the table); an `index_id` value of 1 is always associated with the clustered index on the table, whereas `index_id` values greater than 1 are reserved for non-clustered indexes

- **user_seeks** – the number of times the index has been used in a seek operation (to find a specific row)

- **user_scans** – number of times the index has been used by scanning the leaf pages of the index for data

- **user_lookups** – for clustered indexes only, this is the number of times the index has been used in a "bookmark lookup" to fetch the full row; this is because non-clustered indexes use the clustered indexes key as the pointer to the base row

- **user_updates** – number of times the index has been modified due to a change in the table's data.

For each of the user actions (user_* columns), there is also a corresponding last_user_* column (e.g. last_user_seek), which records the date and time the action last occurred. Also, there is a system_* and last_system_* equivalent for each of these columns, providing statistics regarding use of the index by a system operation.

Data in this DMV is cumulative, and is refreshed when the server is restarted or when the index is dropped and recreated. Statistics live on when an index is rebuilt or reorganized, and even when it is disabled and rebuilt. Queries against this DMV return all indexes (including heaps and the clustered index) that have been read or written to at least once. If an index exists but has never been used since creation, or since the statistics were refreshed, then there will be no entry for this index row in sys.dm_db_index_usage_stats. It's an instance-wide DMV and so will return indexes for every database on the instance, but you will almost always want to limit it per database, using the database_id to retrieve the index names for that database, via sys.indexes (as shown in Listing 5.1). Note also that the DMV does not distinguish between partitions, so if an index is physically manifested in two or more partitions, the DMV only returns a single record.

Listing 5.3 provides a listing of indexes for the database that have been used at least once during a query execution, with those indexes that have been scanned the most listed first. A high number of scans may indicate a need to update your statistics for a given table or index. Equally, however, a high number of scans will result if the query optimizer decides that the table is small enough that it is quicker to scan the index rather than perform a seek operation. Hence, the output of this query should not be considered in isolation, but rather in conjunction with data regarding the selectivity and the size of the index (which can be returned via a query against sys.dm_db_index_physical_stats, covered later in the chapter).

```
SELECT   OBJECT_NAME(ddius.[object_id], ddius.database_id) AS [object_name] ,
         ddius.index_id ,
         ddius.user_seeks ,
         ddius.user_scans ,
         ddius.user_lookups ,
         ddius.user_seeks + ddius.user_scans + ddius.user_lookups
                                               AS user_reads ,
         ddius.user_updates AS user_writes ,
         ddius.last_user_scan ,
         ddius.last_user_update
FROM     sys.dm_db_index_usage_stats ddius
WHERE    ddius.database_id > 4 -- filter out system tables
         AND OBJECTPROPERTY(ddius.object_id, 'IsUserTable') = 1
         AND ddius.index_id > 0  -- filter out heaps
ORDER BY ddius.user_scans DESC
```

	object_name	index_id	user_seeks	user_scans	user_lookups	user_reads
1	Product	1	0	1610	0	1610
2	Contact	1	0	211	0	211

user_writes	last_user_scan	last_user_update
0	2010-07-28 08:50:45.710	NULL
0	2010-07-28 09:37:30.403	NULL

Listing 5.3:   Usage stats for indexes that have been used to resolve a query.

You will see that, in this query and all the ones that follow, we use the following formula to calculate the total number of times that the index is used by the optimizer to resolve a user query:

```
[user_seeks] + [user_scans] + [user_lookups] = [user reads]
```

The user_updates column on its own provides the total number of times the index has been updated as a result of data modifications (writes). From a performance tuning perspective, this DMV is invaluable as it shows exactly how the indexes are being used and, critically, it tells us something that no previous version of SQL Server did: which indexes are *not* being used or, more pertinently, not being used but being frequently

187

updated. A similar calculation can be used to get the total system reads of an index. However, we'll ignore any system activity from this point forward as it is almost always negligible in comparison to user-driven activity.

Over the coming sections, we'll present scripts to:

- find indexes on your system that have never been read or written
- find indexes that have never been read but are being maintained (i.e. updated in response to modification of the underlying table data)
- get detailed read/write stats on all indexes, looking for those where the maintenance burden may outweigh their usefulness in boosting query performance.

These indexes are candidates for removal, **after thorough investigation**. You should never blindly drop indexes, and you must be certain that an index really isn't used (e.g. by infrequent, yet critical, monthly or quarterly reporting queries) before dropping it.

Identify indexes that have never been accessed

Listing 5.4 uses **sys.indexes** and **sys.objects** to find tables and indexes in the current database that do not show up in **sys.dm_db_index_usage_stats**. This means that these indexes have had no reads or writes since SQL Server was last started, or since the current database was closed or detached, whichever is shorter.

```
-- List unused indexes
SELECT   OBJECT_NAME(i.[object_id]) AS [Table Name] ,
         i.name
FROM     sys.indexes AS i
         INNER JOIN sys.objects AS o ON i.[object_id] = o.[object_id]
WHERE    i.index_id NOT IN ( SELECT  ddius.index_id
                            FROM     sys.dm_db_index_usage_stats AS ddius
                            WHERE    ddius.[object_id] = i.[object_id]
                            AND i.index_id = ddius.index_id
```

```
                                    AND database_id = DB_ID() )
         AND o.[type] = 'U'
ORDER BY OBJECT_NAME(i.[object_id]) ASC ;
```

Listing 5.4: Finding unused indexes.

If SQL Server has been running long enough for you to have a complete, representative workload, there is a good chance that those indexes (and perhaps tables) are "dead," meaning they are no longer used by your database and can potentially be dropped, after some further investigation.

Identify indexes that are being maintained but not used

Listing 5.5 identifies clustered and non-clustered indexes that are consuming resources, in terms of writes and maintenance, but are never being selected for use by the optimizer, so have never been read, at least since the last time the cache was cleared of accumulated usage data. It uses a fully-qualified naming convention and is identified as "statement," in order to conform to the output that you will see when querying the missing indexes DMOs. We identify the name of the index via a join to the **sys.indexes** system catalog view, on the **object_id** and **index_id** columns, and we join to the **sys.partitions** system view on the same columns in order to return the **total_rows** metric (the total number of rows in the index).

```
SELECT   '[' + DB_NAME() + '].[' + su.[name] + '].[' + o.[name] + ']'
             AS [statement] ,
         i.[name] AS [index_name] ,
         ddius.[user_seeks] + ddius.[user_scans] + ddius.[user_lookups]
             AS [user_reads] ,
         ddius.[user_updates] AS [user_writes] ,
         SUM(SP.rows) AS [total_rows]
FROM     sys.dm_db_index_usage_stats ddius
         INNER JOIN sys.indexes i ON ddius.[object_id] = i.[object_id]
                              AND i.[index_id] = ddius.[index_id]
         INNER JOIN sys.partitions SP ON ddius.[object_id] = SP.[object_id]
                              AND SP.[index_id] = ddius.[index_id]
```

```
          INNER JOIN sys.objects o ON ddius.[object_id] = o.[object_id]
          INNER JOIN sys.sysusers su ON o.[schema_id] = su.[UID]
WHERE     ddius.[database_id] = DB_ID() -- current database only
          AND OBJECTPROPERTY(ddius.[object_id], 'IsUserTable') = 1
          AND ddius.[index_id] > 0
GROUP BY su.[name] ,
          o.[name] ,
          i.[name] ,
          ddius.[user_seeks] + ddius.[user_scans] + ddius.[user_lookups] ,
          ddius.[user_updates]
HAVING    ddius.[user_seeks] + ddius.[user_scans] + ddius.[user_lookups] = 0
ORDER BY ddius.[user_updates] DESC ,
          su.[name] ,
          o.[name] ,
          i.[name ]
```

	statement	index_name	user_reads	user_writes	total_rows
1	[demo].[sch1].[au_trail]	NDX_auil_1	0	89993	996452
2	[demo].[sch1].[au_trail]	PK_audrail	0	89993	996452
3	[demo].[sch1].[SC_Audit]	IX_SCRster	0	50349	235493
4	[demo].[sch1].[CTeTrack]	PK_CTCrack	0	44394	646058
5	[demo].[sch1].[vivisit]	extendn_ix	0	43555	11210312
6	[demo].[sch1].[SCJobLog]	IX_SCRtjob	0	42625	521551
7	[demo].[sch1].[SC_Audit]	IX_SCRtamp	0	22031	950625
8	[demo].[sch1].[SC_Audit]	IX_SCRtity	0	22031	950625
9	[demo].[sch1].[SC_Audit]	IX_SCRvity	0	22031	950625
10	[demo].[sch1].[SC_Audit]	IX_SCRster	0	22031	950625
11	[demo].[sch1].[SC_Audit]	IX_SCRuser	0	22031	950625
12	[demo].[sch1].[BBResult]	IX_BBTlt_3	0	21481	105
13	[demo].[sch1].[ct_visit]	ctc_vim_ix	0	20991	5874156
14	[demo].[sch1].[VStenLog]	PK_DSJnLog	0	19894	1555227
15	[demo].[sch1].[SCortJob]	IX_SCRtype	0	17325	206312
16	[demo].[sch1].[SCmogDoc]	IX_SCRphys	0	16241	94940
17	[demo].[sch1].[SCmogDoc]	IX_SCR_api	0	16215	94940
18	[demo].[sch1].[SCmogDoc]	IX_SCR_epi	0	16215	94940
19	[demo].[sch1].[SCmogDoc]	IX_SCRrule	0	16215	94940
20	[demo].[sch1].[SCmogDoc]	IX_SCRssub	0	16215	94940

Listing 5.5: Querying sys.dm_db_index_usage_stats for indexes that are being maintained but not used.

I ran this query recently in my production environment against a database supplied and administered by a third party; I knew I would see some scary things, but I was amazed when it returned over 120 indexes that had not been read. It is possible, at the same time as listing these high-write/zero-read indexes, to generate the commands to drop them, simply by inserting the following at the end of the **SELECT** clause:

```
'DROP INDEX [' + i.[name] + '] ON [' + su.[name] + '].[' + o.[name]
+ '] WITH ( ONLINE = OFF )' AS [drop_command]
```

Having verified the need to drop an index from the database, simply copy the **DROP INDEX** command text from the result set into a new query window and execute it. As always, we advocate testing such processes in your development environment first, before running against a production database. Furthermore, it is recommended you take a backup of the database before running such a command.

As noted earlier, I would not like to encourage readers to go around wildly dropping large numbers of indexes without proper investigation. For a start, it is always advisable to check how recently the usage stats were cleared, by querying **sys.sysdatabases**, as shown in Listing 5.6.

```
SELECT  DATEDIFF(DAY, sd.crdate, GETDATE()) AS days_history
FROM    sys.sysdatabases sd
WHERE   sd.[name] = 'tempdb' ;
```

Listing 5.6:   How old are the index usage stats?

Also, an index may not have been used recently simply because its functionality is cyclical in nature (perhaps only used in a month-end process), or simply because it is a recently-implemented index. Once again, it is important not to drop or create indexes, without first performing adequate testing in a non-production environment.

Identify inefficient indexes

Our final `sys.dm_db_index_usage_stats` query filters by the current database, and only includes non-clustered indexes. It can help you decide whether the cost of maintaining a particular index outweighs the benefit you are receiving from having it in place.

```
-- Potentially inefficient non-clustered indexes (writes > reads)
SELECT   OBJECT_NAME(ddius.[object_id]) AS [Table Name] ,
         i.name AS [Index Name] ,
         i.index_id ,
         user_updates AS [Total Writes] ,
         user_seeks + user_scans + user_lookups AS [Total Reads] ,
         user_updates - ( user_seeks + user_scans + user_lookups )
             AS [Difference]
FROM     sys.dm_db_index_usage_stats AS ddius WITH ( NOLOCK )
         INNER JOIN sys.indexes AS i WITH ( NOLOCK )
             ON ddius.[object_id] = i.[object_id]
             AND i.index_id = ddius.index_id
WHERE    OBJECTPROPERTY(ddius.[object_id], 'IsUserTable') = 1
         AND ddius.database_id = DB_ID()
         AND user_updates > ( user_seeks + user_scans + user_lookups )
         AND i.index_id > 1
ORDER BY [Difference] DESC ,
         [Total Writes] DESC ,
         [Total Reads] ASC ;
```

Listing 5.7: Finding rarely-used indexes.

Make sure that the SQL Server instance has been running long enough to ensure that the complete, typical workload will be represented in the reported statistics. Again, don't forget about periodic, reporting workloads that might not show up in the day-to-day workload. Even though the indexes that facilitate such workloads will be infrequently used, their presence will be critical.

Determine usage patterns of current indexes (index_operational_stats)

The `sys.dm_db_index_operational_stats` is a DMF; it accepts `database_id`, `object_id`, `index_id`, and `partition_number` as parameters, in order to identify the object (heap, clustered or non-clustered index) in question, and returns detailed "operational stats" for each partition of that object. It provides index usage statistics at a more detailed level than those provided by the `sys.dm_db_index_usage_stats` DMV, as well as evidence of potential lock or latch contention on the objects, or of excessive I/O being issued by the object. All the parameters can be `NULL` or `DEFAULT` if you want to return all rows, in which case the DMF will return a row for every partition in every database.

Data in this DMV is cumulative, and is refreshed when the server is restarted or when the index is dropped and recreated. Statistics live on when an index is rebuilt or reorganized, and even when it is disabled and rebuilt.

Whereas an index will always appear in the `index_usage_stats` DMV as long as it has been used, the data returned by the `index_operational_stats` DMF is slightly more "transient" in nature. As detailed in Books Online, at HTTP://MSDN.MICROSOFT.COM/EN-US/LIBRARY/MS174281.ASPX:

> The data returned by `sys.dm_db_index_operational_stats` exists only as long as the metadata cache object that represents the heap or index is available...an active heap or index will likely always have its metadata in the cache, and the cumulative counts may reflect activity since the instance of SQL Server was last started. The metadata for a less active heap or index will move in and out of the cache as it is used. As a result, it may or may not have values available...

Since the "grain" of the function is the partition level, a table that is partitioned into five parts will have five rows in this DMF, whereas `sys.dm_db_index_usage_stats` will see the object as only a single row. Use usage stats if you want counts of each usage, as each usage in counted once. The operational stats object may have multiple values set for each type of activity recorded. Finally, note that we cannot use **APPLY** operators with this DMF.

Whereas the usage stats give a feel for how an index is used by the optimizer to satisfy the needs of certain queries, the operational stats offer more detailed information about how the index is used at a physical level, via columns such as `leaf_insert_count`, `leaf_update_count` and `leaf_delete_count` (the cumulative number of leaf-level inserts, updates and deletes), as well as the `nonleaf_*` equivalents, for modifications above the leaf level.

For diagnosis of resource contention on the object, the following columns are particularly useful:

- **row_lock_count** – number of row locks that have been requested against this index

- **row_lock_wait_count** – number of times a session has waited on a row lock against this index

- **row_lock_wait_in_ms** – amount of time a session had to wait on a row lock against this index

- **page_lock_count**, **page_lock_wait_count**, **page_lock_wait_in_ms** – same as **row_lock** values at the page grain

- **index_lock_promotion_attempt_count**, **index_lock_promotion_count** – number of times the lock grain for an operation using this index was attempted or granted to be escalated (like from row to page)

- **page_latch_wait_count**, **page_latch_wait_in_ms** – number of waits and time waited on the physical page of the object to have the latch removed

- **page_io_latch_wait_count**, **page_io_latch_wait_in_ms** – number of waits and time while SQL loads pages from disk into memory for an index operation.

This DMF offers many more columns; for example, to investigate use of row overflow data, LOB data, and so on. For a full listing, see Books Online. Let's take a look at this DMF in action.

Detailed activity information for indexes not used for user reads

The script in Listing 5.8 isolates just those indexes that are not being used for user reads, courtesy of sys.dm_db_index_usage_stats, and then provides detailed information on the type of writes still being incurred, using the leaf_*_count and nonleaf_*_count columns of sys.dm_db_index_operational_stats. In this way, you gain a deep feel for how indexes are being used, and just exactly how much the index is costing you.

```
SELECT   '[' + DB_NAME() + '].[' + su.[name] + '].[' + o.[name] + ']'
                                              AS [statement] ,
         i.[name] AS [index_name] ,
         ddius.[user_seeks] + ddius.[user_scans] + ddius.[user_lookups]
            AS [user_reads] ,
         ddius.[user_updates] AS [user_writes] ,
         ddios.[leaf_insert_count] ,
         ddios.[leaf_delete_count] ,
         ddios.[leaf_update_count] ,
         ddios.[nonleaf_insert_count] ,
         ddios.[nonleaf_delete_count] ,
         ddios.[nonleaf_update_count]
FROM     sys.dm_db_index_usage_stats ddius
         INNER JOIN sys.indexes i ON ddius.[object_id] = i.[object_id]
                                 AND i.[index_id] = ddius.[index_id]
         INNER JOIN sys.partitions SP ON ddius.[object_id] = SP.[object_id]
                                 AND SP.[index_id] = ddius.[index_id]
         INNER JOIN sys.objects o ON ddius.[object_id] = o.[object_id]
         INNER JOIN sys.sysusers su ON o.[schema_id] = su.[UID]
         INNER JOIN sys.[dm_db_index_operational_stats](DB_ID(), NULL, NULL,
                                              NULL)
                AS ddios
                   ON ddius.[index_id] = ddios.[index_id]
```

```
                          AND ddius.[object_id] = ddios.[object_id]
                          AND SP.[partition_number] = ddios.[partition_number]
                          AND ddius.[database_id] = ddios.[database_id]
WHERE OBJECTPROPERTY(ddius.[object_id], 'IsUserTable') = 1
        AND ddius.[index_id] > 0
        AND ddius.[user_seeks] + ddius.[user_scans] + ddius.[user_lookups] = 0
ORDER BY ddius.[user_updates] DESC ,
          su.[name] ,
          o.[name] ,
          i.[name ]
```

	statement	index_name	user_reads	user_writes	leaf_insert_count	leaf_delete_count
1	[demo].[sch1].[mmrspace]	IX_mmsdate	0	69064440	21684066	1726
2	[demo].[sch1].[mmrspace]	IX_mmsdate	0	14331153	14319292	8934
3	[demo].[sch1].[mmrspace]	IX_mmsmber	0	78277	46464	5408
4	[demo].[sch1].[mmrspace]	IX_mmsdate	0	52529	28685	3731
5	[demo].[sch1].[mmntries]	IX_mmstype	0	36144	6778	0

	leaf_update_count	nonleaf_insert_count	nonleaf_delete_count	nonleaf_update_count
1	0	64362	22	0
2	0	42560	30601	612
3	0	482	542	1476
4	0	7	0	0
5	0	0	0	0

Listing 5.8: Detailed write information for unused indexes.

Upon review of the output it's quite clear that some of these indexes are still being hammered by inserts even though the users are not benefiting from their existence in regard to reads. If I encountered metadata like this in the real world (wink, wink) you could be sure that I would do something about it.

Identify locking and blocking at the row level

We can also return information about locking, latching, and blocking from **sys.dm_db_index_operational_stats**. Listing 5.9 returns records that relate to locking and blocking at the row level for the indexes of the active database.

```sql
SELECT   '[' + DB_NAME(ddios.[database_id]) + '].[' + su.[name] + '].['
         + o.[name] + ']' AS [statement] ,
         i.[name] AS 'index_name' ,
         ddios.[partition_number] ,
         ddios.[row_lock_count] ,
         ddios.[row_lock_wait_count] ,
         CAST (100.0 * ddios.[row_lock_wait_count]
         / ( ddios.[row_lock_count] ) AS DECIMAL(5, 2)) AS [%_times_blocked] ,
         ddios.[row_lock_wait_in_ms] ,
         CAST (1.0 * ddios.[row_lock_wait_in_ms]
         / ddios.[row_lock_wait_count] AS DECIMAL(15, 2))
             AS [avg_row_lock_wait_in_ms]
FROM     sys.dm_db_index_operational_stats(DB_ID(), NULL, NULL, NULL) ddios
         INNER JOIN sys.indexes i ON ddios.[object_id] = i.[object_id]
                                 AND i.[index_id] = ddios.[index_id]
         INNER JOIN sys.objects o ON ddios.[object_id] = o.[object_id]
         INNER JOIN sys.sysusers su ON o.[schema_id] = su.[UID]
WHERE    ddios.row_lock_wait_count > 0
         AND OBJECTPROPERTY(ddios.[object_id], 'IsUserTable') = 1
         AND i.[index_id] > 0
ORDER BY ddios.[row_lock_wait_count] DESC ,
         su.[name] ,
         o.[name] ,
         i.[name ]
```

	statement	index_name	page_latch_wait_count	page_io_latch_wait_count
1	[demo].[sch1].[MSTable0]	IX_MSSocID	24377499	549
2	[demo].[sch1].[MScProps]	IX_MSSrops	8266	2884072
3	[demo].[sch1].[MScSdids]	IX_MSSdids	2084875	1716
4	[demo].[sch1].[MSIQueue]	IX_MSSeqID	896558	94
5	[demo].[sch1].[MSawlURL]	IX_MSSocID	764105	52279
6	[demo].[sch1].[MSopsAlt]	IX_MSSsAlt	674592	16
7	[demo].[sch1].[MScProps]	IX_MSSrops	629314	7
8	[demo].[sch1].[MSIQueue]	IX_MSSocID	299937	86
9	[demo].[sch1].[MSTable0]	IX_MSSwllD	293126	549
10	[demo].[sch1].[MShesAlt]	IX_MSSsAlt	267941	1

Listing 5.9:   Retrieving locking and blocking details for each index.

Notice that in the calculations of both the [%_times_blocked] and avg_row_lock_wait_in_ms columns, we've had to use a decimal multiplication factor:

```
CAST (100.0 * ddios.[row_lock_wait_count] / (ddios.[row_lock_count])
    AS decimal(5,2))

CAST (1.0 * ddios.[row_lock_wait_in_ms] / ddios.[row_lock_wait_count]
    AS decimal(15,2)).
```

This is due to an unfortunate glitch in the data type conversion process within T-SQL that you are never aware of until it sneaks up on you, and you spend hours trying to figure out why your results don't follow basic mathematical rules. Unless a mathematical formula includes a decimal, float, or other non-integer numeric data type, the results will only produce an integer result, even when the math warrants a non-integer result. You can try this for yourself. What do you get when you execute the code "SELECT 3/2" in a query window?

I bet you the answer is not 1.5. The way to fix this is to force a conversion to decimal form by including a constant that best fits your formula, in the form of a decimal, as demonstrated in the previous calculations.

Identify latch waits

Listing 5.10 highlights which of our indexes are encountering latch contention using the `page_io_latch_wait_count` and `page_io_wait_in_ms` columns.

```
SELECT   '[' + DB_NAME() + '].[' + OBJECT_SCHEMA_NAME(ddios.[object_id])
         + '].[' + OBJECT_NAME(ddios.[object_id]) + ']' AS [object_name] ,
         i.[name] AS index_name ,
         ddios.page_io_latch_wait_count ,
         ddios.page_io_latch_wait_in_ms ,
         ( ddios.page_io_latch_wait_in_ms / ddios.page_io_latch_wait_count )
                                     AS avg_page_io_latch_wait_in_ms
FROM     sys.dm_db_index_operational_stats(DB_ID(), NULL, NULL, NULL) ddios
         INNER JOIN sys.indexes i ON ddios.[object_id] = i.[object_id]
                              AND i.index_id = ddios.index_id
WHERE    ddios.page_io_latch_wait_count > 0
         AND OBJECTPROPERTY(i.object_id, 'IsUserTable') = 1
ORDER BY ddios.page_io_latch_wait_count DESC ,
         avg_page_io_latch_wait_in_ms DESC
```

	object_name	index_name	page_io_latch_wait_count	page_io_latch_wait_in_ms	avg_page_io_latch_wait_in_ms
375	[demo].[dbo].[Customers]	Data	20	2297	114
376	[demo].[dbo].[Customers]	345C	20	1267	63
377	[demo].[dbo].[Customers]	Phys	20	264	13
378	[demo].[dbo].[Customers]	FA00	20	233	11
379	[demo].[dbo].[Customers]	e_ix	20	219	10

Listing 5.10: Investigating latch waits.

Latching occurs when the engine reads a physical page. Upon doing so, it issues a latch, scans the page, reads the row, and then releases the latch when, and this is important, the page is needed for another process. This process is called *lazy latching*. Though latching is quite a benign process, it is of interest to have handy such information as this query provides. It allows us to identify which of our indexes are encountering significant waits when trying to issue a latch, because another latch has already been issued. I/O latching occurs on disk-to-memory transfers, and high I/O latch counts could be a reflection of a disk subsystem issue, particularly when you see average latch wait times of over 15 milliseconds.

Identify lock escalations

As discussed in *Chapter 4*, SQL Server may attempt to escalate locks in response to a need to reduce the total number of locks being held and the memory therefore required to hold and manage them. For example, individual row locks may be escalated to a single table lock, or page locks may be escalated to a table lock. While this will result in lower overhead on SQL Server, the downside is lower concurrency. If processes are running on your servers that are causing lock escalation, it's worth investigating whether the escalation is justified, or if SQL tuning can be performed to prevent it.

The `sys.dm_db_index_operational_stats` DMV can be queried to return information on the count of attempts made by SQL Server to escalate row and page locks to table locks for a specific object. The query in Listing 5.11 provides information regarding how frequently these escalation attempts were made, and the percentage success in performing the escalation.

```
SELECT   OBJECT_NAME(ddios.[object_id], ddios.database_id) AS [object_name] ,
         i.name AS index_name ,
         ddios.index_id ,
         ddios.partition_number ,
         ddios.index_lock_promotion_attempt_count ,
         ddios.index_lock_promotion_count ,
         ( ddios.index_lock_promotion_attempt_count
           / ddios.index_lock_promotion_count ) AS percent_success
FROM     sys.dm_db_index_operational_stats(DB_ID(), NULL, NULL, NULL) ddios
         INNER JOIN sys.indexes i ON ddios.object_id = i.object_id
                                 AND ddios.index_id = i.index_id
WHERE    ddios.index_lock_promotion_count > 0
ORDER BY index_lock_promotion_count DESC ;
```

	object_name	index_name	index_id	partition_number	index_lock_promotion_attempt_count	index_lock_promotion_count	percent_success
1	TBL_SEC...	PK_TBL_SE...	1	1	206	53	3
2	tmpEmp	NULL	0	1	117	26	4
3	TBL_TMX...	PK_TBL_T...	1	1	59	16	3
4	TBL_TMX...	PK_TBL_T...	1	1	33	15	2
5	TBL_TMX...	PK_TBL_T...	1	1	68	14	4

Listing 5.11: Investigating lock escalation.

Identify indexes associated with lock contention

The `sys.dm_os_wait_stats` DMV, discussed in detail in *Chapter 7*, is a great "first hit" resource for drilling into issues that may instigate those "Hey, the database is slow" phone calls that we all know and love at 3 a.m. If the outcome of your queries into `sys.dm_os_wait_stats` points to locking problems, the query in Listing 5.12 makes a good next step in the investigation. This original idea comes from the Microsoft "SQL Server Premier Field Engineer" blog, at HTTP://BLOGS.MSDN.COM/B/SQL_PFE_BLOG/ARCHIVE/2009/06/11/ THREE-USAGE-SCENARIOS-FOR-SYS-DM-DB-INDEX-OPERATIONAL-STATS.ASPX with a few enhancements to identify the indexes by name in the results.

```
SELECT  OBJECT_NAME(ddios.object_id, ddios.database_id) AS object_name ,
        i.name AS index_name ,
        ddios.index_id ,
        ddios.partition_number ,
        ddios.page_lock_wait_count ,
        ddios.page_lock_wait_in_ms ,
        CASE WHEN DDMID.database_id IS NULL THEN 'N'
            ELSE 'Y'
        END AS missing_index_identified
FROM    sys.dm_db_index_operational_stats(DB_ID(), NULL, NULL, NULL) ddios
        INNER JOIN sys.indexes i ON ddios.object_id = i.object_id
                            AND ddios.index_id = i.index_id
        LEFT OUTER JOIN ( SELECT DISTINCT
                            database_id ,
                            object_id
                    FROM    sys.dm_db_missing_index_details
                ) AS DDMID ON DDMID.database_id = ddios.database_id
```

```
                                      AND DDMID.object_id = ddios.object_id
WHERE     ddios.page_lock_wait_in_ms > 0
ORDER BY ddios.page_lock_wait_count DESC ;
```

	object_nm	index_name	index_id	partition_number	page_lock_wait_count	page_lock_wait_in_ms	missing_index_identified
1	TBL_N...	IDX_NTF...	3	1	2	31	Y

Listing 5.12: Indexes associated with lock contention.

Notice the very useful outer join to `sys.dm_db_missing_index_details` to identify if there was a potential suggestion for a missing index that might resolve the locking. Of course, before implementing any new index, you should first test it thoroughly in your test environment, which we discuss in depth as we move on to look at the missing index DMOs.

Find missing indexes

When the query optimizer generates an execution plan for a query, it determines the optimal data access path that will satisfy the search criteria, and then checks to see if any existing indexes offer this path (or something close). If the ideal index does not exist, the optimizer chooses the best one available, or simply does a table scan, but it stores the details of the "missing index." This information is exposed via four `sys.dm_db_missing_index_*` DMOs, which are rarely used individually, but as a group. They are:

- **`sys.dm_db_missing_index_details`** – a DMV that provides detailed information regarding indexes the optimizer would have chosen to use, had they been available

- **`sys.dm_db_missing_index_columns`** – a DMF that accepts an `index_handle` parameter and returns a table providing details of columns that would comprise the suggested missing index

- **`sys.dm_db_missing_index_group_stats`** – a DMV that returns detailed information pertaining to metrics on groups of missing indexes

- **sys.dm_db_missing_index_groups** – a DMV that provides details of missing indexes in a specific group; this is the intermediate join table between sys.dm_db_missing_index_details and sys.dm_db_missing_index_group_stats.

Napoleon Bonaparte stated that *a good sketch is better than a long speech*. I promise that this is my one and only quote from a 19th century French dictator in this book, but the adage is quite appropriate in this case. Figure 5.4 shows the many-to-many relationship between missing_index_details and index_group_stats, via missing_index_groups.

The first thing to note is that there is no index_id in any of the missing index DMOs. This is because the returned results are recommendations for indexes which have yet to be created, and are therefore non-materialized. The unique identifier for the records in these DMVs is the index_handle column, which is unique across the entire SQL Server instance.

The data stored by each of these DMOs is reset on a server restart. This is why it is so important to preserve this cumulative data and keep your instances in a constantly running state; you need to make sure, when you use this data, that the stored statistics are fully representative of your normal query workload. One service restart, and your accrued history (and the ability to generate meaningful results for this and other DMV-based queries) is, pardon the pun, history.

Furthermore, the data stored in these DMOs is also volatile and based on active queries. By implementing a single new index on a given table or view, the results of the DMO query for that object may no longer be valid.

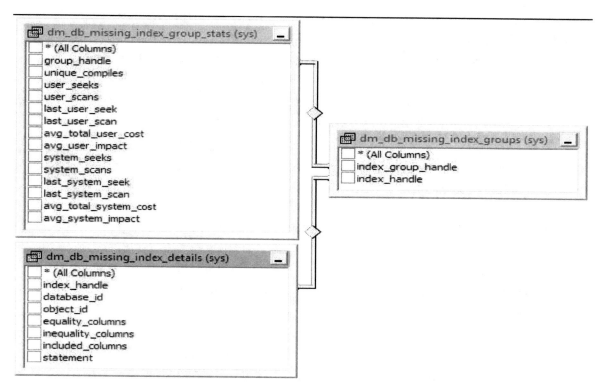

Figure 5.4: The many-to-many relationship: `missing_index_details` and `index_group_stats`, via `missing_index_groups`.

The columns returned by each one are well covered on MSDN (HTTP://MSDN.MICROSOFT. COM/EN-US/LIBRARY/MSI87974.ASPX) so we'll only review the most significant columns here, for each DMO.

Missing index details

The `sys.dm_db_missing_index_details` DMV, which identifies our missing indexes, returns the identifier columns `index_handle`, `object_id` and `database_id`, along with the following:

- **`equality_columns`** – the columns that would have been useful, based on an equality predicate

- **`inequality_columns`** – the columns that would have been useful, based on an inequality predicate (i.e. any comparison other than "column = value")

- **`included_columns`** – columns that, if included, would have been useful to cover the query

- **`statement`** – database and schema qualified object name of the object identified by `database_id` and `object_id`.

Missing index columns

The `sys.dm_db_missing_index_columns` DMF accepts the `index_handle` as a parameter (retrieved from `sys.dm_db_missing_index_details` or `sys.dm_db_missing_index_group`) and returns a table containing a record for each of the individual columns that would make up the identified index. This makes it easier for tools to use the columns to build a `CREATE INDEX` statement. It returns only three columns, `column_id`, `column_name` and `column_usage`, the latter taking the self-explanatory values of either `EQUALITY`, `INEQUALITY` or `INCLUDE`. There may be duplicate `column_name` values for the case where a column would be useful for both an equality and an inequality predicate.

It's important to note that the columns in this list are not ordered in a way that reflects the optimal column ordering for the index key, so you may have to do some additional tweaking to get the best result.

Missing index groups

The `sys.dm_db_missing_index_groups` DMV simply resolves the many-to-many relationship between `sys.dm_db_missing_index_details` and `sys.dm_db_missing_index_group_stats`. It identifies a missing index to its missing index group via the following columns:

- **index_group_handle** – the id of the index group, which is used to relate the row to the `sys.dm_db_missing_index_group_stats` view

- **index_handle** – the handle of the index, used to relate the row to `sys.dm_db_missing_index_details` and `sys.dm_db_missing_index_columns`.

Currently, there is only one index to a group but, for future compatibility, you should consider the key of this object to be comprised of both columns.

Missing index group statistics

The `sys.dm_db_missing_index_group_stats` DMV provides all the detail statistics regarding the size of the benefit that SQL Server would expect from the missing index, including how often it would have been used in scans and seeks, and how many compiled plans could use it.

Its identifier column is `group_handle`, which joins to `index_group_handle` in `sys.dm_db_missing_index_groups`. As noted, for the time being there is only one index per group. It also returns the following statistical columns:

- **unique_compiles** – the number of plans that have been compiled that might have used the index

- **user_seeks** – the number of seek operations in user queries that might have used the index

- **user_scans** – the number of scan operations in user queries that might have used the index

- **last_user_seek** – the last time that a seek operation might have used the index

- **last_user_scan** – the last time that a scan operation might have used the index

- **avg_total_user_cost** – average cost saving for the queries that could have been helped by the index in the group

- **avg_user_impact** – the estimated percentage by which the average query cost would drop, for the queries that could use this index.

For each of the user statistics columns there are equivalent system columns, which record when the index is used for a system operation, such as automatic statistics operations.

The last_user_* columns are vital in helping you assess whether you really do need to add the suggested missing index. If this time isn't fairly recent, then it's likely that the query it would have helped was ad hoc, and not part of your normal workload, and so the benefit of creating the index is likely to be marginal, or even detrimental, if the table in question is updated frequently.

Limitations of the missing index DMOs

While these DMOs are potentially very useful in optimizing your index strategy and query execution times, the information they provide should be used with caution. Just as we advised against wildly dropping indexes without thorough investigation, so you should never just blindly add every index that these DMOs suggest. This is especially true if you have an OLTP workload, where too many indexes can be just as damaging as too few. Every time data is updated in a table, the data in the indexes must be maintained as well. This can dramatically reduce the performance of these data modifications.

Instead, you need to examine the results of the query carefully and manually filter out results that are not part of your regular workload.

Also, be warned that the order in which these DMOs list missing columns does *not* accurately suggest the correct column order for an index key. Furthermore, in our experience, these DMOs are often over-enthusiastic in suggesting INCLUDE columns. They are best used to find the biggest "holes" in an indexing strategy, not as a fine-tuning tool.

In addition, Microsoft Books Online lists the following specific limitations:

- cannot gather statistics for more than 500 missing index groups
- return less accurate cost information for queries involving only inequality predicates
- reports only include columns for some queries, so index key columns must be manually selected
- return only raw information about columns on which indexes might be missing
- can return different costs for the same missing index group that appears multiple times in XML Showplans.

Finding the most beneficial missing indexes

So how do you go about putting these DMOs to good use? Our goal is clearly to obtain a list of missing indexes, with the most useful ones listed at the top. The SQL Server Query Optimization Team at Microsoft proposed the following formula for calculating the overall benefit of a suggested index, based on the columns in the _group_stats DMV, and it has been widely adopted:

```
(user_seeks + user_scans) * avg_total_user_cost * (avg_user_impact * 0.01)
```

Listing 5.13 provides a quick and useful query, based on this formula, that DBAs can run to identify potentially useful indexes. The results of this query are instance-wide, so be sure to limit your results to just the database in question, in the **WHERE** clause, as demonstrated here. This query provides the DBA with information directly from the query optimizer history, accrued since the last restart of the SQL Server service. It provides information on columns the optimizer would have preferred to have indexed, based upon the original parse of the query upon execution. Equality columns, inequality columns, and included columns are each identified. Also presented are the accrued counts of compiles and seeks, as well as calculated figures that denote the amount of improvement to be gained if the indexes were created.

```
SELECT  user_seeks * avg_total_user_cost * ( avg_user_impact * 0.01 )
                                        AS [index_advantage] ,
        dbmigs.last_user_seek ,
        dbmid.[statement] AS [Database.Schema.Table] ,
        dbmid.equality_columns ,
        dbmid.inequality_columns ,
        dbmid.included_columns ,
        dbmigs.unique_compiles ,
        dbmigs.user_seeks ,
        dbmigs.avg_total_user_cost ,
        dbmigs.avg_user_impact
FROM    sys.dm_db_missing_index_group_stats AS dbmigs WITH ( NOLOCK )
        INNER JOIN sys.dm_db_missing_index_groups AS dbmig WITH ( NOLOCK )
                ON dbmigs.group_handle = dbmig.index_group_handle
        INNER JOIN sys.dm_db_missing_index_details AS dbmid WITH ( NOLOCK )
                ON dbmig.index_handle = dbmid.index_handle
WHERE   dbmid.[database_id] = DB_ID()
ORDER BY index_advantage DESC ;
```

	index_advantage	last_user_seek	statement	equality_columns	inequality_columns
1	323529.372737502	2010-07-28 17:23:01.077	[demo].[dbo].[Patients]	[patient_type]	[facility_code], [discharged]
2	321492.297819951	2010-07-28 16:38:36.937	[demo].[dbo].[Patients]	[facility_code]	[patient_type], [discharged]
3	110785.726366788	2010-07-28 17:24:52.437	[demo].[dbo].[Audit]	[audit_entity]	[fk_auditactivity], [dt_created]
4	109457.795922066	2010-07-28 17:06:11.763	[demo].[dbo].[Patients]	[patient_type], [facility_code]	[discharged]
5	77265.9424917084	2010-07-28 17:24:52.437	[demo].[dbo].[Demog]	NULL	[fk_reportstatus]

	included_columns	unique_compiles	user_seeks	avg_total_user_cost	avg_user_impact
1	[patient_id], [visit_id]	278	1585	567.31372447978	35.98
2	[patient_id], [visit_id]	84	861	890.093144512649	41.95
3	[pk_audit], [audit_id], [fk_cut], [fk_scruser], [fk...	52	19223	22.7344619260618	25.35
4	[patient_id], [visit_id]	96	642	201.60223391794	84.57
5	[pk_udn], [mrn], [lastname], [firstname], [middle...	52	19223	22.7344619260618	17.68

Listing 5.13: Finding beneficial missing indexes.

This query represents a powerful tool in helping DBAs to identify pathways for performance improvement. However, the SQL Server Query Optimization Team have taken this a step or two further, and offer a "missing index" tool, available at HTTP://BLOGS. MSDN.COM/QUERYOPTTEAM/ARCHIVE/2006/06/01/613516.ASPX, which generates a lot of details about indexes that might be useful.

In either case, however, we should never simply create each and every index suggested by the results. As discussed at the start of the "Index Strategy" section earlier in this chapter, creating too many indexes on a table can be just as damaging to performance as not creating enough (or creating the wrong) indexes. We recommend that you create a duplicate environment for your test and development work that represents the hardware and SQL Server configurations of your production environment. You should then go through the process of creating indexes recommended through these results, and testing performance in a simulated production load.

Index Maintenance (index_physical_stats)

The sys.dm_db_index_physical_stats DMF is, in this author's opinion, the most important of all the index-related DMOs. I use the scripts that will be provided in this section on a daily basis, on every SQL Server 2005 and 2008 instance I administer, to seek out and fix index fragmentation issues. It can be used to identify fragmentation in non-clustered indexes, clustered tables (a table with a clustered index) and heaps (a table with no clustered index). The latter two will be covered in further detail in *Chapter 6*.

I think most of us had our start as DBAs using the SQL Server Maintenance Plans Wizard built into Enterprise Manager or SQL Server Management Studio. This is how we cut our teeth when backing up data and log files, checking our databases for errors, and rebuilding our indexes. The issue with using maintenance plans, particularly for index maintenance, is that it is an all-or-nothing process: you either rebuild all the indexes in your database (and all the databases in the maintenance plan) or you rebuild none of them. There is no middle ground.

Even now, many years and editions later, this rather large hammer is the only built-in tool at our disposal for performing index maintenance. However, with the help of this DMF, at least we can find out which indexes really are suffering from fragmentation and then, based on this, build our own index maintenance plans, which limit rebuilds to just those indexes that need them, or just clustered or non-clustered indexes, indexes of a certain size, or of a specific table, and so on. In short, this DMF gives the DBA an element of control over the index maintenance process that is sadly lacking in the current Maintenance Plans tool.

A brief overview of index fragmentation

The leaf level of a clustered index is implemented as a doubly-linked list. This means that every leaf level of the index includes a pointer to both the previous and the next page in the index. The data will be stored in the logical order dictated by the clustering key and new data will be added in its correct place on the relevant page. So, assuming there is room on that page, the logical order will match the physical order.

The pointers in the doubly-linked list make it easy to scan ranges of data and, when the data is ordered as described above, this becomes a very efficient operation. In turn, non-clustered indexes on a table with a clustered index, are implemented as a doubly-linked list, and have the same benefits (by contrast, indexes on heaps are not implemented this way, and have no knowledge of which page to scan next).

This idyllic picture begins to break down, unfortunately, as a natural by-product of data modifications. As data is inserted, deleted, and updated, index fragmentation can occur. When data is deleted, gaps appear in data pages that create wasted empty space. When data is updated or added on a page that has become full, a page split will occur and one of the split pages will be stored "at the end," and so out of logical sequence. Now we have a logical ordering of the data that no longer matches the physical ordering of the data (referred to as logical fragmentation).

As a result, disk I/O is affected because the disk head must now jump all over the disk following a fragmented chain of records and pointers as opposed to a sequential listing. Wasted space reduces the number of rows that can be stored in SQL Server's data cache, which can also lead to increased disk I/O. Do keep in mind that, as a result, this only pertains to data/index pages that are not residing within memory, in the cache.

SQL Server doesn't automatically correct index fragmentation problems. The only way to remove wasted space and restore the correct page ordering is to rebuild or reorganize the indexes on a regular basis. Rebuilding an index is the process by which the existing index is dropped and recreated. The process can occur either offline or online (if hosting on Enterprise Edition SQL Server). Since the index is recreated, all fragmentation is removed. The indexes are recreated under the mandate of the existing fill factor percentage and the index is rebuilt in continuous pages. Meanwhile, reorganizing only defragments the leaf level of an index by physically reordering them to match the logical order of the leaf nodes.

The first step is to identify the indexes that are fragmented beyond an acceptable percentage, and this is where our _index_physical_stats DMF comes in very useful.

Fragmentation statistics (index_physical_stats)

The `sys.dm_db_index_physical_stats` DMF provides invaluable information regarding the state of your index partitions, including type of index, index depth, and degree of fragmentation. An index in this context can mean several things: a clustered index, heap, index, or a partition of either of these. These physical stats all serve to tell you of the condition of an index. Even the most potentially beneficial index in terms of optimizing query execution can become useless if it is not maintained properly.

Data stored in this DMF is cumulative but refreshed when the server is restarted or when the index is dropped and recreated. Statistics live on when the index is rebuilt or reorganized, and even when it is disabled and rebuilt.

Like the `operational_stats` DMF, the `physical_stats` DMF accepts the `database_id`, `object_id`, `index_id`, and `partition_number` as parameters, in order to identify the object (heap, index or partition) in question, and returns detailed "physical stats" for each partition. All the parameters can be `NULL` or `DEFAULT` if you want to return all rows, in which case the DMF will return a row for every partition in every database. It also accepts a `mode` parameter, which determines the thoroughness with which the statistics are collected. Possible values are:

- **LIMITED** is the default and the least costly, but it also will leave a lot of the columns as `NULL`; `LIMITED` will not scan the leaf level of the indexes and the data pages of heaps are not scanned

- **SAMPLED** mode returns statistics based only upon a 1% sample of all pages of the indexes and heaps in the scope of the function call; if any page or heap within the scope of the function call has less than 10,000 pages, then `DETAILED` is automatically used

- **DETAILED** provides the most complete result set from this function of the three, but can require ample resources; it scans all pages; it returns all statistics.

The DMF returns a large number of columns and we'll only review a subset of them here. It returns a number of columns that describe the physical structure of the index, including:

- **index_type_desc** – describes the physical type of the index (clustered index, non-clustered index, heap, primary xml index, xml index)

- **alloc_unit_type_desc** – describes the type of pages in the index object (IN_ROW_DATA, LOB_DATA, ROW_OVERFLOW_DATA)

- **index_depth** – the number of levels in the b-tree of the index

- **index_level** – 0 for the leaf level of the index, counting up the levels of the leaf levels; for example, if index depth is 3, then you will have 0 = leaf level, 2 for the middle page, and 1 for the top level page in the index; note that leaf/heap pages are processed when the mode parameter = 'DETAILED'; leaf pages are ignored in 'LIMITED' mode

- **page_count** – the number of pages in the index or data pages level; for heaps, LOB_DATA and ROW_OVERFLOW_DATA allocation unit types, it is the count of all pages

- **avg_page_space_used_in_percent** – the average percentage of space used in the index or data pages level; for heaps, LOB_DATA and ROW_OVERFLOW_DATA allocation unit types, it is the average space used on all pages

- **record_count** – the number of records that are represented in the current object.

Most significantly, the DMF returns much valuable information regarding the degree of fragmentation of the index, including:

- **avg_fragmentation_in_percent** – the percentage of logical fragmentation for indexes, and of extent fragmentation for heaps

- **fragment_count** – the number of fragments in the leaf level of IN_ROW_DATA allocation units

- **avg_fragment_size_in_pages** – the average number of pages in a fragment for IN_ROW_DATA allocation unity types

- **forwarded_record_count** – for heaps, the number of forwarding pointers; forwarding pointers are very bad for performance when using heaps, because they are always resolved immediately as they are encountered.

Detecting and fixing fragmentation

Every index encounters some level of fragmentation, and its resolution is a two-part process. Part 1 is detecting unacceptable fragmentation levels. The query in Listing 5.14 will return fragmentation information for each index in the current database, where the **average_fragmentation_in_percent** column is greater than 15% and where the page count is greater than 500. On a busy system, this can be a resource-intensive query so please keep that in mind when setting the scope of your query (via the parameters for the DMF) and the time of day when you are going to execute the query.

```
SELECT   '[' + DB_NAME() + '].[' + OBJECT_SCHEMA_NAME(ddips.[object_id],
                                          DB_ID()) + '].['
         + OBJECT_NAME(ddips.[object_id], DB_ID()) + ']' AS [statement] ,
         i.[name] AS [index_name] ,
         ddips.[index_type_desc] ,
         ddips.[partition_number] ,
         ddips.[alloc_unit_type_desc] ,
         ddips.[index_depth] ,
         ddips.[index_level] ,
         CAST(ddips.[avg_fragmentation_in_percent] AS SMALLINT)
             AS [avg_frag_%] ,
         CAST(ddips.[avg_fragment_size_in_pages] AS SMALLINT)
             AS [avg_frag_size_in_pages] ,
         ddips.[fragment_count] ,
         ddips.[page_count]
FROM     sys.dm_db_index_physical_stats(DB_ID(), NULL,
                                  NULL, NULL, 'limited') ddips
         INNER JOIN sys.[indexes] i ON ddips.[object_id] = i.[object_id]
                                  AND ddips.[index_id] = i.[index_id]
WHERE    ddips.[avg_fragmentation_in_percent] > 15
         AND ddips.[page_count] > 500
```

```
ORDER BY ddips.[avg_fragmentation_in_percent] ,
         OBJECT_NAME(ddips.[object_id], DB_ID()) ,
         i.[name ]
```

	statement	index_name	index_type_desc	partition_number	alloc_unit_type_desc
1	[demo].[sch1].[tsgnosis]	PK_NCLosis	CLUSTERED INDEX	1	IN_ROW_DATA
2	[demo].[sch1].[DB917734]	NULL	HEAP	1	IN_ROW_DATA
3	[demo].[sch1].[DB712179]	NULL	HEAP	1	IN_ROW_DATA
4	[demo].[sch1].[tsgnosis]	IX_NU_Text	NONCLUSTERED INDEX	1	IN_ROW_DATA
5	[demo].[sch1].[tsements]	PK_tstents	CLUSTERED INDEX	1	IN_ROW_DATA
6	[demo].[sch1].[tsdvisor]	IX_tstisor	NONCLUSTERED INDEX	1	IN_ROW_DATA
7	[demo].[sch1].[tsaps]	PK_tsts	CLUSTERED INDEX	1	IN_ROW_DATA
8	[demo].[sch1].[tsaphics]	PK_tsthics	CLUSTERED INDEX	1	IN_ROW_DATA
9	[demo].[sch1].[tsObject]	PK_tstject	CLUSTERED INDEX	1	IN_ROW_DATA
10	[demo].[sch1].[DB340534]	NULL	HEAP	1	IN_ROW_DATA

	index_depth	index_level	avg_frag_%	avg_frag_size_in_pages	fragment_count	page_count
1	3	0	16	3	1926	7115
2	1	0	16	19	4	76
3	1	0	16	36	10	361
4	3	0	18	3	1621	5553
5	2	0	18	3	41	143
6	2	0	21	3	31	103
7	3	0	23	2	16106	48070
8	3	0	34	2	7858	18141
9	3	0	37	2	12769	28328
10	1	0	40	10	7	74

Listing 5.14: Investigating fragmented indexes.

Note that this query does not ignore heaps. Fragmentation occurs in heaps just as in indexes; but fixing this fragmentation in heaps is a little different than in clustered and non-clustered indexes (as will be explained shortly).

The rule of thumb for index reorganization is 15–30% fragmentation. The often-recommended process for indexes with fragmentation greater than 30% is a rebuild of the index. These standards should be taken lightly, as a more heavily trafficked index may need to be rebuilt at a lower fragmentation level, and a less active index could conceivably wait until its fragmentation reaches the rebuild range, and so is never reorganized.

I tend to stick with these standards, except in extreme cases. If we go by those standards, it is a decent assessment to state that our demo database is in decent shape from an index fragmentation angle. I would recommend running reorganization commands against the clustered and non-clustered indexes with less than 30% fragmentation, and rebuilding the two clustered indexes with fragmentation in excess of 30%.

For the fragmented heap (**demo.sch1.DB340534**), I would identify a clustering key and create the clustered index. If, for some reason, a heap is warranted, then I'd still identify a clustering key, create the clustered index, and then drop the index. The data will remain ordered based upon the clustering key identified, but will revert back to a heap object once you drop the clustered index. Alternatively, if I'm lucky enough to be using a SQL Server 2008 instance, I can issue **ALTER TABLE...REBUILD**.

Now that we've shown you how to identify fragmentation in your indexes and heaps, how do you go about resolving it, without manually crafting a reorganization or rebuild command for each index identified as being fragmented beyond acceptable levels? I've created many iterations of such a script over the years, but I've scrapped it in favor of one created by Andrew Kelly, published in the July 2008 issue of SQL Server Magazine (WWW.SQLMAG.COM/ARTICLE/ARTICLEID/99019/REBUILD_ONLY_THE_INDEXES_THAT_ NEED_HELP.HTML). Based on his code, I generated a SQL Agent job that I schedule and run against selected databases, and rebuild/reorganize indexes accordingly.

Summary

This chapter has covered the DMOs that can help the DBA to define an effective SQL Server indexing strategy, since this is one of the best ways to ensure that the most significant and frequent queries are able to read the required data in a logical, ordered fashion, and so avoid unnecessary I/O. Finding the correct balance between too many and too few indexes, and having in place the appropriate set of "useful" indexes is extremely important for a DBA who wants to get the best performance from SQL Server.

This chapter showed how to:

- use the `sys.dm_db_index_usage_stats` DMV to uncover those indexes that exist but have never been used, or where the maintenance cost of the index, (perhaps because the table data is regularly updated), is high but the index is rarely used as a data access path, and so is offering relatively little in terms of query performance benefit

- use the `sys.dm_db_index_operational_stats` DMF to obtain "physical" usage statistics for a clustered index, heap or index, so that we can investigate potential lock or latch contention on the object, or excessive I/O being issued by the object, all of which may cause users to wait a significant amount of time in order to read data from the object

- use the `sys.dm_db_missing_` group of DMOs to identify indexes that the optimizer would have liked to have had available when seeking out the optimal data access path for a given query

- use the `sys.dm_db_index_physical_stats` DMV to investigate fragmentation in indexes and heaps, and to determine a rebuild/reorganize strategy based on real need, rather than just the "better safe than sorry" approach of defragmenting as often as available maintenance windows allow.

Throughout the chapter, we've stressed the need for the DBA to apply judgment, and their knowledge of their database, its data, and the normal query workload, before creating or removing any of the indexes identified by the DMO queries presented in this chapter. In particular, make sure that the SQL Server instance has been running long enough for the complete, typical workload to be represented in the reported statistics, and don't forget to account for the indexes required by periodic reporting jobs that might not show up in the day-to-day workload.

Chapter 6: Physical Disk Statistics and Utilization

A critical aspect of SQL Server performance is how the engine uses the disk I/O subsystem, and the ability of that subsystem to cope with the I/O throughput (I/Os per second) demanded by the system workload. Physical I/O, in other words writing to disk or reading from disk, when the required data page does not reside in cache memory, is an expensive operation. The DBA must work to minimize the occurrence of physical reads from disk, for example, by ensuring that there is adequate RAM for cache data, and configuring the disk subsystem to cope smoothly with the total I/O load.

During busy periods, or when performing I/O-intensive maintenance operations (such as backup/restore or index rebuild), physical reads can be very high, and if the speed or configuration of the disk subsystem is inadequate for the generated I/O throughput, the DBA will to notice an immediate and often dramatic impact on performance. It is vital that the DBA has a means to identify this I/O pressure and its root cause, and respond appropriately, by tuning queries, adding indexes, defragmenting indexes, better distributing the I/O workload across the file system, or by adding more RAM, or more and faster disks.

In order to diagnose various I/O-related issues relating directly to the performance and condition of the files and disks in your databases, we'll be putting into action views and functions from several of the 17 categories of dynamic management objects listed on MSDN (HTTP://MSDN.MICROSOFT.COM/EN-US/LIBRARY/MS188754.ASPX). Following is a list and brief description of each view or function that we'll use, with the category to which it belongs indicated in brackets:

- **sys.dm_db_partition_stats** (**database related**) – returns disk space oriented statistics (row count, page counts, and so on) for each object in a partition

- **sys.dm_db_index_physical_stats** (**index related**) – provides health information (size and fragmentation stats) regarding your clustered tables, non-clustered indexes (covered in more detail in *Chapter 5*) and heaps, which directly relates to how reads will affect I/O

- **sys.dm_io_virtual_file_stats** (**I/O related**) – provides statistics on how all database files have been utilized; both data and log files are represented; excellent resource for discovering hotspots, and identifying opportunities to spread I/O over different channels

- **sys.dm_io_pending_io_requests** (**I/O related**) – provides a list of all I/O operations that SQL Server is currently waiting to complete

- **sys.dm_db_file_space_usage** (**database related**) – gives information on how tempdb is being used.

Keep in mind that interpretation of the statistics you obtain from these DMVs must be done with care. They will give you a deeper understanding of the characteristics and usage of your data structures, and of how the disk I/O subsystem is being used or abused by your programming (or by other processes that share use of the disk subsystem with SLQ Server). However, this data must not be taken in isolation when making decisions about the necessary remedial action. An overtaxed CPU can make I/O take longer, just as readily as slow disks, or a malfunctioning controller.

Minimizing I/O

Physical I/O is simply a request to read data from, or write data to, physical disk. It is an expensive operation. SQL Server does not directly manage reading and writing data to disk; whenever it needs to read or write to an MDF or LDF file, it passes off the I/O request to the Windows I/O Manager (part of the OS kernel) which, in turn, passes it to a device driver to perform the actual reads from, and writes to, disk.

A certain amount of physical I/O is inevitable. It will occur when data modifications, written to the data cache in memory, need to be "hardened" to disk. The write-ahead logging mechanism used by SQL Server means that the details of INSERT, UPDATE and DELETE transactions are always first written to the transaction log (LDF) file on disk. A data page that contains data that has been committed to the transaction log file but not to the data (MDF) file is referred to as a "dirty page." A process called the "lazy writer" manages the writing of dirty pages to physical disk when there is time, or when no more data can be placed into the cache, while another process, called the "checkpoint" process, makes sure the number of dirty pages is kept to a level such that, if you needed to recover the database, a relatively small number of pages would need to be read from the log.

In addition, physical I/O will occur each time a requested data page is not found in the data cache, and so needs to be first read into memory from the underlying disks. Logical I/O is a less expensive operation than physical I/O, so the DBA will want as many queries as possible to be served from the cache. This often means having as much RAM as can be afforded, up to and perhaps slightly over the amount of data on the server. However, this is frequently an unrealistic proposition. Even medium-sized organizations can store hundreds of gigabytes of data, and their appetite for data is growing rapidly. While RAM costs start out cheap, we aren't likely to have terabytes of cheap RAM any time soon.

While the focus of this chapter is disk (i.e. physical) I/O, it's worth remembering that logical I/O, while cheaper, is far from free. Logical I/O occurs when a data request (read) can be satisfied by serving up a page residing in memory, in the data cache. Writes are also first written to the data cache, before later being written to disk. If your query workload results in unnecessarily high logical I/O, then your performance will suffer. The best way to ensure that as many data requests as possible are served from memory is to avoid **all** unnecessary I/O. This means tuning the query workload so that each query returns the minimum necessary data, reads the data as few times as possible, and uses solid, set-based logic to manipulate the data set.

One of the most effective ways to minimize both logical and physical I/O is to create an appropriate set of indexes, as discussed in *Chapter 5*. A scan of even a moderately-sized table could easily result in reading 100,000 pages, even if you only need to return a small fraction of that data. The appropriate index, allowing data to be returned by an index seek operation, can reduce the I/O load by many orders of magnitude. Queries that are returning large amounts of data, or are returning only moderate amounts, but without use of an index, are likely to be the ones that are causing the heaviest I/O load on SQL Server. As described in *Chapters 2* and *3*, you can isolate the most I/O-intensive queries (or connections or sessions) using the execution-related DMOs, notably `sys.dm_exec_query_stats`.

Indexes reduce physical as well as logical I/O. A scan of a large table will result in a large volume of data being read into the cache. This may well result in other data being flushed from the cache to make room, causing increased physical I/O for queries that need that data.

Another critical aspect of minimizing I/O overhead is ensuring that your data structures, heaps, and indexes, are properly maintained, i.e. not fragmented. When gaps appear in data pages, or they become logically fragmented, so that the physical ordering of the data does not match the logical order, the engine has to perform a lot more I/O to retrieve the disordered data pages, especially when performing scans.

Ultimately, however, on busy OLTP systems subject to a high volume of data modifications, there may be a high level of unavoidable physical I/O. Aside from query tuning, indexing and so on, the DBA must ensure that the I/O subsystem is correctly configured to handle the required I/O throughput. If I/O bottlenecks are observed, the DBA can use the DMOs described in this chapter to find out where the hotspots are on the file system, and look for ways to distribute the workload more evenly, perhaps by using table and index partitioning, and spreading the partitions across multiples files, for better I/O balancing.

Tuning the Disk I/O Subsystem

In keeping with the other chapters in this book, our focus is on how to retrieve the information that will indicate how the disk I/O subsystem is being used from SQL Server's perspective. We do not, and cannot, spend time suggesting how the disk I/O subsystem might be tuned as a result. Certain advice, pertaining, for example, to the use of separate drives for random I/O (data files) and sequential I/O (log files), separate drives for tempdb, optimal RAID configurations for various data access patterns, and so on, is well documented. However, in general, it is a vast topic with many variables.

The disk I/O subsystem may range from straightforward direct attached storage to highly elaborate architectures involving the use of SANs, RAID, and so on. In either case, SQL Server treats the disk I/O subsystem as a black box. It creates a file, and asks to write and read from that file. If SQL Server's I/O throughput requirements are not being adequately catered for, this will be reflected in the statistics returned by the DMOs covered in this chapter, in the form, for example, of high I/O stalls (covered in the section, *Diagnosing I/O Bottlenecks*).

If you are lucky enough to have a simple disk subsystem dedicated solely to SQL Server, then such problems indicate a need to find ways to minimize the amount of I/O SQL Server performs, and/or increase disk speed, and so on, as described in the previous section.

If your disk I/O subsystem is complex and/or shared by other applications, as is common when using SANs, the situation is less straightforward. You need to consider the possibility that other, non-SQL Server processes are causing the problem, along with the fact that the problem may be anywhere along the path from the cache manager to the physical disks on the SAN, and caused by incorrect array configuration, insufficient cache on the controller, problems with drive controllers, and network or interface cards, and so on.

In any event, it is vital that, before even installing SLQ Server, you gain a good understanding of the I/O capacity of your disk subsystem, using tools such as SQLIO (see, for example, HTTP://TECHNET.MICROSOFT.COM/EN-US/LIBRARY/CC966412.ASPX), and then, once SQL Server is up and running, closely monitor its disk I/O usage via tools such as the PerfMon counters, Profiler, and the DMOs covered in this chapter.

Getting Physical Statistics on your Tables and Indexes

In the fight to minimize I/O overhead, DBAs need detailed knowledge of the size and structure of the objects in their databases, and their state of physical health – in other words, the degree to which their data structures are fragmented. In this section, we are going to take a look at the tools that will provide us with statistics on the physical structures of the tables and indexes, focusing mainly on clustered tables and heaps (since indexes were covered in detail in *Chapter 5*).

- A **clustered table** is simply a table with a clustered index. The leaf pages of the clustered index, which are the actual data pages of the table, are implemented as a doubly-linked list, ordered by the clustered index key, referred to as the clustering key. Any non-clustered index defined on this table will hold this clustering key value, in addition to any other columns defined in the index. If a non-clustered index does not hold all the columns required for a query, a bookmark lookup is performed on the clustered index, using the clustering key.

- A **heap structure** has no clustered index. The storage engine inserts all rows at the end of the table, in order of arrival. Any non-clustered index defined on a heap uses a pointer to the physical location of the row in the heap, if data is required but not stored in the index itself.

We'll start by investigating the size and structure of partitioned and non-partitioned objects, using the `sys.dm_db_partition_stats` DMV, then we'll deal with fragmentation separately, using the `sys.dm_db_index_physical_stats` DMF. The latter is mainly used for obtaining index fragmentation information, but is also useful for investigating tables; it can provide valuable information on the degree of fragmentation of the extents that comprise your tables, the number of forward pointers, and so on.

Note that, structurally, a table resembles an index, since the data pages of any tables are, in essence, index leaf pages. Even a heap can be thought of as a "brute force," scan-only index. This is why the same tools can be used to manage indexes and tables.

Size and structure

It is critical that DBAs have a simple means to monitor the size of the tables and indexes in their databases and the number of rows stored for each object, for each partition. With this information, they can find the largest objects and partitions, especially those that are subject to heavy updates, monitor the effectiveness of their partitioning scheme, or investigate the need to upgrade/configure the disk I/O subsystem appropriately.

In the text, we have referred to a "table," but in the engine of SQL Server, the unit of measure for dealing with objects physically is a partition. Conceptually, it helps to think of every table as being partitioned, even if you have only a single partition. `sys.dm_db_partition_stats` provides statistics regarding the pages that store your tables and indexes, in a given partition. It shows the number of pages used by that object for in-row, Large Object (LOB) and row overflow data, along with the total number of rows stored for that object.

It returns one row per partition; if no tables or indexes are partitioned, you'll simply see one row per object, with a partition number of 1. Note that, even in a newly created database, you will start out with nearly 100 partitions for the system objects. In many of our queries we will filter out system objects using the `objectproperty` function like this: `objectproperty(ddps.object_id,'IsMSShipped')`.

sys.dm_db_partition_stats, sysindexes *and* **sp_spaceused**

The sys.dm_db_partition_stats *DMV resembles* sysindexes *in versions of SQL Server before 2005, but provides a lot more information. It also contains a lot of the raw information that is aggregated for you in the* sp_spaceused *system stored procedure.*

The view supplies the following "identifier" columns:

- **partition_id** – numeric identifier of the partition (relates to **sys.partitions**)

- **object_id** – numeric identifier of the object, associated with the partition identified above

- **index_id** – identifies the index on the table; 0 = heap, 1 = clustered, other values are indexes

- **partition_number** – will have a value of 1 for non-partitioned objects; for partitioned tables it will be the number of the partition starting with 1.

Note that, as of now, only SQL Server Enterprise Edition supports partitioning, so the partition_number will always have a value of 1 in editions other than Enterprise. For those people who normally use Standard Edition or lower, the need to deal with partitions in all management code can seem a bit tedious, since it feels like an extra, unnecessary layer of complexity. However, the problem with omitting partition_id from queries when using a Standard Edition server, is that if you execute the same script against another, Enterprise Edition server, then the table and index names will be duplicated. In the example code here, we always include the partition information, or group by and sum the rows if we want to know the total number of items (row count for a table, perhaps), regardless of whether or not partitioning is being used.

The view returns the statistical columns below.

- **`in_row_data_page_count`** – number of pages being used for in-row object data in the partition. For an index, this is the number of leaf pages; for a clustered table or heap, it is the number of data pages.

- **`in_row_used_page_count`** – all pages in use for the object, including non-leaf index and index allocation map pages.

- **`in_row_reserved_page_count`** – all pages in use plus any pages reserved for the object, even if the pages are not currently in use. For example, when a table grows, it grows in 8 x 8 K page extents, so all these pages could be allocated to the table, even though only a single page is used.

- **`lob_used_page_count`** – count of pages in use for the object to store out-of-row values such as `varchar(max)`, `varbinary(max)`, and so on.

- **`lob_reserved_page_count`** – count of out-of-row pages including any that are reserved but not in use.

- **`row_overflow_used_page_count`** – count of pages that are in use for storing overflow data, for rows that are larger than will fit on a single ~8 K page.

- **`row_overflow_reserved_page_count`** – count of overflow pages that includes any pages that are reserved but not in use.

- **`used_page_count`** – total number of pages in use in the partition for any reason.

- **`reserved_page_count`** – total number of pages in use or reserved in the partition for any reason.

- **`row_count`** – number of rows in the object (or partition of an object).

Total number of rows in a table

The query in Listing 6.1 will provide the total number of rows in all clustered indexes and heaps on a given SQL Server instance. System objects such as `sys.dm_db_partition_stats` are updated asynchronously, for performance reasons, so the counts may not be completely up to date. The values are far more reliable than those obtained from the old system tables in SQL Server 2000 and earlier, but just bear in mind that the only way to get a perfectly accurate count is to use `SELECT count(*) FROM tablename`.

```
SELECT   object_schema_name(ddps.object_id) +
               '.' + OBJECT_NAME(ddps.object_id) AS name ,
         SUM(ddps.row_count) AS row_count
FROM     sys.dm_db_partition_stats AS ddps
         JOIN sys.indexes ON indexes.object_id = ddps.object_id
                           AND indexes.index_id = ddps.index_id
WHERE    indexes.type_desc IN ( 'CLUSTERED', 'HEAP' )
   and   objectproperty(ddps.object_id,'IsMSShipped') = 0
GROUP    BY ddps.object_id
```

Listing 6.1:   Number of rows in clustered tables and heaps.

Note that we group on the `object_id` because, for a partitioned table, we'd need to include all the rows in all partitions. Even if none of your objects are partitioned, I would suggest you always build your queries the "right" way, just in case you do ever need to partition a table.

Number of rows per partition

Let's now take a look at an example where we have some partitioning. The script in Listing 6.2 creates a sample partitioned table. The partition function, `PFdateRange`, uses `RANGE LEFT` to create three partitions: one for all date values less than, or equal to, 20020101; one for all dates greater than 20020101 but less than, or equal to, 20030101; and one for all values greater than 20030101. We then assign rows to each partition according to the value in the `orderDate` column.

```
CREATE PARTITION FUNCTION PFdateRange (SMALLDATETIME)
AS RANGE LEFT FOR VALUES ('20020101','20030101') ;
GO
CREATE PARTITION SCHEME PSdateRange
AS PARTITION PFdateRange ALL TO ( [PRIMARY] )
GO

CREATE TABLE salesOrder
    (
        salesOrderId INT ,
        customerId INT ,
        orderAmount DECIMAL(10, 2) ,
        orderDate SMALLDATETIME ,
        CONSTRAINT PKsalesOrder PRIMARY KEY NONCLUSTERED ( salesOrderId )
          ON [Primary] ,
        CONSTRAINT AKsalesOrder UNIQUE CLUSTERED ( salesOrderId, orderDate )
    )
--the ON clause causes this clustered table to be partitioned by orderDate
--using the partition function/scheme
ON  PSdateRange(orderDate)
GO
--Generate some random data
INSERT  INTO salesOrder
        SELECT  SalesOrderId ,
                CustomerId ,
                TotalDue ,
                OrderDate
        FROM    AdventureWorks.Sales.SalesOrderHeader
```

Listing 6.2:   Creating a three-partition salesOrder table.

To find out how many rows are in each partition, we can use the query shown in
Listing 6.3.

```
SELECT  indexes.name ,
        indexes.type_desc ,
        dps.row_count AS row_count ,
        partition_id
FROM    sys.dm_db_partition_stats AS dps
        JOIN sys.indexes ON indexes.object_id = dps.object_id
                        AND indexes.index_id = dps.index_id
WHERE   OBJECT_ID('salesOrder') = dps.object_id
```

Listing 6.3: Number of rows in each object, per partition.

The results reveal a clustered index named **AKsalesOrder**, broken into three partitions, and a **PKsalesOrder PRIMARY KEY** constraint that is not partitioned, and shows the total number of rows in the three partitions.

```
name            type_desc       row_count       partition_id
--------------  -------------   ------------    --------------------
AKsalesOrder    CLUSTERED       1424            72057594038714368
AksalesOrder    CLUSTERED       3720            72057594038779904
AksalesOrder    CLUSTERED       26321           72057594038845440
PksalesOrder    NONCLUSTERED    31465           72057594038910976
```

Finally, we can expand this query, as shown in Listing 6.4, to get the information about some of the physical characteristics of the partition, as well as the definition of the structure.

```
SELECT  OBJECT_NAME(indexes.object_id) AS Object_Name ,
        ddps.index_id AS Index_ID ,
        ddps.partition_number ,
        ddps.row_count ,
        ddps.used_page_count ,
        ddps.in_row_reserved_page_count ,
        ddps.lob_reserved_page_count ,
        CASE pf.boundary_value_on_right
          WHEN 1 THEN 'less than'
          ELSE 'less than or equal to'
        END AS comparison ,
```

```
          value
FROM      sys.dm_db_partition_stats ddps
          JOIN sys.indexes ON ddps.object_id = indexes.object_id
                          AND ddps.index_id = indexes.index_id
          JOIN sys.partition_schemes ps
                  ON ps.data_space_id = indexes.data_space_id
          JOIN sys.partition_functions pf ON pf.function_id = ps.function_id
          LEFT OUTER JOIN sys.partition_range_values prv
                  ON pf.function_id = prv.function_id
                      AND ddps.partition_number = prv.boundary_id
WHERE     OBJECT_NAME(ddps.object_id) = 'salesOrder '
          AND ddps.index_id IN ( 0, 1 ) --CLUSTERED table or HEAP
```

Listing 6.4: Physical characteristics of each partition.

This returns the following results, broken up into three sets for ease of viewing:

```
Object_Name     Index_ID     partition_number row_count
--------------- ------------ ---------------- ------------------
salesOrder      1            1                1424
salesOrder      1            2                3720
salesOrder      1            3                26321


used_page_count         in_row_reserved_page_count       lob_reserved_page_count
----------------------- -------------------------------- -------------------------
1928                    25                               1905
5024                    57                               4969
35494                   393                              35113


comparison              value
----------------------- -------------------------
less than or equal to   2002-01-01 00:00:00.000
less than or equal to   2003-01-01 00:00:00.000
less than or equal to   NULL
```

This query provides a lot of useful information on the structure of a partitioned table, including the relative sizes of the partitions (are there too many rows in the third partition?) and the inclusion of the ranges makes it clear how the partitions are structured.

Investigating fragmentation

Arguably the most important aspect of managing the health of your tables and indexes, partitioned or otherwise, is minimizing and, if necessary, rectifying fragmentation. The coming sections will explain how fragmentation can occur in both clustered tables and heaps. In either case, when the rows that constitute the pages of an object become disordered and non-contiguous, the disk heads have to skip around performing short, random reads rather than long, contiguous reads, which causes significantly increased disk I/O. Disk head latency is a costly operation that most of us will have to live with until solid state disks become cost effective and we can replace all the mechanical disks that are currently in use. Don't underestimate the impact of fragmentation; it can be terrible for performance, especially when doing table scans which, bad as they sound, are really done quite often. Also, don't underestimate how quickly fragmentation can occur. If your tables are subject to frequent modifications, you can very quickly end up with a table with 10,000 pages and 10,000 fragments, meaning that SQL Server can never perform a sequential read on the pages of the table, and any scans on the object will be very inefficient.

We'll show how to investigate and hopefully rectify each problem, using the `sys.dm_db_index_physical_stats` DMF. As noted in the previous chapter, where this DMF was first introduced, many DBAs rebuild indexes as often as they can get away with it, but this tends to be an all-or-nothing operation, with indexes being rebuilt even if they are suffering no fragmentation. Such operations can bloat transaction logs and, when using differential backups, it means that all the pages in the index/tables will have changed since the last full backup. *Chapter 5* described how to set up an index maintenance scheme based on need rather than expediency, and the same criteria should be considered for the base table rows, i.e. the data pages for a clustered index or the rows in the heap, which are the focus of the discussion here.

The sys.dm_db_index_physical_stats DMF

In order to investigate table fragmentation, we will use the `sys.dm_db_index_physical_stats` DMF. It belongs to the index-related category of DMOs, but since every table is considered either a clustered or heap "index," there is a good amount of overlap. When dealing with a heap, we'll get valuable information regarding the fragmentation of the extents (an **extent** is a group of eight contiguous 8K data pages, and is the basic allocation unit for pages), and the number of forwarding pointers (discussed in detail shortly) in use due to this fragmentation. Since the columns provided by the `sys.dm_db_index_physical_stats` DMF were covered in detail in *Chapter 5*, we'll only provide a very brief recap here.

The DMF has several parameters:

- **database_id**, **object_id**, **index_id**, **partition_number** – each parameter can be NULL or DEFAULT if we want to return all rows; if `database_id is NULL` or DEFAULT, we get stats for all tables in all databases, without having to loop through each one

- **mode** – determines how rigorous is the scan performed on the object(s) to return the fragmentation statistics; aside from NULL or DEFAULT, valid values are:

  - **LIMITED** – the default and the least costly, but will return NULL for many of the columns

  - **SAMPLED** – will not do as thorough a job of checking all of the pages as LIMITED, but will give you an idea of the situation by sampling some of the table

  - **DETAILED** – the most thorough and most costly of the choices.

The level chosen will depend on the size of your tables, the amount of time you have in your maintenance window and, simply, on whether you need the values that LIMITED won't provide. In this chapter, we will be concerned with only four of the columns returned by this function:

- **avg_fragmentation_in_percent** – for indexes, the percentage of logical fragmentation; for heaps, the percentage of extent fragmentation

- **fragment_count** – the number of fragments in the leaf level of the index, of IN_ROW_DATA allocation units; this includes the leaf pages of all types of indexes, including clustered, non-clustered, and even heaps

- **avg_fragment_size_in_pages** – the average number of pages in a fragment for IN_ROW_DATA allocation unity types

- **forwarded_record_count** – for heaps, the number of forwarding pointers; forwarding pointers are very bad for performance because they are always resolved immediately, as they are encountered.

The first three give you a feel for the degree of fragmentation in your indexes, clustered tables, and heaps, whereas the final one pertains only to heaps.

Fragmentation in clustered tables

As discussed earlier, the leaf pages of the clustered table (a table with a clustered index), which are the actual data pages of the table, are implemented as a doubly-linked list, ordered by the clustering key. Range scans using this linked list structure are highly efficient, but become less so as the index becomes fragmented as a result of data inserts, deletes, and updates. When data is deleted, gaps appear in the pages; when data is inserted, or an updated row increases in size, and there is no space on the appropriate page to accommodate it, then a page split occurs, with 50% of the data staying on the page, and 50% moving to a new page. These two pages will still be linked together in the linked list, but the new page is unlikely to be contiguous with the existing page, and may be placed in a different extent.

These types of fragmentation, especially page splits, can drastically increase the amount of physical I/O required to retrieve the data since, rather than perform long, sequential reads the disk heads will need to perform shorter, more random reads. If the data on the split page is placed in a different extent, fetching the data will require a completely separate physical I/O operation. The occurrence of page splits can be minimized to some degree, though not avoided altogether, by setting the appropriate fill factor for the clustered table (e.g. 90%) thus allowing space for new data on each page. In fact, a common cause of fragmentation is rebuilding clustered tables and indexes and forgetting to set the fill factor appropriately. By default, the fill factor will be 0 (meaning zero spare space). This can end up causing a lot more subsequent fragmentation than was resolved by rebuilding!

Let's start with a simple example, a small table where we cluster on an IDENTITY column, the value of which will increase monotonically. It is generally considered good practice to use narrow, integer, ever-increasing columns, such as afforded by an IDENTITY column for the clustering key. Note, though, that this IDENTITY column should not be the only primary key on the table, as the value has no relationship to the data in the table. Some form of natural key should also be enforced.

Clustering on an IDENTITY (or similar) column means that each row will be inserted in the logical order dictated by the clustering key, i.e. at the end of the table (that is, in order of arrival). This avoids the need to insert new rows into the middle of a page, which can dramatically increase page splits and fragmentation. Bear in mind, though, that clustering by time of arrival is not necessarily commensurate with the needs of your critical queries where, ideally, the goal would be to cluster on the key(s) that will gather together data that is most likely to be queried together.

We insert 100 rows into the table, using a clever trick with GO, in SSMS, which allows us to execute a batch multiple times, in a loop. Each row is 1 KB in size, so we're limited to about 8 rows per page (and 64 rows per extent).

```
CREATE TABLE testClusteredIdentity
    (
        testClusteredId INT
            IDENTITY
            CONSTRAINT PKtestClusteredIdentity PRIMARY KEY CLUSTERED ,
```

```
      value VARCHAR(1000)
    )
GO

INSERT INTO testClusteredIdentity(value)
SELECT replicate('a',1000) --only allows 8 rows per page.
GO 100
```

Listing 6.5:   The testClusteredIdentity clustered table, with an IDENTITY clustering key.

Next, we check the fragmentation using the sys.dm_db_index_physical_stats
DMV, as shown in Listing 6.6.

```
SELECT   avg_fragmentation_in_percent AS avgFragPct ,
         fragment_count AS fragCount ,
         avg_fragment_size_in_pages AS avgFragSize
FROM     sys.dm_db_index_physical_stats(DB_ID(), NULL, NULL, NULL, 'DETAILED')
WHERE    index_type_desc = 'CLUSTERED INDEX'
         AND index_level = 0 -- the other levels are the index pages
         AND OBJECT_NAME(object_id) = 'testClusteredIdentity'
```

Listing 6.6:   Fragmentation statistics for the testClusteredIdentity clustered table.

The results show that there is little fragmentation, though not zero. While the data is
always placed into the clustered index in order, this concentrates all inserts on the one
page. When this page fills up, it splits, leaving a fragment.

```
avgFragPct          fragCount     avgFragSize
----------------    ------------- -----------
13.3333333333333    3             5
```

Unfortunately, however, many designers persist in the habit of using GUIDs for surrogate
keys, and clustering on them. GUIDs are random in nature, and tend not to be created
sequentially and, as a result, insertions of data into the middle of the table are common.

238

The NEWSEQUENTIALID() *function*

This function will ensure that GUID values are ever increasing. However, it can only be used in a DEFAULT constraint, and one of the main reasons people like GUIDs is that they can be created anywhere.

To see the dramatic effect this has on fragmentation, consider the small table in Listing 6.7 where, this time, we cluster on a GUID, then insert 100 rows, using the same GO <number> technique.

```
CREATE TABLE testClustered
    (
        testClusteredId UNIQUEIDENTIFIER
         CONSTRAINT PKtestClustered PRIMARY KEY CLUSTERED ,
        value VARCHAR(1000)
    )

INSERT INTO testClustered
SELECT NEWID(), replicate('a',1000)
GO 100
```

Listing 6.7: The testClustered clustered table, with a GUID clustering key.

Check the fragmentation using the **sys.dm_db_index_physical_stats** DMV, as shown in Listing 6.6 (changing the target object to **testClustered**), and you'll see that just by adding 100 rows, our small table is already heavily fragmented with 21 fragments, and an average of only one page per fragment.

```
avgFragPct          fragCount      avgFragSize
------------------  -------------  -----------
95.2380952380952    21             1
```

Fragmentation in heaps

With heaps, the storage engine inserts all rows at the end of the table, in order of arrival. This is the same behavior as we'll see when clustering on an IDENTITY key, as described previously, and if the heap is not subject to modifications, fragmentation will not be a problem.

However, if the heap data is subsequently modified, fragmentation can become a very big problem indeed. With clustered tables, we discussed fragmentation in the form of the non-contiguous pages that arise as a result of page splits. This occurs on all types of data pages other than heap data pages, which are managed differently. On heap data pages, when a row increases in size and can no longer fit on the current page, a forwarding pointer is used. Instead of splitting the row, the row that pushes the byte count above the 8060 byte limit is moved to a new location, and a pointer to where the row has been moved is placed in the original location.

This makes inserting into a heap super-fast, as all external references to that data can remain the same. As such, many people use heaps as a place to drop rows (for instance, when logging operations, and even when loading data using bulk copy), while avoiding the performance impact of index maintenance.

Reading from a fragmented heap, however, is a performance nightmare. SQL Server has to follow the pointer to get the row, then back to the page that contained the pointer, often immensely increasing I/O. The situation is exacerbated by the fact that, unlike on an index, we cannot specify a fill factor for a heap, meaning that zero free space will be left on each page, so any inserts (or updates that increase row size) on already filled pages will inevitably result in fragmentation.

To demonstrate the problem, consider the testHeap table shown in Listing 6.8, with 100 rows containing a single character value.

```
CREATE TABLE testHeap
    (
      testHeapId UNIQUEIDENTIFIER
        CONSTRAINT PKtestHeap PRIMARY KEY NONCLUSTERED ,
      value VARCHAR(100)
    )

INSERT INTO testHeap
SELECT NEWID(),'a'
GO 100
```

Listing 6.8: The `testHeap` heap structure.

If we take a look at the fragmentation stats, we will see that the table is almost perfect.

```
SELECT   avg_fragmentation_in_percent AS avgFragPct ,
         fragment_count AS fragCount ,
         avg_fragment_size_in_pages AS avgFragSize ,
         forwarded_record_count AS forwardPointers
FROM     sys.dm_db_index_physical_stats(DB_ID(), NULL, NULL, NULL, 'DETAILED')
WHERE    index_type_desc = 'HEAP'
         AND index_level = 0 -- the other levels are the index pages
         AND OBJECT_NAME(object_id) = 'testHeap'
```

Listing 6.9: Fragmentation statistics for `testHeap`.

This reports one page, with no fragmentation, and no forwarding pointers.

avgFragPct	fragCount	avgFragSize	forwardPointers
0	1	1	0

The problem with heaps only starts when we modify the data. Let's make the value in our `value` column 100 times bigger.

```
UPDATE testHeap
SET    value = REPLICATE('a',100)
```

Listing 6.10: Updating the value column in **testHeap** with bigger values.

Now, let's check the stats again.

```
avgFragPct        fragCount avgFragSize    forwardPointers
----------------- --------- -------------- ----------------
50                2         1              41
```

Not horribly fragmented, and only one new page was added to the structure, but 41 of the 100 rows had to be moved to this new page. Now, to really see the damage that these forwarding pointers can cause, consider this: there are two pages in this table (two fragments, of average size one page, means there are two pages; or you can check the page_count column of sys.dm_db_index_physical_stats).

If this table is scanned, how many logical reads would you expect? No more than two, right? While it's true that we only have to read two pages, and the entire table will be in cache if you don't clear it, there are, unfortunately, many more logical reads performed.

```
SET STATISTICS I/O ON
SELECT  *
FROM    testHeap
SET STATISTICS I/O OFF
```

Listing 6.11: Capturing I/O statistics when reading the **testheap** table.

This returns 100 rows and the following:

```
Table 'testHeap'. Scan count 1, logical reads 43, physical
reads 0, read-ahead reads 0, lob logical reads 0, lob physical
reads 0, lob read-ahead reads 0.
```

So, 43 logical reads? For a table with 2 pages?! Unfortunately, yes, one read for each page and one read for each of the 41 forwarding pointers. In an actual usage scenario this can really be a very costly activity, even if all of the data being read was in RAM. This is one of the major reasons that heaps are generally avoided by most architects of OLTP systems.

The only way to correct forwarding pointers is to rebuild the table. Unfortunately for SQL Server 2005 users, there is no "simple" way to correct this. You have to either move all the data into a new table, or add a clustered index and drop it (which seems like a really silly set of operations). Fortunately, SQL Server 2008 added syntax to let you rebuild the heap and eliminate the forwarding pointers, as shown in Listing 6.12. Of course, this does not indicate that heaps are now the way to go, but it is better than adding the type of index you have specifically (and wisely) avoided.

```
ALTER TABLE testHeap REBUILD
```

Listing 6.12: Rebuilding a heap to remove fragmentation (SQL 2008 only).

Diagnosing I/O Bottlenecks

There are many tools available for diagnosing I/O bottlenecks on a system. A good place to start is the OS PerfMon counters, such as `PhysicalDisk Object: Avg. Disk Queue Length` and `Avg. Disk Reads/Sec`, which can help you work out the number of I/Os per disk, per second, and how many physical I/O requests are being queued, on a given disk.

In addition, the OS-related DMV, `sys.dm_os_wait_stats`, covered in *Chapter 7*, can provide strong corroborating evidence of a disk I/O bottleneck. For example, if the top cumulative wait types are disk I/O related, such as `PAGEIOLATCH_EX` or `PAGEIOLATCH_SH`, this indicates that many sessions are experiencing delays in obtaining a latch for a buffer, since the buffer is involved in physical I/O requests.

Having diagnosed possible I/O pressure, the next step for the DBA is to find out where (i.e. to which files on a given disk) the pressure is being applied. This is the extra granularity provided by the disk I/O-related DMOs discussed in this section, namely `sys.dm_io_virtual_file_stats` and `sys.dm_io_pending_io_requests`.

An overview of sys.dm_io_virtual_file_stats

For each database file that SQL Server uses, including not only the data files but also the log and full text files, the `sys.dm_io_virtual_file_stats` DMF gives cumulative physical I/O statistics, indicating how frequently the file has been used by the database for reads and writes since the server was last rebooted. It also provides a very useful metric in the form of the "I/O stall" time, which indicates the total amount of time that user processes have waited for I/O to be completed on the file in question. Note that this DMF measures physical I/O only. Logical I/O operations that read from cached data will not show up here.

The `sys.dm_io_virtual_file_stats` DMO is a function, and has the following parameters. Each is used to filter the set of data being returned, and you can use `NULL` or `DEFAULT` to retrieve all:

- **database_id** – surrogate key of the database, retrieved from `sys.databases`

- **file_id** – surrogate key of a file in a database; can be retrieved from `sys.database_files` if you are working in the context of a database, or `sys.master_files` will give you all files in all databases.

The columns returned are all pretty interesting and useful for getting a handle on your SQL I/O, in terms of how the actual files in your databases are being used:

- **database_id**, **file_id** – same as the parameter descriptions

- **sample_ms** – the number of milliseconds that have passed since the values for `sys.dm_io_virtual_file_stats` were reset (the only way to reset the values is to restart the server)

- **num_of_reads** – number of individual read operations that were issued to the file; note that this is physical reads, not logical reads; logical reads would not be registered

- **num_of_bytes_read** – the number of bytes that were read, as opposed to the number of reads; the size of a read is not a constant value that can be calculated by the number of reads

- **io_stall_read_ms** – total time user processes waited for I/O; note that this number can be much greater than the `sample_ms`; if ten processes are trying to use the file simultaneously, but the disk is only able to serve one of them, then you might get nine seconds waiting over a ten-second time period

- **num_of_writes**, **num_of_bytes_written**, **io_stall_write_ms** – the same as the read values, but for writes

- **io_stall** – sum of `io_stall_write_ms` and `io_stall_read_ms`

- **size_on_disk_bytes** – the size of the file in bytes

- **file_handle** – the Windows file handle of the file.

Using sys.dm_io_virtual_file_stats

Generally speaking, multiple concurrent users will need to access SQL Server, and with those users trying to access data in the same physical files, there will likely be some contention. Therefore, the I/O stalls value, showing the amount of time that processes are waiting on the file system because of excessive physical I/O, is probably the most interesting piece of information provided by this DMF. This is one of the primary DMFs that I use often when a new system is being started up as, despite all efforts to predict the required I/O throughput, and to spec configure the disk subsystem appropriately, it seems that disk setup is one of the most difficult things to get right first time (unless you have the luxury of taking the easy route, and over-specifying the disk subsystem from the start).

Pinpointing the cause of high I/O stalls and resolving the problem is sometimes a complex process. As noted earlier, you can use data from the execution- and index-related DMOs to attempt to reduce the overall I/O load on the server through tuning and indexing. You could also increase the amount of RAM, so that more data can be held in the data cache, so reducing the occurrence of physical file reads. Armed with stall rate, and the amount of data read and written, you can also identify opportunities to implement partitioning, or to at least separate tables onto different file groups.

Of course, ultimately, high stall rates could simply indicate that the disk I/O subsystem is inadequate to handle the required I/O throughput. Hard disk drives generally have only a single head per platter, and if you have five platters, with four heads, that means that, physically, only 20 pages of data can be read simultaneously (and the four heads are not usually independent of one another, either). If you have more than 20 users executing queries simultaneously (plus processes other than SQL Server that may be accessing the data), then some of those users will definitely have to wait to retrieve their required data. While those DBAs with enterprise architecture will be scoffing at such small amounts of disk hardware, many smaller organizations would love to have five hard drives on their main business server.

However, if stall rates are causing severe issues, and all attempts to reduce the overall I/O load fail to bring them down to acceptable levels, there is little choice but to consider adding more or faster disks, or to investigate potential problems with the configuration of the I/O subsystem, as discussed earlier.

Finally, remember that the data in this DMO reflects SQL Server's perspective of disk I/O. If the disk subsystem is shared at a server level with other applications, the actual cause of poor disk performance may be another application, not SQL Server. Also, as discussed earlier, with the increasing use of SANs, virtualization software, and so on, there are often several "intermediary" layers between SQL Server and the actual disk storage. An issue with disk I/O could, in fact, be caused by one of these intermediary layers rather than the disk drives. In short, give careful consideration to data obtained from this DMO, and consider it in conjunction with data obtained from Windows OS counters, Profiler, and other DMOs, before deciding on a course of action.

Investigating physical I/O and I/O stalls

As noted previously, the data provided by this DMO is cumulative from when the server is restarted; in other words, the values in the data columns increment continuously from the point when the server was last restarted. To get a really accurate view of the data, you'd need to reboot the server at same time every day, and take a snapshot at the same time so you could compare day-to-day activity and trends. Since this isn't really practical, we can, instead, take a baseline measurement followed by the actual measurement, then subtract the two, to see where I/O is accumulating.

Let's take a look at an example. To see any interesting data, you'll need an active test system, or a handy, overtaxed server to try it out on. Happily, thanks to previous remedial action, based on results collected from this DMO, such servers seem to be fewer and farther between, in my case. First, I put the initial baseline into a temp table (or you could use a permanent table, if desired), as shown in Listing 6.13.

```
SELECT   DB_NAME(mf.database_id) AS databaseName ,
         mf.physical_name ,
         divfs.num_of_reads ,
         divfs.num_of_bytes_read ,
         divfs.io_stall_read_ms ,
         divfs.num_of_writes ,
         divfs.num_of_bytes_written ,
         divfs.io_stall_write_ms ,
         divfs.io_stall ,
         size_on_disk_bytes ,
         GETDATE() AS baselineDate
INTO     #baseline
```

```
FROM      sys.dm_io_virtual_file_stats(NULL, NULL) AS divfs
          JOIN sys.master_files AS mf ON mf.database_id = divfs.database_id
                                      AND mf.file_id = divfs.file_id
```

Listing 6.13: Capturing baseline disk I/O statistics from `sys.dm_io_virtual_file_stats`
in a temporary table.

Listing 6.14 shows a query against the #baseline table, returning read statistics for a
particular database.

```
SELECT    physical_name ,
          num_of_reads ,
          num_of_bytes_read ,
          io_stall_read_ms
FROM      #baseline
WHERE     databaseName = 'DatabaseName'
```

Listing 6.14: Querying the #baseline temporary table.

This returns the following data:

physical_name	num_of_reads	num_of_bytes_read	io_stall_read_ms
F:\MSSQ...DATABASE.mdf	1560418	381784449024	176090340
E:\MSSQ...BASE_log.LDF	925	592683008	7000
I:\MSSQ...SE_index.ndf	398504	310491209728	39664904
k:\mssq...TABASE2A.mdf	540176	155267350528	319640508

This data, taken on a server that was restarted about 12 hours previously, is not especially
interesting or meaningful in its own right. However, the next step is where we turn this
data into information.

Having captured the baseline, wait a set amount of time, or for some process to complete,
and then take a second measurement, from which the baseline values are subtracted, as

shown in Listing 6.15. On a busy server, you may wait as little as 10 seconds before taking the second measurement, as is the case in this example.

```
WITH  currentLine
      AS ( SELECT    DB_NAME(mf.database_id) AS databaseName ,
                     mf.physical_name ,
                     num_of_reads ,
                     num_of_bytes_read ,
                     io_stall_read_ms ,
                     num_of_writes ,
                     num_of_bytes_written ,
                     io_stall_write_ms ,
                     io_stall ,
                     size_on_disk_bytes ,
                     GETDATE() AS currentlineDate
           FROM      sys.dm_io_virtual_file_stats(NULL, NULL) AS divfs
                     JOIN sys.master_files AS mf
                        ON mf.database_id = divfs.database_id
                           AND mf.file_id = divfs.file_id
         )
SELECT  currentLine.databaseName ,
        LEFT(currentLine.physical_name, 1) AS drive ,
        currentLine.physical_name ,
        DATEDIFF(millisecond,baseLineDate,currentLineDate) AS elapsed_ms,
        currentLine.io_stall - #baseline.io_stall AS io_stall_ms ,
        currentLine.io_stall_read_ms - #baseline.io_stall_read_ms
                                                AS io_stall_read_ms ,
        currentLine.io_stall_write_ms - #baseline.io_stall_write_ms
                                                AS io_stall_write_ms ,
        currentLine.num_of_reads - #baseline.num_of_reads AS num_of_reads ,
        currentLine.num_of_bytes_read - #baseline.num_of_bytes_read
                                                AS num_of_bytes_read ,
        currentLine.num_of_writes - #baseline.num_of_writes AS num_of_writes ,
        currentLine.num_of_bytes_written - #baseline.num_of_bytes_written
                                                AS num_of_bytes_written
FROM  currentLine
      INNER JOIN #baseline ON #baseLine.databaseName = currentLine.databaseName
        AND #baseLine.physical_name = currentLine.physical_name
WHERE #baseline.databaseName = 'DatabaseName'
```

Listing 6.15: Capturing 10 seconds of disk I/O statistics, since the baseline measurement.

Following is a sampling of the result, again focusing only on the read statistics:

```
physical_name    elapsed_ms num_of_reads num_of_bytes_read  io_stall_read_ms
--------------   ---------- ------------ ------------------  ------------------
F:\MSSQ.SE.mdf 10016          915        128311296          34612
E:\MSSQ.og.LDF 10016          0          0                  0
I:\MSSQ.ex.ndf 10016          344        172933120          8000
k:\mssq.2A.mdf 10016          0          0                  0
```

These results show that, over the 10-second sampling period, read operations against the data file on the F: drive had to wait a combined total of 34 seconds. Of course, this data would have to be assessed in the light of how many processes ran during the sampling period; if it was 4, the result would be very worrying; if it was 100, then perhaps less so.

It is interesting that more data was read from the 1: drive, with fewer I/O stalls, which is most likely explained by different usage patterns. The 1: drive is subject to a smaller number of, mostly sequential, reads, whereas the F: drive is subject to many more reads that are mainly random in nature. Obviously, one can only know for sure given some knowledge of the activity that was occurring during the sampling. In any event, it is certainly worrying to see that the stall times on the F: drive are substantially greater than the elapsed time, and I'd want to investigate further, to find out why.

This was just a simple example of how performance bottlenecks might be identified using this data. By comparing this data to that obtained routinely from performance counters, Profiler traces, and other DMV snapshots, we can really start to get an idea of how our disks are being utilized for a given server workload.

Viewing pending I/O requests

Whereas the data in the the `sys.dm_io_virtual_file_stats` DMF is cumulative, the `sys.dm_io_pending_io_requests` DMV returns a row for each *currently pending* I/O request, so it is interesting from the standpoint of seeing what is happening right now, at the file level. This is a useful tool for analyzing disk I/O at a more granular level than is allowed by tools such as Profiler, which will summarize I/O activity at the drive level.

Each time you query this DMV, it's likely that a different set of processes will be pending, so the returned data will vary each time. However, if you frequently see what seems like a high number of pending I/Os, this is evidence of some level of I/O bottleneck. Obviously, "high" is a matter of interpretation, but more than two or three could indicate an issue.

This DMV returns several columns that are occasionally useful, including:

- **io_completion_request_address** – address of the I/O request

- **io_type** – type of I/O, for example 'disk'

- **scheduler_address** – relates to `sys.dm_os_schedulers` to get information about the scheduler coordinating this I/O request

- **io_handle** – handle for the file that is the target of the I/O request; relates to `sys.dm_id_virtual_file_stats.file_handle` to get the file information.

However, the most interesting columns returned by this view, and the ones we'll use in our script, are:

- **io_pending** – an integer value that indicates whether an I/O request is pending (returns 1) or has been completed by Windows but not yet processed by SQL Server, since it has not yet performed the context switch (returns 0); we know that the item is pending for the SQL Server storage engine, as this is the purpose of the DMV

- **io_pending_ms_ticks** – represents the total time individual I/Os are waiting in the pending queue; Books Online lists this as internal use only, but it is useful for comparing the magnitude of the waits on each file.

Using the query in Listing 6.16, we can view the file name, the status, and how long the operation has been waiting.

```
SELECT   mf.physical_name ,
         dipir.io_pending ,
         dipir.io_pending_ms_ticks
FROM     sys.dm_io_pending_io_requests AS dipir
         JOIN sys.dm_io_virtual_file_stats(NULL, NULL) AS divfs
                              ON dipir.io_handle = divfs.file_handle
         JOIN sys.master_files AS mf ON divfs.database_id = mf.database_id
                              AND divfs.file_id = mf.file_id
ORDER BY dipir.io_pending , --Show I/O completed by the OS first
         dipir.io_pending_ms_ticks DESC
```

Listing 6.16: Returning pending I/O requests.

This will return results such as the following:

```
physical_name                         io_pending  io_pending_ms_ticks
-----------------------------------   ----------  --------------------
h:\sqlfiles\data\dbname_index.ndf     0           15
h:\sqlfiles\data\dbname_data.mdf      1           15
h:\sqlfiles\data\dbname_log.ldf       1           0
```

In this case, there are pending I/O operations on the log and data files stored on the H: drive. On the secondary data file (judging by the name, one that contains most of the indexes), there is an I/O request that has been completed by Windows but not yet fetched by SQL Server.

If you regularly observe a high number of pending I/O requests on a single drive, you should consider moving some of the files onto a separate drive, on a different access channel.

Finding the Read:Write Ratio

In an OLTP database, the goal of every read is to touch as few data pages as possible in order to return the required data, and the goal of every write is to modify only one page of data, though this number will be higher if the page is in an index, since the index will need to be updated as well as the underlying table.

An interesting metric for the DBA is the read ratio compared to the write ratio at the file, database, or even table level. In other words, we calculate physical reads as a proportion of total physical reads and writes, and compare it to physical writes, again as a proportion of total physical reads and writes. We can use the `sys.dm_io_virtual_file_stats` DMF to calculate two different forms of this ratio:

- **amount of data read versus written** – in other words, the number of bytes read in from disk, compared to the number of bytes of data written out to the file system

- **number of read versus write operations** – in this view of the ratio, reading 1 GB of data is indistinguishable from reading 10 KB; as long as each occurs in a single read, each will register as a single operation.

For example, consider a full table scan of a single table that contains a gigabyte of data. In the first method, the scan will register as a gigabyte of data, and in the second method it will register as a single operation. Bear in mind that these ratios refer purely to physical I/O. If a column value is updated ten times, by ten separate transactions, in memory it will record as ten operations in the log file, but only one operation in the data file.

In an optimized OLTP system, user requests should read as little data as possible to perform any required update and so the read:write ratio, in either form, would ideally be close to 50:50. In reality, however, there are almost always more reads than writes; even an update that fetches data with the clustered primary key may read a few pages of index and the data page in order to find the single page to modify. Nevertheless, you'd still like to see reads minimized to only four or five reads per one or two writes. A higher ratio than around 80:20, and most DBAs will start to suspect non-optimal queries, or insufficient cache memory to avoid physical disk access.

Let's say you find a heavily used table, where you expect the ratio to be close to 50:50, but, instead, find that it is heavily weighted towards reads (perhaps 99:1). This could indicate a problem such as an application looping a row at a time instead of doing relational operations. It is also very interesting to look out for cases where the two ratios return very different results. For example, and clearly this is an oversimplification, but if you find that the read:write ratio is 50:50 based on counts, and 99:1 based on data, this indicates that you are reading a lot of data to write a little data, which could be caused by inefficient database code, perhaps allowing users to search in a very inefficient manner, resulting in table scans.

In general, these ratios are a useful tool in helping you to find opportunities to optimize the I/O via tuning, and to help you make decisions about how to optimize your disk subsystem. By finding which files, database, and tables are subject to the most read and write activity, and in what ratio, you can make better decisions regarding the need, for example, to move objects to different disks (e.g. making sure write-intensive objects are situated on hardware specially configured for this purpose), add spindles, use a SAN versus direct attached storage, and so on. It is also very useful to determine the read:write ratio for a given batch of operations.

Amount of data read versus written

The script in Listing 6.17 simply calculates the number of bytes read as a proportion of the total number of bytes read or written (RatioOfReads), and then the number of bytes written as a proportion of the total bytes read or written (RatioOfWrites), and presents them alongside the total number of bytes read and written, for the files associated with the selected database(s). Bear in mind that this includes only actual writes to the files, or reads from the file, and will not reflect data read from the cache, or written to the cache and not yet flushed to the disk.

```
--uses a LIKE comparison to only include desired databases, rather than
--using the database_id parameter of sys.dm_io_virtual_file_stats
--if you have a rather large number of databases, this may not be the
--optimal way to execute the query, but this gives you flexibility
--to look at multiple databases simultaneously.
DECLARE @databaseName SYSNAME
SET @databaseName = '%'
 --'%' gives all databases

SELECT  CAST(SUM(num_of_bytes_read) AS DECIMAL)
        / ( CAST(SUM(num_of_bytes_written) AS DECIMAL)
            + CAST(SUM(num_of_bytes_read) AS DECIMAL) ) AS RatioOfReads ,
        CAST(SUM(num_of_bytes_written) AS DECIMAL)
        / ( CAST(SUM(num_of_bytes_written) AS DECIMAL)
            + CAST(SUM(num_of_bytes_read) AS DECIMAL) ) AS RatioOfWrites ,
        SUM(num_of_bytes_read) AS TotalBytesRead ,
        SUM(num_of_bytes_written) AS TotalBytesWritten
FROM    sys.dm_io_virtual_file_stats(NULL, NULL) AS divfs
WHERE   DB_NAME(database_id) LIKE @databaseName
```

Listing 6.17: The read:write ratio, by database, for amount of data transferred.

The results of this query will give you an idea of how much data has been read from and written to all of the files in the system or database. The following is a set of results from an OLTP system that had been up and running for four days. In total, it is about 81:19, which is a fairly good ratio, considering it is for all databases on your server:

```
RatioOfReads             RatioOfWrites              TotalBytesRead     TotalBytesWritten
--------------------     ----------------------     ----------------   ------------------
0.81449639341533276910   0.18550360658466723089     5612056879616      1278160099840
```

Capturing these ratios for all files, or even at the database level, is not necessarily very useful, but we can easily add in a reference to the **sys.master_files** catalog view and start to slice the data in various interesting ways. As an example, consider the slicing shown in Listing 6.18, grouping on the drive letter to give the ratios for each drive on the server that is used by the selected databases.

```
DECLARE @databaseName SYSNAME
SET @databaseName = '%'
 --'%' gives all databases

SELECT  LEFT(physical_name, 1) AS drive ,
        CAST(SUM(num_of_bytes_read) AS DECIMAL)
        / ( CAST(SUM(num_of_bytes_written) AS DECIMAL)
            + CAST(SUM(num_of_bytes_read) AS DECIMAL) ) AS RatioOfReads ,
        CAST(SUM(num_of_bytes_written) AS DECIMAL)
        / ( CAST(SUM(num_of_bytes_written) AS DECIMAL)
            + CAST(SUM(num_of_bytes_read) AS DECIMAL) ) AS RatioOfWrites ,
        SUM(num_of_bytes_read) AS TotalBytesRead ,
        SUM(num_of_bytes_written) AS TotalBytesWritten
FROM    sys.dm_io_virtual_file_stats(NULL, NULL) AS divfs
        JOIN sys.master_files AS mf ON mf.database_id = divfs.database_id
                                    AND mf.file_id = divfs.file_id
WHERE   DB_NAME(divfs.database_id) LIKE @databaseName
GROUP BY LEFT(mf.physical_name, 1)
```

Listing 6.18: The read:write ratio, by drive, for amount of data transferred.

The results are as follows:

drive	RatioOfReads	RatioOfWrites	TotalBytesRead	TotalBytesWritten
E	0.509947179620...	0.49005282037...	324253917696	311603933184
F	0.953302196684...	0.04669780331...	2213262221312	108417335296
H	0.376100820227...	0.62389917977...	344707538944	571822073344
I	0.922886044827...	0.07711395517...	1316300808192	109986668544
J	0.708701451352...	0.29129854864...	381697171456	156889522176
K	0.974068440224...	0.02593155977...	1040343924736	27695939584

As you can see, some of the drives are heavily skewed towards reads (92:8 for the I: drive), whereas H: is skewed towards writes. Do any of these values indicate a potential problem? As the old DBA saying goes: "It depends." In this case, the H: drive contains `tempdb`, so heavy writes are to be expected. The E: drive, with a ratio of 51:49, is where all the `tempdb` logs reside.

Of considerable concern are the I:, F:, and K: drives, where we have a tremendous amount of reading taking place in each case. These drives house the data for one of our heavy use databases and I would certainly like to investigate further to see if the amount of data being read could be reduced. The next step is to obtain the read:write ratios for this database in terms of the number of read and write operations. If this method reveals a ratio much closer to 50:50 then we know that reads are reading a disproportionately high amount of data.

Number of read and write operations

Listing 6.19 takes exactly the same form as Listing 6.17, except that it returns the number of reads and writes as a proportion of the total number of reads and writes.

```
DECLARE @databaseName SYSNAME
SET @databaseName = 'BusyDatabase'
 --obviously not the real name
 --'%' gives all databases

SELECT   CAST(SUM(num_of_reads) AS DECIMAL)
         / ( CAST(SUM(num_of_writes) AS DECIMAL)
             + CAST(SUM(num_of_reads) AS DECIMAL) ) AS RatioOfReads ,
         CAST(SUM(num_of_writes) AS DECIMAL)
         / ( CAST(SUM(num_of_reads) AS DECIMAL)
             + CAST(SUM(num_of_writes) AS DECIMAL) ) AS RatioOfWrites ,
         SUM(num_of_reads) AS TotalReadOperations ,
         SUM(num_of_writes) AS TotalWriteOperations
FROM     sys.dm_io_virtual_file_stats(NULL, NULL) AS divfs
WHERE    DB_NAME(database_id) LIKE @databaseName
```

Listing 6.19: The read:write ratio, by database, for number of read/write operations.

For the database that spanned the I:, F:, and K: drives, from the previous section, the following results were returned:

RatioOfReads	RatioOfWrites	TotalReadOperations	TotalWriteOperations
0.669141428931…	0.330858571068…	49582510	24516190

So, for this database, reads account for about 67% of all operations, and about 90% in terms of the actual amount of physical I/O performed. In my experience, this is not "horrible," but there might seem to be scope to reduce the amount of data each read is retrieving.

Number of reads and writes at the table level

Using the sys.dm_db_index_usage_stats DMV, covered in *Chapter 5*, we can get another view of the read:write ratio, this time down to the table level. Note that counts returned by this DMV will include logical operations, so the ratio obtained here is not necessarily directly comparable to the previous count-based ratio, obtained from `sys_dm_io_virtual_file_stats`. These numbers, however, provide a better representation of the actual number of read and write operations, as they are counted at the object level, whether or not the utilization is logical or physical. Note, too, that only objects that have been used in a DML statement will be included, so after a reboot, you may get not get any results for some objects.

The query shown in Listing 6.20 is based on one first suggested by Jamie Massie, in his blog entry entitled *Is 80/20 a 90's Estimate?* For all objects in a given database, it sums seeks, scans and lookups as read operations, and updates as changes to the data (the `CASE` expressions prevent divide by zero errors when the table has never been used).

```
DECLARE @databaseName SYSNAME
SET @databaseName = 'BusyDatabase' --obviously not the real name
 --'%' gives all databases


SELECT   CASE
            WHEN ( SUM(user_updates + user_seeks + user_scans + user_lookups) = 0 )
               THEN NULL
               ELSE ( CAST(SUM(user_seeks + user_scans + user_lookups)
                                                           AS DECIMAL)
                    / CAST(SUM(user_updates + user_seeks + user_scans
                                 + user_lookups) AS DECIMAL) )
            END AS RatioOfReads ,
            CASE
            WHEN ( SUM(user_updates + user_seeks + user_scans + user_lookups) = 0 )
               THEN NULL
               ELSE ( CAST(SUM(user_updates) AS DECIMAL)
                       / CAST(SUM(user_updates + user_seeks + user_scans
                                 + user_lookups) AS DECIMAL) )
            END AS RatioOfWrites ,
            SUM(user_updates + user_seeks + user_scans + user_lookups)
                                                   AS TotalReadOperations ,
            SUM(user_updates) AS TotalWriteOperations
FROM     sys.dm_db_index_usage_stats AS ddius
WHERE    DB_NAME(database_id) LIKE @databaseName
```

Listing 6.20: Read:write ratio for all objects in a given database.

On the same busy server as used in the previous two sections, the following results were obtained, which are within the same range as the previous results.

RatioOfReads	RatioOfWrites	TotalReadOperations	TotalWriteOperations
0.73322906464778...	0.26677093535221...	297209079	79286744

Listing 6.21 breaks down the ratio data to the object level, simply by grouping on the object_id.

```
--only works in the context of the database due to sys.indexes usage
USE BusyDatabase
 --obviously not the real name

SELECT   OBJECT_NAME(ddius.object_id) AS object_name ,
         CASE
           WHEN ( SUM(user_updates + user_seeks + user_scans + user_lookups) = 0 )
           THEN NULL
           ELSE ( CAST(SUM(user_seeks + user_scans + user_lookups) AS DECIMAL)
                      / CAST(SUM(user_updates + user_seeks + user_scans
                          + user_lookups) AS DECIMAL) )
           END AS RatioOfReads ,
         CASE
           WHEN ( SUM(user_updates + user_seeks + user_scans + user_lookups) = 0 )
           THEN NULL
           ELSE ( CAST(SUM(user_updates) AS DECIMAL)
                      / CAST(SUM(user_updates + user_seeks + user_scans
                          + user_lookups) AS DECIMAL) )
           END AS RatioOfWrites ,
         SUM(user_updates + user_seeks + user_scans + user_lookups)
                                                AS TotalReadOperations ,
         SUM(user_updates) AS TotalWriteOperations
FROM     sys.dm_db_index_usage_stats AS ddius
         JOIN sys.indexes AS i ON ddius.object_id = i.object_id
                           AND ddius.index_id = i.index_id
```

```
WHERE    i.type_desc IN ( 'CLUSTERED', 'HEAP' ) --only works in Current db
GROUP BY ddius.object_id
ORDER BY OBJECT_NAME(ddius.object_id)
```

Listing 6.21: Read:write ratio per object.

Getting Stats about tempdb Usage

In the earlier section, *Diagnosing I/O Bottlenecks*, we discussed how to investigate activity levels at the file level. This will have included activity on files associated with the tempdb database. However, in many respects, tempdb is a special case and merits individual attention.

The tempdb database is a global resource that is used by all sessions connected to a given SQL Server instance, and it holds many objects that you can't "see" in the system tables. For example, it stores internal objects (work tables), created by SQL Server to hold the intermediate results of sorts and spools, as well as user temporary objects such temporary tables, table variables, cursors, and so on. It also holds row versioning information when using snapshot isolation (see *Chapter 4*, for full details) as well as triggers and online indexing.

As such, sizing and configuration of the tempdb database is crucially important to the overall performance of SQL Server, especially if you are running transactions using SNAPSHOT, or READ_COMMITTED_SNAPSHOT isolation. Thorough coverage of how to set up tempdb is beyond the scope of this book, but a good place to start is the MSDN article, *tempdb Size and Placement Recommendations* (HTTP://MSDN.MICROSOFT.COM/ EN-US/LIBRARY/MS175527.ASPX), which recommends placing tempdb files on very fast disks, independent of other databases, and broken up into multiple files (even if they are in one filegroup), depending on the number of CPUs in your system. A common starting place, as stated in the aforementioned article, is to have one file per CPU core.

The **sys.dm_db_file_space_usage** DMV returns data that reflects the current state of file usage, including the following columns:

- **database_id** – surrogate key of the database (relates to **sys.databases**)

- **file_id** – the file identifier (relates to **sys.database_files**)

- **unallocated_extent_page_count** – extents that are reserved in the file but not currently allocated to objects

- **version_store_reserved_page_count** – number of pages that are reserved to support snapshot isolation transactions

- **user_object_reserved_page_count** – number of pages reserved to user tables

- **internal_object_reserved_page_count** – number of pages reserved to internal objects, such as work tables, that SQL Server creates to hold intermediate results, such as for sorting data

- **mixed_extent_page_count** – number of extents that have pages of multiple types – user objects, version store, or internal objects, Index Allocation Map (IAM) pages, etc.

Listing 6.22 demonstrates how to get an overview of **tempdb** utilization.

```
SELECT  mf.physical_name ,
        mf.size AS entire_file_page_count ,
        dfsu.version_store_reserved_page_count ,
        dfsu.unallocated_extent_page_count ,
        dfsu.user_object_reserved_page_count ,
        dfsu.internal_object_reserved_page_count ,
        dfsu.mixed_extent_page_count
FROM    sys.dm_db_file_space_usage dfsu
        JOIN sys.master_files AS mf ON mf.database_id = dfsu.database_id
                                   AND mf.file_id = dfsu.file_id
```

Listing 6.22: An overview of **tempdb** utilization.

If you are using database snapshots, snapshot isolation level, or even triggers, the `version_store_reserved_page_count` can be really interesting. The biggest worry with snapshot isolation level is `tempdb` utilization. Using this query you can see how much of the data being stored in the `tempdb` is for the version store. Version store usage can be investigated in much more detail using the dedicated DMOs covered in *Chapter 4*.

One thing to also note is that, since the storage engine uses a proportional fill algorithm to choose which files to put data in first, every file that is returned ought to have the same value for `entire_file_page_count`, as we see in the following sample results:

physical_name	entire_file_page_count	version_store_reserv...
H:\MSSQL\DATA\tempdb.mdf	524288	208
H:\MSSQL\DATA\tempdev_2.ndf	524288	208
H:\MSSQL\DATA\tempdev_3.ndf	524288	200
H:\MSSQL\DATA\tempdev_4.ndf	524288	176

That looks like a well configured set of files (there were 16 files in total on the system from which these results were taken). However, on a different server, a far less palatable result was returned:

physical_name	entire_file_page_count	version_store_reserved...
H:\MSSQL\DATA\tempdb.mdf	1024	0
H:\MSSQL\DATA\tempdata2.ndf	65536	64

The `tempdata2` file will be used approximately 60 times more than the other, which is apparent, not only in the version store column, but also in the others.

In addition, the query in Listing 6.23 provides an overview of the entire `tempdb` file size and version store utilization, in pages.

```
SELECT   SUM(mf.size) AS entire_page_count ,
         SUM(dfsu.version_store_reserved_page_count) AS version_store_reserved_page_
count
FROM     sys.dm_db_file_space_usage dfsu
         JOIN sys.master_files AS mf ON mf.database_id = dfsu.database_id
                                     AND mf.file_id = dfsu.file_id
```

Listing 6.23: `tempdb` file size and version store usage.

The `sys.dm_db_file_space_usage` DMV may not be a "marquee name" in DMVs but, like so many of the DMVs, it is there to cover some facet of the system's internals that you just can't get any other way.

Summary

In this chapter, we have looked at a lot of very useful queries and techniques that allow us to understand the physical characteristics of our objects and their usage statistics. We used the `sys.dm_db_partition_stats` DMV to return the size and structure characteristics of our clustered tables and heaps (and their underlying partitions), and then the `sys.dm_db_index_physical_stats` DMV to diagnose fragmentation in these objects. If even the simplest process appears to be taking way more time than seems reasonable, it may well be caused by page splits in your clustered tables and non-clustered indexes, or by fragmentation, and the subsequent use of forwarding pointers, in heaps.

Next, we looked at how to get I/O statistics from the `sys.dm_io_virtual_file_stats` DMF, which, at a file level, shows us how many reads and writes are issued to a file as well as providing important information regarding how long processes have had to wait for I/O operations to be completed (I/O stalls). This is an amazingly useful tool for seeing where your I/O system is performing poorly, from SQL Server's perspective. Note that if the data returned indicates a "disk I/O problem," it may not be SQL Server that is causing this problem. The problem could easily lie elsewhere, especially if you are using a SAN with many other users, or someone is serving web pages from the same physical drives as your database.

We also briefly discussed the use of the `sys.dm_io_pending_io_requests` DMV to see currently pending I/O requests, i.e. to view how much data is currently in the I/O pipeline to be processed by SQL Server but, for some reason, has not been consumed.

Next, we demonstrated two methods of finding the read:write ratio at the file, database, or table level. This information is invaluable when determining, for example, the most appropriate RAID configuration for a given disk (RAID 10 for frequently updated data, RAID 5 for read-only data, and so on). We saw how the value for this ratio could vary dramatically, depending on whether it was based on the amount of data being read or written to disk, or on the number of individual read/write operations. If you see a value of 99:1 in terms of amount of data, but 40:60 in terms of the number of operations, it means that your queries are reading way too much data, and you have some tuning work to do.

Finally, we covered the `sys.dm_db_file_space_usage` DMV, and used it to investigate `tempdb` space usage, an understanding of which is critical since, in SQL Server 2005 and 2008, `tempdb` is central to so much of the query activity on your server.

If you are a newbie to performance tuning from a disk I/O perspective, I know that you are thinking, "Disk I/O tuning is hard!" and that is completely true. In all but the most talented shops, it is a very common practice to guess high and buy too much hardware for small applications, and guess way too low for very active applications. The goal of this chapter and, in fact, the whole book is to help you understand the tools that are available to help you to reach the "right" solution.

Chapter 7: OS and Hardware Interaction

In this final chapter, we reach the lowest level of the SQL Server engine, namely the SQL Server Operating System (SQLOS) layer. The SQLOS manages many functions and services in the engine, but the two primary ones are the scheduling of task execution (i.e. CPU time) and the allocation and management of memory across all SQL Server data engine components.

Books Online lists 29 objects in the "sys.dm_os_" category, which collectively can provide us with a vast amount of detailed data (sometimes too much) regarding the nature of the interaction between SQL Server and the operating system. What we've tried to do in this chapter is to select the ten DMOs in this category that are likely to be the most immediately useful to DBAs in their normal tuning and system management activities. We'll answer common questions, such as those below (relevant DMOs are shown in brackets, minus the sys.dm_os_ prefix).

- What kinds of things have the SQL Server OS threads been waiting on? (**wait_stats**).
- What are the values of the SQL Server performance counters, and how are they decoded? (**performance_counters**).
- What are the characteristics of the machine that SQL Server is running on? (**sys_info**).
- Is there currently CPU pressure? (**schedulers**, **ring_buffers**).
- How is memory as a whole being utilized? (**sys_memory**, **process_memory**).
- How is the cache memory being utilized? (**memory_clerks**, **cache_counters**).
- How much resource locking (latches) has occurred? (**latch_stats**).

With this information we can get a solid view of the SQL Server system and how it is interacting with the hardware, and we can spot potential bottlenecks and pressure points.

A word of warning before we begin: perhaps more so than any other category of DMO, the operating system-related objects provide enough "raw" data to make your head spin. Much of this data needs to be gathered carefully, and tracked over time, in order to draw firm conclusions regarding the nature of the SQL Server-OS interaction. The situation is further complicated by the use of virtualization, where the values you get back from the queries in this chapter may not represent reality, but rather what the virtualization software tells the virtual machine on which your SQL Server is running.

This chapter assumes that you have a reasonable knowledge of the SQL Server Architecture (*SQL Server 2008 Internals,* by Kalen Delaney, is a good book to have open alongside this one) and, metaphorically, attempts to play the role of the flashlight salesperson at the mouth of the cave, allowing you to shine a light on objects of interest. In-depth analysis and interpretation is in the eyes of the spelunker.

Wait Statistics

Arguably the most significant DMV in the Operating System category is `sys.dm_os_wait_stats`. Every time a session has to wait for some reason before the requested work can continue, SQL Server records the length of time waited, and the resource that is being waited on. The `sys.dm_os_wait_stats` DMV exposes these wait statistics, aggregated across all session IDs, to provide a summary review of where the major waits are on a given instance. This same DMV also exposes performance (PerfMon) counters, which provide specific resource usage measurements (disk transfer rates, amount of CPU time consumed and so on). By correlating wait statistics with resource measurements, you can quickly locate the most contested resources on your system, and so highlight potential bottlenecks.

SQL Server 2005 waits and queues

The use of "waits and queues" as the basis for a performance tuning methodology is explained in an excellent white paper by Tom Davidson, which is available at HTTP://SQLCAT.COM/WHITEPAPERS/ ARCHIVE/2007/11/19/SQL-SERVER-2005-WAITS-AND-QUEUES.ASPX.

Essentially, each request to SQL Server will result in the initiation of a number of "worker tasks." A SQL Server Scheduler assigns each task to a worker thread. Normally, there is one SQLOS scheduler per CPU, and only one session per scheduler can be running at any time. It's the scheduler's job to spread the workload evenly between available worker threads. If a session's worker thread is running on the processor, the status of the parent request will be "Running," as exposed by the `Status` column of the `sys.dm_exec_requests` DMV. If a thread is "ready to go" (has been signaled) but the scheduler to which it is assigned currently has another session running, it will be placed in the "runnable" queue, which simply means it is in the queue to get on the processor. This is referred to as a "signal wait." The signal wait time is exposed by the `signal_wait_time_ms` column, and is solely CPU wait time. If a session's request is waiting for another resource, such as a locked page, to become available in order to proceed, or if a running session needs to perform I/O, then it is moved to the waiter list; this is a resource wait and the waiting request's status will be recorded as "suspended." The reason for the wait is recorded, and exposed in the `wait_type` column of the `sys.dm_os_wait_stats` DMV. The total time spent waiting is exposed by the `wait_time_ms` column, so the resource wait time can be calculated simply, as follows:

```
Resource waits = Total waits — Signal waits
               =(wait_time_ms) - (signal_wait_time_ms).
```

Signal waits are unavoidable in OLTP systems, comprising a large number of short transactions. The key metric, with regard to potential CPU pressure, is the signal wait as a percentage of the total waits. A high percentage signal is a sign of CPU pressure (see Listing 7.5). The literature tends to quote "high" as more than about 25%, but it depends on your system.

Overall, the use of wait statistics represents a very effective means to diagnose response times in your system. In very simple terms, you either work, or you wait:

```
Response time = service time + wait time
```

If response times are slow and you find no significant waits, or mainly signal waits, you know you need to focus on the CPU. If, instead, you find the response time is mainly comprised of time spent waiting for other resources (network, I/O, etc.) then, again, you know exactly where to focus your tuning efforts.

Taking the guesswork out of performance profiling

Mario Broodbakker has written an excellent introductory series of articles on using wait events to diagnose performance problems, which you can find at HTTP://WWW.SIMPLE-TALK.COM/AUTHOR/ MARIO-BROODBAKKER/.

A brief overview of sys.dm_os_wait_stats

In the battle against a poorly performing system, the ability to investigate where, and for how long, SQL Server OS threads have been waiting for some other action to complete before proceeding, is one of the most potent weapons that the DBA has available, and these wait times are exposed via the **sys.dm_os_wait_stats** DMV.

This DMV gives us a list of all the different types of wait that threads have encountered, the number of times they have waited on a resource to be available, and the amount of time waited. The values provided are running totals, accumulated across all sessions since the server was last restarted or the statistics were manually reset using the DBCC SQLPERF command shown in Listing 7.1.

```
DBCC SQLPERF ('sys.dm_os_wait_stats', CLEAR);
```

Listing 7.1: Resetting the wait statistics.

If your SQL Server instance has been running for quite a while and you make a significant change, such as adding an important new index, you might consider clearing the old wait stats in order to prevent the old cumulative wait stats masking the impact of your change on the wait times.

The following columns are available in the view (times are all in millisecond units):

- **wait_type** – the type of wait

- **waiting_tasks_count** – the cumulative total number of waits that have occurred for the given wait_type

- **wait_time_ms** – total amount of time that tasks have waited on this given wait type; this value includes the time in the signal_wait_time_ms column

- **max_wait_time_ms** – the maximum amount of time that a task has been delayed, for a wait of this type

- **signal_wait_time_ms** – the total amount of time tasks took to start executing after being signaled; this is time spent on the runnable queue, and is pure CPU wait.

There are many reasons why a certain task within SQL Server may need to wait before proceeding, which means there are many possible values for the wait_type column. Some are quite usual, such as the need to wait for a lock to be released before it can access the required resource (e.g. a data page), and these are indicated by the "normal" lock modes such as shared, intent, exclusive, and so on (see *Chapter 4*, *Transactions*, for more detail). Other common causes of waits include latches, backups, external operations like extended stored procedure execution, replication, resource semaphores (used for memory access synchronization), and many more. There are too many to cover them all in detail, though most of the wait types are at least listed, if not well documented, in Books Online.

Finding the most common waits

The script in Listing 7.2 was run on a particularly busy server that does mostly OLTP transactions. We order the output based on the number of times a task has waited for any `wait_type` except those caused when certain key internal processes, such as the lazy writer, are briefly suspended.

```
SELECT TOP 3
       wait_type ,
       waiting_tasks_count ,
       wait_time_ms / 1000.0 AS wait_time_sec ,
       CASE WHEN waiting_tasks_count = 0 THEN NULL
            ELSE wait_time_ms / 1000.0 / waiting_tasks_count
       END AS avg_wait_time_sec ,
       max_wait_time_ms / 1000.0 AS max_wait_time_sec ,
       ( wait_time_ms - signal_wait_time_ms ) / 1000.0 AS resource_wait_time_sec
FROM   sys.dm_os_wait_stats
WHERE  wait_type NOT IN --tasks that are actually good or expected
                        --to be waited on
( 'CLR_SEMAPHORE', 'LAZYWRITER_SLEEP', 'RESOURCE_QUEUE', 'SLEEP_TASK',
  'SLEEP_SYSTEMTASK', 'WAITFOR' )
ORDER BY waiting_tasks_count DESC
```

wait_type	waiting_tasks_count	wait_time_sec	avg_wait_time_sec ...
OLEDB	2157499031	301112.781000	0.0001395656622197...
CXPACKET	239217887	1086440.015000	0.0045416336906278...
ASYNC_NETWORK_IO	93163538	89125.765000	0.0009566592994783...

Listing 7.2: The most common waits.

Analyzing the output, we see that the type of task causing the most waits is OLEDB. Books Online defines this wait type as follows:

Occurs when SQL Server calls the SQL Server Native Client OLE DB Provider. This wait type is not used for synchronization. Instead, it indicates the duration of calls to the OLE DB provider.

In short, a SQL Server process has made a call to another server via an **OLEDB** and is waiting on the response. On this particular server, there are several daemon-style processes that make calls to a different server. We are using application tier services that do row-by-row processing, which is one of the many possible reasons for these waits. Others include linked server access, CLR functions that access data, and so on.

The average wait time is only about 0.00014 seconds, which is not high, but the fact that the wait has occurred approximately 2.2 billion times is a little disturbing, as was the maximum wait time (omitted from the output for space reasons) of just over 2 minutes.

Is this of sufficient concern that it might warrant an optimization effort? It's difficult to judge using only this data. We'd need to clear the old stats out, gather and closely monitor the fresh data over time, and use Profiler to try to capture what's happening when the worst waits occur. This should tell us whether there really is an issue with the OLTP code, or whether it's some nightly process that, while perhaps inefficient, won't hurt OLTP performance directly.

The second of the most frequently occurring wait types is **CXPACKET**, which is described by Books Online as follows:

> *Occurs when trying to synchronize the query processor exchange iterator. You may consider lowering the degree of parallelism if contention on this wait type becomes a problem.*

Essentially, if the query optimizer believes that a certain long or complex query would benefit from parallel execution (i.e. distributing execution across multiple threads and CPUs), it uses exchange operators, indicated by the parallelism operators in your execution plans, such as `Distribute Streams`, to manage data redistribution, flow control and so on.

In general, parallelism tends to benefit OLAP-style workloads. In an OLTP system such as this, it is certainly worrying to see 239 million waits that occurred while SQL Server parallelized queries. It means there are a lot of queries that are longer, and more complex and CPU-intensive than we would hope. In this particular case, the `max degree of parallelism` option is set to 2, in an attempt to maximize throughput but give those poorly performing queries a bit of a performance boost. Ideally, of course, these queries would be optimized, but they are the product of a third-party system that we can't touch, and it has a habit of generating queries that are ten pages long.

CXPACKET *waits and latch classes*

CXPACKET *waits are often associated with the occurrence of latches of the type* ACCESS_METHODS_ SCAN_RANGE_GENERATOR. *We'll discuss this further in a later section, Investigating Latching.*

The third wait type on our list `ASYNC_NETWORK_IO`, is described in Books Online as:

> *Occurs on network writes when the task is blocked behind the network. Verify that the client is processing data from the server.*

This wait type occurs when sending data back to the client over the network. Often, these waits simply mean that the client is slowly fetching rows as it works on them, rather than fetching all rows into cache and disconnecting (at least logically, using connection pooling). It can also indicate a slow/unreliable network that needs to be upgraded. Although this wait type caused an order of magnitude fewer waits than `CXPACKET`, it will certainly merit further investigation.

Not included in our output here, but worth looking out for nevertheless, are `SOS_SCHEDULER_YIELD` waits, described in Books Online as:

> *Occurs when a task voluntarily yields the scheduler for other tasks to execute. During this wait the task is waiting for its quantum to be renewed.*

If you are experiencing CPU pressure (see Listing 7.5, for example) and observe that the signal wait time is largely composed of SOS_SCHEDULER_YIELD waits, it indicates that the scheduler is experiencing pressure, and regularly swapping out a running session in order to allow another session to proceed, causing the original session to wait a considerable time before getting back on the CPU. Such waits commonly occur when several CPU-intensive queries get assigned to the same scheduler. Consistently increasing signal wait times can also be a sign of scheduler pressure.

In such cases, you will need to further investigate the queries that are running, and to look for opportunities to tune them to reduce expensive sort operations, and so on. You would also want to find out how much plan recompilation is taking place on your system (see *Chapter 3*), as this is a CPU-intensive operation. In addition, more or faster CPUs might help, along with a better balancing of the load across CPUs, or simply better timing of when CPU-heavy queries are run.

Scheduler activity can be investigated further using the sys.dm_os_schedulers DMV, as we will discuss shortly.

Finding the longest cumulative waits

It is useful to dissect the wait_stats data in several different ways, such as by the amount of waiting, or the average wait time, and look for "repeat offenders."

The script in Listing 7.3 will help determine on which resources SQL Server is spending the most time waiting, as a percentage of the total amount of time spent waiting on any wait_type that doesn't appear in the exclusion list.

```
-- Isolate top waits for server instance since last restart
-- or statistics clear
WITH    Waits
        AS ( SELECT    wait_type ,
                       wait_time_ms / 1000. AS wait_time_sec ,
```

```
                              100. * wait_time_ms / SUM(wait_time_ms) OVER ( ) AS pct ,
                              ROW_NUMBER() OVER ( ORDER BY wait_time_ms DESC ) AS rn
                FROM          sys.dm_os_wait_stats
                WHERE         wait_type NOT IN ( 'CLR_SEMAPHORE', 'LAZYWRITER_SLEEP',
                                                'RESOURCE_QUEUE', 'SLEEP_TASK',
                                                'SLEEP_SYSTEMTASK',
                                                'SQLTRACE_BUFFER_FLUSH', 'WAITFOR',
                                                'LOGMGR_QUEUE', 'CHECKPOINT_QUEUE' )
                    )
    SELECT   wait_type ,
             CAST(wait_time_sec AS DECIMAL(12, 2)) AS wait_time_sec ,
             CAST(pct AS DECIMAL(12, 2)) AS wait_time_percentage
    FROM     Waits
    WHERE    pct > 1
    ORDER BY wait_time_sec DESC
```

Listing 7.3: Report on top resource waits.

This script will help you locate the biggest bottleneck, at the instance level, allowing you to focus your tuning efforts on a particular type of problem. For example, if the top cumulative wait types are disk I/O related, then you would want to investigate this issue further using DMVs such as `sys.dm_io_pending_io_requests` and `sys.dm_io_virtual_file_stats`, both covered in *Chapter 6*.

Investigating locking waits

In some cases, it's useful to move in from the big picture, and focus on specific types of wait. For example, if you feel that excessive locking may be the root cause of a performance issue, the query shown in Listing 7.4 will return the cumulative waits for I/O operations.

```
SELECT   wait_type ,
         waiting_tasks_count ,
         wait_time_ms ,
         max_wait_time_ms
FROM     sys.dm_os_wait_stats
```

```
WHERE    wait_type LIKE 'LCK%'
         AND Waiting_tasks_count > 0
ORDER BY waiting_tasks_count DESC
```

Listing 7.4:   Seeking out locking waits.

On the same busy server as used in the previous example, which had been recently rebooted, the following result was obtained (the `signal_wait_time_ms` column was omitted for space reasons only):

wait_type	waiting_tasks_count	wait_time_ms	max_wait_time_ms
LCK_M_U	79219	563343	29718
LCK_M_X	51842	495984	30515
LCK_M_SCH_S	1018	2841578	464031
LCK_M_SCH_M	434	27437	1859
LCK_M_IX	85	431015	137046
LCK_M_IS	59	1517906	111796
LCK_M_S	8	6578	2000
LCK_M_RX_X	5	41093	14812

In this case, this server has been waiting on a lot of update mode locks (`LCK_M_U`), issued when a process is reading data that it might update, as well as exclusive locks. Together, they indicate that the server is performing a lot of data modifications. The amount of time waited on update locks is 563343 / 79219, or about 7.1 ms.

On the whole, not a terrible number, but what might be a bit more concerning are some of the maximum wait times, especially the 29.7 seconds (not milliseconds) maximum wait time on an update lock. However, without knowing when the maximum wait times occurred, we don't know whether the waits were caused by OLTP queries that were blocking one another, or by a set of long-running nightly processes that would be expected to block other processes for their duration. On this particular server, we use the `READ_COMMITTED_SNAPSHOT` setting on the very busy databases and blocking locks are rare, as reflected in the number of shared lock (`LCK_M_S`) waits being very low. This is a strong indication that the waits are originating from the nightly processes, and it is also a good reminder that, like almost every reading we get from the DMVs, these wait times must be taken in the context of the server configuration. The next step would be to run traces on operations that last 20 seconds or more during those times when the longest waits were happening, and start to find out whether or not there really is a problem.

Session-by-session wait times

The difficulty in pulling the fine detail out of a vast set of cumulative statistics, across all sessions, highlights how useful it would be to be able to track wait times on a session-by-session basis. In this way, we'd be able to see exactly what waits were occurring during normal OLTP operation, and exactly what was happening while sessions running the nightly processes were under way. Hopefully, the pioneering work in this regard by the likes of Mario Broodbakker (HTTP://WWW.SIMPLE-TALK.COM/AUTHOR/MARIO-BROODBAKKER/) will eventually make its way into SQL Server.

Ideally, we need to clear the statistics using the aforementioned `DBCC SQLPERF` command, take a baseline reading and then take periodic snapshots of the data so that we can accurately compare the data over a time period.

Investigating CPU pressure

The simple query shown in Listing 7.5 calculates signal waits and resource waits as a percentage of the overall wait time, in order to diagnose potential CPU pressure.

```
-- Total waits are wait_time_ms (high signal waits indicates CPU pressure)
SELECT  CAST(100.0 * SUM(signal_wait_time_ms) / SUM(wait_time_ms)
                        AS NUMERIC(20,2)) AS [%signal (cpu) waits] ,
        CAST(100.0 * SUM(wait_time_ms - signal_wait_time_ms)
        / SUM(wait_time_ms) AS NUMERIC(20, 2)) AS [%resource waits]
FROM    sys.dm_os_wait_stats ;
```

Listing 7.5: Is there any CPU pressure?

This query is useful to help confirm CPU pressure. Since signal waits are time waiting for a CPU to service a thread, if you record total signal waits above roughly 10–15%, this is a pretty good indicator of CPU pressure. These wait stats are cumulative since SQL Server was last restarted, so you need to know what your baseline value for signal waits is, and watch the trend over time.

SQL Server Performance Counters

SQL Server provides a number of database-level and instance-level objects and associated counters which can be used to monitor various aspects of SQL Server performance. These counters are exposed by the **sys.dm_os_performance_counters** DMV. These counters expose the "queues" in your system; the places where there is a lot of demand for a given resource, and the reasons for the excessive demand, via specific resource measurements such as disk writes/sec, processor queue lengths, available memory, and so on.

Generally, these performance counters are investigated using Performance Monitor (PerfMon), a Windows OS monitoring tool that provides a vast range of counters for monitoring memory, disk, CPU, and network usage on a server (for example, see HTTP:// TECHNET.MICROSOFT.COM/EN-US/LIBRARY/CC768048.ASPX), and also exposes the counters maintained by SQL Server. Generally, the DBA or system administrator would set up PerfMon to record statistics from various counters at regular intervals, storing the data in a file and then importing it into Excel for analysis.

However if, like me, you prefer to save the statistics in a database table and interrogate them using SQL, the **sys.dm_os_performance_counters** DMV is a very useful tool. Just write the query to retrieve the data from the DMV, add **INSERT INTO Counter-TrendingTableName...** and you have a rudimentary monitoring system! Also, it's not always possible to get direct access to PerfMon, and accessing it from a different machine can be pretty slow.

Unfortunately, using this DMV is far from plain sailing, and querying it can be plain annoying at times. As has been noted a few times throughout the book, the DMOs are not built with end-user comfort in mind. The data in them is often exposed in a form that's most convenient in terms of data collection efficiency, rather than in order to make it easy for people to read and interpret that data. This is especially true of the `performance_counters` DMV, where some of the code required to present the data in a meaningful way in the queries is kludgy to the point of embarrassment.

With that warning in mind, let's take a look at the columns that the **sys.dm_os_performance_counters** DMV provides.

- **object_name** – name of the object to which the counter refers. This is usually a two-part name, starting with **SQL Server:**. For example, **SQL Server:Databases** or **SQL Server:Locks**.

- **counter_name** – name of the counter. For example, the **SQL Server:Databases** object exposes the **Log Shrinks** counter, to monitor transaction log shrink events.

- **instance_name** – specific instance of a counter, such as the database name for **SQLServer:Databases:LogShrinks** or user errors for **SQLServer:SQL Errors:Errors/sec**.

- **cntr_value** – most recent value of the counter.

- **cntr_type** – type of counter.

Note that only SQL Server counters are represented in the DMV, not any Windows or other counters.

Most of these columns look innocuous enough, but don't be deceived – the `cntr_value` and the `cntr_type` values, in particular, are a nest of vipers. The `cntr_type` column exposes WMI Performance Counter Types and, for the most part, the values provided for each type of counter in `cntr_value` will need to be decoded before we can use them. To get the list of counter types, we can execute the query shown in Listing 7.6.

```
SELECT DISTINCT
        cntr_type
FROM    sys.dm_os_performance_counters
ORDER BY cntr_type

cntr_type
```

```
-----------
65792
272696576
537003264
1073874176
1073939712
```

Listing 7.6:   Returning a list of PerfMon counter types.

The cntr_type values returned are not documented in Books Online, but my research on MSDN and elsewhere revealed the following:

- **65792 = PERF_COUNTER_LARGE_RAWCOUNT** – provides the last observed value for the counter; for this type of counter, the values in cntr_value can be used directly, making this the most easily usable type

- **272696576 = PERF_COUNTER_BULK_COUNT** – provides the average number of operations per second. Two readings of cntr_value will be required for this counter type, in order to get the per second averages.

- **537003264 = PERF_LARGE_RAW_FRACTION** – used in conjunction with PERF_LARGE_RAW_BASE to calculate ratio values, such as the cache hit ratio.

- **1073874176 = PERF_AVERAGE_BULK** – used to calculate an average number of operations completed during a time interval; like PERF_LARGE_RAW_FRACTION, it uses PERF_LARGE_RAW_BASE to do the calculation

- **1073939712 = PERF_LARGE_RAW_BASE**, used in the translation of PERF_LARGE_RAW_FRACTION and PERF_AVERAGE_BULK values to readable output; should not be displayed alone.

Frankly, the `performance_counters` DMV is one of the least documented, and almost every article I have read uses it in the simplest way possible, one counter at a time.

Based on all research and testing that we have been able to do, these are the only types in use today with 2008 RTM, 2005 SP2, and 2005 SP2 Express, and each of these types should work on all of the cited SQL Server editions and versions, although some materials uncovered during our research suggested that the values were not always LARGE (64-bit) values. Please check the errata and code downloads page for this book, at WWW.SIMPLE-TALK.COM/COMMUNITY/FORUMS/590/SHOWFORUM.ASPX where we'll report any cases of malfunction on a user's system.

For the purpose of this discussion, we'll break these counter types down into four subsections, as follows:

- directly usable values (`PERF_COUNTER_LARGE_RAWCOUNT`)

- ratios (`PERF_LARGE_RAW_FRACTION`)

- average number of operations per second (`PERF_COUNTER_BULK_COUNT`)

- average number of operations (`PERF_AVERAGE_BULK`).

Directly usable counter types

Let's start with the most easily usable counter types, which provide the current count for a given metric, for example, the number of times a log file has grown or shrunk, or the number of pages of data in a database, the number of entries in a given cache, the number of active transactions, and so on. These values need no consideration of how long the machine has been running, nor how often the values are captured.

The code in Listing 7.7 filters for performance counters of type `PERF_COUNTER_LARGE_RAWCOUNT`.

```
DECLARE @PERF_COUNTER_LARGE_RAWCOUNT INT
SELECT  @PERF_COUNTER_LARGE_RAWCOUNT = 65792

SELECT  object_name ,
        counter_name ,
        instance_name ,
        cntr_value
FROM    sys.dm_os_performance_counters
WHERE   cntr_type = @PERF_COUNTER_LARGE_RAWCOUNT
ORDER BY object_name ,
         counter_name ,
         instance_name
```

Listing 7.7: Returning the values of directly usable PerfMon counters.

This query will return the current value for counters such as page life expectancy, current data and log file sizes for database on the instance, and so on.

Monitoring shrinkage and growth of the transaction log

Let's say that we want to closely monitor any auto-grow or auto-shrink events for the transaction log on our most important server, as shown in Listing 7.8.

```
--the default instance reports as SQLServer, but other
--instances as MSSQL$InstanceName
DECLARE @object_name SYSNAME
SET @object_name = CASE WHEN @@servicename = 'MSSQLSERVER' THEN 'SQLServer'
                       ELSE 'MSSQL$' + @@serviceName
                  END + ':Databases'

DECLARE @PERF_COUNTER_LARGE_RAWCOUNT INT
SELECT  @PERF_COUNTER_LARGE_RAWCOUNT = 65792

SELECT  object_name ,
        counter_name ,
        instance_name ,
        cntr_value
FROM    sys.dm_os_performance_counters
```

```
WHERE      cntr_type = @PERF_COUNTER_LARGE_RAWCOUNT
           AND object_name = @object_name
           AND counter_name IN ( 'Log Growths', 'Log Shrinks' )
           AND cntr_value > 0
ORDER BY object_name ,
         counter_name ,
         instance_name
```

Listing 7.8:   Monitoring changes in the size of the transaction log.

Log size adjustments aren't problematical in all cases but it is quite costly to have users on a busy server waiting while space is being allocated to the log, and an excessive number of small auto-grow events will fragment the log. Shrinking the log (i.e. removing any unused space) is, as a general habit, a bad idea as it just means that you are likely to see a log growth event very soon. The best practice is to have log space pre-allocated and not to adjust it; free log space is not harmful to performance, but a full log is.

Deprecated feature use

In 2008, a new set of counters was added to show deprecated feature utilization. You can get to them using a query of the form shown in Listing 7.9. In cases where you've recently upgraded a system, it's useful to know what deprecated features are still being used, so that you can plan on updating them, to avoid having them fail when you are upgrading again in a few years.

```
DECLARE @object_name SYSNAME
SET @object_name = CASE WHEN @@servicename = 'MSSQLSERVER' THEN 'SQLServer'
                        ELSE 'MSSQL$' + @@serviceName
                   END + ':Deprecated Features'
DECLARE @PERF_COUNTER_LARGE_RAWCOUNT INT
SELECT  @PERF_COUNTER_LARGE_RAWCOUNT = 65792

SELECT  object_name ,
        counter_name ,
        instance_name ,
        cntr_value
```

```
FROM     sys.dm_os_performance_counters
WHERE    cntr_type = @PERF_COUNTER_LARGE_RAWCOUNT
         AND object_name = @object_name
         AND cntr_value > 0
```

Listing 7.9: Which deprecated features are still in use?

You may be interested to discover that you are using some of these deprecated features. Apparently, on my laptop, I am using Hindi, Korean Wansung Unicode, and other collations that, to my knowledge, I've never touched, at least not directly.

However, it does note that I am using **sp_dbcmptlevel** and string literals as column aliases, which is true to the extent that a script I downloaded when researching this chapter used them.

Ratios

The second group of counters, PERF_LARGE_RAW_FRACTION, provides ratios, such as cache hit ratios for log and data caches, as well as a few pertaining to the Resource Governor and one for worktables from the cache.

These counters are trickier to use because, obviously, we need to retrieve two values in order to calculate the ratio, and we need to marry the counter name from the PERF_LARGE_RAW_BASE row to the PERF_LARGE_RAW_FRACTION row. This trivial-sounding task is made more complex by the fact that the names don't exactly match. You have to remove 'base' from the _BASE row. One of the counters, Worktables from Cache, is an exception and has to be treated differently (see Listing 7.10).

Having worked through these issues, however, the code to get these ratio values is pretty simple, and is shown in Listing 7.10. If the _BASE value is 0, we return NULL rather than cause a divide-by-zero error. The cases where I have seen this have, generally, corresponded to cases where a resource had not been used.

```
DECLARE  @PERF_LARGE_RAW_FRACTION INT ,
    @PERF_LARGE_RAW_BASE INT
SELECT   @PERF_LARGE_RAW_FRACTION = 537003264 ,
         @PERF_LARGE_RAW_BASE = 1073939712


SELECT   dopc_fraction.object_name ,
         dopc_fraction.instance_name ,
         dopc_fraction.counter_name ,
         --when divisor is 0, return I return NULL to indicate
         --divide by 0/no values captured
         CAST(dopc_fraction.cntr_value AS FLOAT)
         / CAST(CASE dopc_base.cntr_value
                  WHEN 0 THEN NULL
                  ELSE dopc_base.cntr_value
                END AS FLOAT) AS cntr_value
FROM     sys.dm_os_performance_counters AS dopc_base
         JOIN sys.dm_os_performance_counters AS dopc_fraction
            ON dopc_base.cntr_type = @PERF_LARGE_RAW_BASE
               AND dopc_fraction.cntr_type = @PERF_LARGE_RAW_FRACTION
               AND dopc_base.object_name = dopc_fraction.object_name
               AND dopc_base.instance_name = dopc_fraction.instance_name
               AND ( REPLACE(dopc_base.counter_name,
                 'base', '') = dopc_fraction.counter_name
              --Worktables From Cache has "odd" name where
              --Ratio was left off
               OR REPLACE(dopc_base.counter_name,
                 'base', '') = ( REPLACE(dopc_fraction.counter_name,
                 'ratio', '') )
                 )
ORDER BY dopc_fraction.object_name ,
         dopc_fraction.instance_name ,
         dopc_fraction.counter_name
```

Listing 7.10: Returning the values of ratio PerfMon counters.

Admittedly, manually calculating cache hit ratios in this manner does not seem like the easiest way to go. Again, though, once you have the script you can maintain it in your DMV script library in SSMS and it does provide a very quick means of getting the values. Also, as noted earlier, you can easily modify the script to dump the data into a reporting table, for trend analysis.

As an example usage, the query in Listing 7.11 will return the cache hit ratio from the buffer manager.

```
DECLARE @object_name SYSNAME
SET @object_name = CASE WHEN @@servicename = 'MSSQLSERVER' THEN 'SQLServer'
                       ELSE 'MSSQL$' + @@serviceName
                  END + ':Buffer Manager'
DECLARE
    @PERF_LARGE_RAW_FRACTION INT ,
    @PERF_LARGE_RAW_BASE INT
SELECT  @PERF_LARGE_RAW_FRACTION = 537003264 ,
        @PERF_LARGE_RAW_BASE = 1073939712


SELECT  dopc_fraction.object_name ,
        dopc_fraction.instance_name ,
        dopc_fraction.counter_name ,
    --when divisor is 0, return I return NULL to indicate
    --divide by 0/no values captured
        CAST(dopc_fraction.cntr_value AS FLOAT)
        / CAST(CASE dopc_base.cntr_value
                WHEN 0 THEN NULL
                ELSE dopc_base.cntr_value
               END AS FLOAT) AS cntr_value
FROM    sys.dm_os_performance_counters AS dopc_base
        JOIN sys.dm_os_performance_counters AS dopc_fraction
            ON dopc_base.cntr_type = @PERF_LARGE_RAW_BASE
                AND dopc_fraction.cntr_type = @PERF_LARGE_RAW_FRACTION
                AND dopc_base.object_name = dopc_fraction.object_name
                AND dopc_base.instance_name = dopc_fraction.instance_name
                AND ( REPLACE(dopc_base.counter_name,
                'base', '') = dopc_fraction.counter_name
    --Worktables From Cache has "odd" name where
    --Ratio was left off
                OR REPLACE(dopc_base.counter_name,
                'base', '') = ( REPLACE(dopc_fraction.counter_name,
                'ratio', '') )
                )
WHERE   dopc_fraction.object_name = @object_name
        AND dopc_fraction.instance_name = ''
        AND dopc_fraction.counter_name = 'Buffer cache hit ratio'
```

```
ORDER BY dopc_fraction.object_name ,
        dopc_fraction.instance_name ,
        dopc_fraction.counter_name
```

Listing 7.11: Returning the current value for the buffer cache hit ratio.

Per second averages

The next set of counters, `PERF_COUNTER_BULK_COUNT`, is used to get average actions per second. Some interesting values to look out for in this category include:

- **Server:Buffer Manager - Page lookups/sec**
  gives an indication of cache activity; higher numbers indicate a more active buffer pool (the definition of "higher" is largely dependent on your hardware and usage)

- **Server:Databases-<databaseName> - Log Bytes Flushed/sec**
  gives an indication of how much data has been written to the log for the database

- **SQLServer:Locks-_Total - Lock Requests/sec**
  provides the number of locks being taken on a server per second, usually to compare to other time periods, to see when the server is being inundated with queries that might block other users.

As "point-in-time" values, these counters do not necessarily tell you very much but, when tracked over time, they can help the DBA to quickly identify worrying events, trends, or changes. For example, let's say that users start experiencing performance problems at a given time of day, and that you notice that this coincides with spikes in the number of lock requests per second which, in turn, coincides with the time that Joe Doofus, the manager with more rights than brains, issues a major query in `SERIALIZABLE` isolation level.

Nearly all of the counters in this group are named with a suffix of '/sec', but a few are actually prefixed '(ms)'. However, the latter will be interpreted as "number of milliseconds waited per second." So, for example, `Total Latch Wait Time (ms)` is the average amount of time per second that a certain process had to wait to acquire a latch, over the time the sample was taken. Basically, these counters are constantly incrementing values, though if they ever hit the maximum value, they would reset to zero.

The way to deal with these counters is pretty much the same as with any accumulating counter DMV. Take a baseline value, wait some number of seconds, then sample again; the number of seconds to wait should be varied based on your needs. For ad hoc monitoring of a given operation you would set the delay such that you could capture a suitable number of samples over the period of time the operation is taking place.

The example in Listing 7.12 uses a simple **WAITFOR** statement to implement the delay, in this case, 5 seconds. It uses a `datetime` column, with a default of `getdate()`, in order to capture the exact time the values were sampled (since the delay may not be exactly 5 seconds each time; for example, it might actually take 5020 milliseconds to execute the query).

```
DECLARE @PERF_COUNTER_BULK_COUNT INT
SELECT  @PERF_COUNTER_BULK_COUNT = 272696576

--Holds initial state
DECLARE @baseline TABLE
    (
        object_name NVARCHAR(256) ,
        counter_name NVARCHAR(256) ,
        instance_name NVARCHAR(256) ,
        cntr_value BIGINT ,
        cntr_type INT ,
        time DATETIME DEFAULT ( GETDATE() )
    )

DECLARE @current TABLE
    (
        object_name NVARCHAR(256) ,
        counter_name NVARCHAR(256) ,
        instance_name NVARCHAR(256) ,
        cntr_value BIGINT ,
        cntr_type INT ,
```

```
      time DATETIME DEFAULT ( GETDATE() )
    )

--capture the initial state of bulk counters
INSERT  INTO @baseline
        ( object_name ,
          counter_name ,
          instance_name ,
          cntr_value ,
          cntr_type
        )
        SELECT  object_name ,
                counter_name ,
                instance_name ,
                cntr_value ,
                cntr_type
        FROM    sys.dm_os_performance_counters AS dopc
        WHERE   cntr_type = @PERF_COUNTER_BULK_COUNT

WAITFOR DELAY '00:00:05' --the code will work regardless of delay chosen

--get the followon state of the counters
INSERT  INTO @current
        ( object_name ,
          counter_name ,
          instance_name ,
          cntr_value ,
          cntr_type
        )
        SELECT  object_name ,
                counter_name ,
                instance_name ,
                cntr_value ,
                cntr_type
        FROM    sys.dm_os_performance_counters AS dopc
        WHERE   cntr_type = @PERF_COUNTER_BULK_COUNT

SELECT  dopc.object_name ,
        dopc.instance_name ,
        dopc.counter_name ,
        --ms to second conversion factor
        1000 *
        --current value less the previous value
        ( ( dopc.cntr_value - prev_dopc.cntr_value )
```

```
                    --divided by the number of milliseconds that pass
                    --casted as float to get fractional results. Float
                    --lets really big or really small numbers to work
                / CAST(DATEDIFF(ms, prev_dopc.time, dopc.time) AS FLOAT) )
                                                        AS cntr_value
            --simply join on the names of the counters
FROM        @current AS dopc
            JOIN @baseline AS prev_dopc ON prev_dopc.object_name = dopc.object_name
                              AND prev_dopc.instance_name = dopc.instance_name
                              AND prev_dopc.counter_name = dopc.counter_name
WHERE       dopc.cntr_type = @PERF_COUNTER_BULK_COUNT
            AND 1000 * ( ( dopc.cntr_value - prev_dopc.cntr_value )
                      / CAST(DATEDIFF(ms, prev_dopc.time, dopc.time) AS FLOAT) )
/* default to only showing non-zero values */ <> 0
ORDER BY dopc.object_name ,
         dopc.instance_name ,
         dopc.counter_name
```

Listing 7.12:   Returning the values of "per second average" PerfMon counters.

This code can be easily adapted to a specific counter type, such as one of those listed previously but we won't show it here, as Listing 7.12 is pretty cumbersome. Notice that we default to only showing non-zero values, since that is almost always what you will be interested in when using this set of data.

Average number of operations

The final type of performance counter, PERF_AVERAGE_BULK, is used to calculate an average number of operations completed during a time interval (SQL Server chooses the sampling time). The most commonly-used counter of the PERF_AVERAGE_BULK type belongs to the Locks object, and shows the average wait time for different types of locks, such as database lock, application lock, page lock, key lock (which is essentially a row lock), and so on.

The query to return these counter values, shown in Listing 7.13, is pretty much exactly the same as the ratio query (Listing 7.10), but this time using the PERF_AVERAGE_BULK type.

```
DECLARE @PERF_AVERAGE_BULK INT ,
    @PERF_LARGE_RAW_BASE INT

SELECT  @PERF_AVERAGE_BULK = 1073874176 ,
        @PERF_LARGE_RAW_BASE = 1073939712

SELECT  dopc_avgBulk.object_name ,
        dopc_avgBulk.instance_name ,
        dopc_avgBulk.counter_name ,
        CAST(dopc_avgBulk.cntr_value AS FLOAT)
         --when divisor is 0, return NULL to indicate
         --divide by 0
        / CAST(CASE dopc_base.cntr_value
                WHEN 0 THEN NULL
                ELSE dopc_base.cntr_value
              END AS FLOAT) AS cntr_value
FROM    sys.dm_os_performance_counters dopc_base
        JOIN sys.dm_os_performance_counters dopc_avgBulk
            ON dopc_base.cntr_type = @PERF_LARGE_RAW_BASE
            AND dopc_avgBulk.cntr_type = @PERF_AVERAGE_BULK
            AND dopc_base.object_name = dopc_avgBulk.object_name
            AND dopc_base.instance_name = dopc_avgBulk.instance_name
        --Average Wait Time has (ms) in name,
        --so it has handled "special"
            AND ( REPLACE(dopc_base.counter_name,
              'base', '') = dopc_avgBulk.counter_name
            OR REPLACE(dopc_base.counter_name,
              'base', '') = REPLACE(dopc_avgBulk.counter_name,
              '(ms)', '')
              )
ORDER BY dopc_avgBulk.object_name ,
        dopc_avgBulk.instance_name ,
        dopc_avgBulk.counter_name
```

Listing 7.13: Returning the values for the "average number of operations" PerfMon counters.

Returned will be values such as the following:

```
object_name                     instance_name  counter_name                    cntr_value
------------------------------  -------------  ------------------------------  --------------
--
SQLServer:Latches                              Average Latch Wait Time (ms)    3.84907340420574
SQLServer:Locks                 _Total         Average Wait Time (ms)          188.428878069211
SQLServer:Locks                 AllocUnit      Average Wait Time (ms)          NULL
SQLServer:Locks                 Application    Average Wait Time (ms)          263.055555555556
SQLServer:Locks                 Database       Average Wait Time (ms)          NULL
SQLServer:Locks                 Extent         Average Wait Time (ms)          NULL
SQLServer:Locks                 File           Average Wait Time (ms)          471.392592592593
SQLServer:Locks                 HoBT           Average Wait Time (ms)          NULL
SQLServer:Locks                 Key            Average Wait Time (ms)          150.459888113501
SQLServer:Locks                 Metadata       Average Wait Time (ms)          95.7042253521127
SQLServer:Locks                 Object         Average Wait Time (ms)          610.405089408528
SQLServer:Locks                 Page           Average Wait Time (ms)          399.793103448276
SQLServer:Locks                 RID            Average Wait Time (ms)          1860
```

From this output, we can see that we've no waiting on `Database`, `Extent`, and `HoBT` (heap or B-tree) objects, but have spent an average of 263 milliseconds on `Application` locks (which are used on this particular system to implement single-threaded reads from a queue), 150 milliseconds on `Key` locks, and 399 on `Page` locks, amongst others.

Monitoring Machine Characteristics

A common task for DBAs is to monitor the configurations and characteristics of their servers, as well as to track changes to these settings over time. The `sys.dm_os_sys_info` DMV contains a host of values that will give you a basic understanding of how the interface between the OS and SQL Server is configured. It returns a single row, summarizing the characteristics of a given machine, in terms of static configuration, such as the number of processors, as well as how long a server has been running. Columns represented in the view include those listed below.

- **cpu_count** – number of logical processors on the computer.

- **hyperthread_ratio** – ratio of logical to physical processors (cores). For example, on a dual-core processor with hyper-threading turned off, this value would be 2. If hyper-threading were enabled, the value would be 4. Note that this ratio value does not discern between hyper-threading and multi-core (e.g. a quad-core processor with no hyper-threading would also return a value of 4).

- **physical_memory_in_bytes** – total amount of physical RAM installed on the computer or, at least, the amount of RAM that the OS believes it has available (a distinction that is particularly relevant when dealing with virtual environments).

- **virtual_memory_in_bytes** – amount of virtual RAM available to the process in user mode. This can differ depending on the OS. On a 32-bit OS, variations can be based on the 3-GB switch or, in Vista and later, the **IncreaseUserVa** switch (set using the **bcdedit** utility).

- **max_workers_count** – maximum number of workers that can be created. Workers do the work for SQL Server and are generally equivalent to threads, unless running in "lightweight pooling" server configuration, in which case it corresponds to a fiber (for a deeper understanding, go to HTTP://MSDN.MICROSOFT.COM/EN-US/LIBRARY/MS189267.ASPX).

- **scheduler_total_count** – total number of schedulers configured, including the system schedulers, such as the one that handles Dedicated Administrator Connection (DAC) connections (corresponds to the result of: `select count(*) from sys.dm_os_schedulers`).

- **scheduler_count** – current number of schedulers that are visible to user processes (corresponds to the result of `select count(*) from sys.dm_os_schedulers where status = 'VISIBLE ONLINE'`).

- **os_priority_class** – Windows scheduling priority for the SQL Server process. Essentially, a high value will allow SQL Server to use a higher than normal allocation of OS resources. Domain: 64 (low), 16384 (below normal), 32 (normal), 32768 (above normal), 256 (real-time), 128 (high). The default is "normal," unless the priority boost option is enabled, which isn't to be advised unless you have a server dedicated to SQL Server and specific needs.

- **sql_server_start_time** – date and time SQL Server was started (new for SQL Server 2008).

- **bpool_committed** – number of 8-K pages in the buffer pool that are in use.

- **bpool_commit_target** – number of 8-K pages that SQL Server needs. If this value is greater than the committed value, SQL Server may try to acquire more memory.

- **bpool_visible** – number of 8-K pages in the buffer pool that are directly accessible in RAM. The number of pages that are visible is limited by the memory structure and OS. On a 32-bit system using AWE, memory is accessed in "windows" and the visible amount of memory can be less than the committed amount of memory.

- **cpu_ticks_in_ms** – the number of CPU ticks per millisecond. Can be used as a conversion factor in calculations, for example, with the cpu_ticks column that is also presented in the results of this DMV.

- **ms_ticks** – number of milliseconds since server was started.

Other columns include: deadlock_monitor_serial_number, os_quantum, os_error_mode, sqlserver_start_time_ms_ticks (new for SQL Server 2008), cpu_ticks, stack_size_in_bytes, and os_quantum, which I mention for completeness, but won't cover.

I capture the values in most of these columns periodically, and hope to find that they remain unchanged over time. This DMV is also quite useful for getting a feel for an unfamiliar server that you need to troubleshoot. A simple query such as that shown in Listing 7.14 will provide basic CPU configuration details.

```
-- Hardware information from SQL Server 2008
-- (Cannot distinguish between HT and multi-core)
SELECT  cpu_count AS [Logical CPU Count] ,
        hyperthread_ratio AS [Hyperthread Ratio] ,
        cpu_count / hyperthread_ratio AS [Physical CPU Count] ,
        physical_memory_in_bytes / 1048576 AS [Physical Memory (MB)] ,
        sqlserver_start_time
FROM    sys.dm_os_sys_info ;
```

Listing 7.14: CPU configuration details.

The script in Listing 7.15 is useful when interrogating memory configuration.

```
--Determine if this is a 32- or 64-bit SQL Server edition
DECLARE @ServerAddressing AS TINYINT
SELECT  @serverAddressing = CASE WHEN CHARINDEX('64',
                                               CAST(SERVERPROPERTY('Edition')
                                                    AS VARCHAR(100))) > 0
                            THEN 64
                            ELSE 32
                     END ;

SELECT  cpu_count / hyperthread_ratio AS SocketCount ,
        physical_memory_in_bytes / 1024 / 1024 AS physical_memory_mb ,
        virtual_memory_in_bytes / 1024 / 1024 AS sql_max_virtual_memory_mb ,
            -- same with other bpool columns as they are page oriented.
            -- Multiplying by 8 takes it to 8K, then / 1024 to convert to mb
        bpool_committed * 8 / 1024 AS buffer_pool_committed_mb ,
            --64 bit OS does not have limitations with addressing as 32 did
        CASE WHEN @serverAddressing = 32
            THEN CASE WHEN virtual_memory_in_bytes / 1024 /
                                                ( 2048 * 1024 ) < 1
                        THEN 'off'
                        ELSE 'on'
                 END
            ELSE 'N/A on 64 bit'
        END AS [/3GB switch]
FROM    sys.dm_os_sys_info
```

Listing 7.15: Interrogating memory configuration.

On the Vista Pro laptop that I am using to write this book, this query returned the following:

```
SocketCount      physical_memory_mb     sql_max_virtual_memory_mb
-------------    --------------------   -------------------------
1                3571                   2047


buffer_pool_committed_mb    /3GB switch
------------------------    -----------
228                         off
```

I have a single dual-core processor, hence one socket; the physical memory matched the memory shown in task manager on the performance tab, and I do not have the IncreaseUserVa turned on, so my virtual memory is limited to less than 2 GB. Thankfully, 32-bit processors are on the way out these days, and we can stop worrying about the limitations of 32-bit addressing.

Investigating CPU Usage

In terms of complexity, SQL Server is almost an operating system in its own right and its resource utilization patterns are, likewise, pretty complex. When a request is submitted to SQL Server, it is assigned to a worker thread. Each of these threads is assigned to a CPU by what is known as the SQL Server OS scheduler. For each CPU, there is only one scheduler available for use by SQL Server, to execute user code, and only one request (SPID or session_id) per scheduler can be running at any time.

Threads waiting for CPU time will be placed in the runnable queue; the longer the queue, the higher the CPU pressure (see Listing 7.5). Threads whose associated request is waiting for a resource to become free, or that have to perform I/O, will be moved to the waiter list. If there are simply no available worker threads, a process will be blocked until one becomes available, and moved to the work queue.

The **max worker threads** *option.*

It is best to let SQL Server automatically configure the number of worker threads at startup, but this number can be adjusted for extremely busy systems, using **max worker threads** *option.*

In order to identify or rule out CPU pressure as a potential cause of slow execution times, we can use **sys.dm_os_schedulers** to investigate the kind of load being applied to our CPUs. It provides information on the current activity of the schedulers that are being used to apportion work to CPUs, along with a few cumulative counters that reveal how often certain events, such as context switches, have occurred since the computer was last started.

The root cause of CPU pressure is, unfortunately, not always easy to nail down. The CPU is used for many operations, not just doing computations. It is used to move data in and out of memory, for disk access, and pretty much everything that is done on the server. Hence, when CPUs are taxed, the server will experience massive slowdowns. We will look at ways to monitor CPU usage and investigate CPU pressure, by finding out such things as how many threads are waiting in the runnable queue, and whether or not a substantial amount of context switching is occurring, meaning that SQL Server is jumping around working on many different tasks at once, and not completing tasks in a reasonable amount of time.

An overview of sys.dm_os_schedulers

Each row returned by the **sys.dm_os_schedulers** DMV represents a scheduler that is being used to assign tasks to an individual CPU. Rows with a **scheduler_id** of less than 255 represent schedulers for CPU activity, and are used to schedule user queries. Row 255 is the DAC, which provides access when the server is hung, and higher values are used for other system objects, such as Non-Uniform Memory Access (NUMA) modules. We will only concern ourselves with the CPU schedulers between 0 and 255.

The columns returned by this view fall into three broad categories, as shown below. (I have omitted columns for internal use only and those that provide addresses to a memory location.)

- **Identification columns** identify the scheduler and, in some conditions, the CPU being used.

  - **scheduler_id** – the ID of the scheduler. Schedulers with an ID of 255 or less execute user queries; others execute system processes.

  - **cpu_id** – if the affinity mask is set, this is the CPU on which the query is scheduled to run.

- **Status columns** reveal the current activity of the scheduler.

  - **status** – status of the scheduler. ONLINE schedulers are available to process requests, OFFLINE ones aren't, and would be set as OFFLINE via the affinity mask. HIDDEN schedulers run external requests, and VISIBLE schedulers run user requests. Possible domain values for status are: HIDDEN ONLINE, HIDDEN OFFLINE, VISIBLE ONLINE, VISIBLE OFFLINE, VISIBLE ONLINE DAC.

  - **is_online** – indicates whether a scheduler is (1) or isn't (0) available to process requests.

  - **is_idle** – indicates whether or not the scheduler is actually being used to process queries or batches. A value of 1 indicates that no workers are running and the scheduler is idle.

  - **current_tasks_count** – number of tasks that the scheduler is managing at this point in time.

  - **runnable_tasks_count** – number of workers with tasks waiting to be assigned to the runnable queue; high, sustained values for this column are an indication of CPU pressure.

  - **current_workers_count** – current number of workers assigned to this queue.

  - **active_workers_count** – number of workers actively processing.

- **work_queue_count** – number of tasks waiting on a worker.

- **pending_disk_io_count** – total number of disk I/O operations upon which the scheduler is waiting, before the worker thread to which this I/O is assigned can be added to the runnable tasks queue.

- **load_factor** – strictly speaking, this is an "internal use only" column, and is used by SQL Server to assess the load on an individual CPU and so decide which scheduler should be assigned the next task. Ideally, the load_factor value should be roughly the same across all active schedulers.

- **History columns** are the cumulative counters storing information regarding the number of times an activity has occurred since the computer has been restarted.

- **preemptive_switches_count** – number of times this scheduler has switched to pre-emptive mode in order to execute code external to SQL Server, such as external stored procedures and distributed queries.

- **context_switches_count** – number of times the scheduler has switched from one task to another because the worker relinquished control of the scheduler.

- **idle_switches_count** – number of times the scheduler has been idle, waiting for work to do.

- **failed_to_create_worker** – number of times an attempt to create a worker failed. Although no definite cause is indicated, this event generally occurs because of memory constraints, and the existence of any failed_to_create_worker rows is a cause for concern, especially if you already have any memory issues on the server.

CPU waits

The query in Listing 7.16 calculates the average number of tasks being managed, and tasks waiting in the runnable queue, across all available schedulers.

```
-- Get Avg task count and Avg runnable task count
SELECT   AVG(current_tasks_count) AS [Avg Task Count] ,
         AVG(runnable_tasks_count) AS [Avg Runnable Task Count]
FROM     sys.dm_os_schedulers
WHERE    scheduler_id < 255
         AND [status] = 'VISIBLE ONLINE' ;
```

Listing 7.16: Investigating scheduler activity.

High, sustained values for the current_tasks_count column usually indicate a blocking issue, and you can investigate this further using the DMOs described in *Chapter 4, Transactions*. It can also be a secondary indicator of I/O pressure. High, sustained values for the runnable_tasks_count column are usually a very good indicator of CPU pressure, since this means that many tasks are waiting for CPU time. The longer the queue, and the greater the number of schedulers with requests waiting, the more stressed is the CPU subsystem. For most systems, a sustained runnable task queue length of more than about 10–20 is a cause for concern.

For individual schedulers, we can employ the query shown in Listing 7.17, which uses various status columns to investigate potential CPU pressure or, by a simple variation of the WHERE clause, to indicate whether or not I/O pressure is the root cause of the system slowdown.

```
SELECT   scheduler_id ,
         cpu_id ,
         Status ,
         is_online ,
         is_idle ,
         current_tasks_count ,
         runnable_tasks_count ,
         current_workers_count ,
         active_workers_count ,
         work_queue_count ,
         pending_disk_io_count ,
         load_factor
FROM     sys.dm_os_schedulers
```

```
WHERE    scheduler_id < 255
         AND runnable_tasks_count > 0
    -- AND pending_disk_io_count > 0
```

Listing 7.17: Investigating potential disk I/O or CPU pressure.

Insufficient threads

If the system isn't experiencing CPU pressure, is not I/O bound, and there aren't too many other types of waits on the system, then you may need to investigate the possibility that there are simply too few threads available to the server. The query in Listing 7.18 comes courtesy of Slava Oks (HTTP://BLOGS.MSDN.COM/SLAVAO/ARCHIVE/2006/09/28/776437.ASPX) and investigates the possible need to adjust the server threads system configuration, by checking the average value of work_queue_count. In the absence of CPU pressure, values of more than one for the average of the work_queue_count column can mean that you need to increase the number of threads allowable to the server.

```
SELECT   AVG(work_queue_count)
FROM     sys.dm_os_schedulers
WHERE    status = 'VISIBLE ONLINE'
```

Listing 7.18: Are there sufficient worker threads for the workload?

Context switching

Context switching occurs when a process fails to complete in a reasonable time, and the process has to give up control of the scheduler (again, representing a CPU) to let another process complete. SQL Server generally operates in a non-preemptive mode, where threads voluntarily give up access to the CPU at the appropriate moment. Some operations, however, such as calling an extended stored procedure, distributed query, and so on, cause the scheduler to preempt a context switch. A high number of context switches, indicating that many SQL Server tasks are giving up control before completing, is not ideal as it increases load on the CPU simply to allow more users to feel as if they are being served.

With the values from the query in Listing 7.19 we can get the counts of the various operations related to context switching that have occurred since the last reboot.

```
SELECT   scheduler_id ,
         preemptive_switches_count ,
         context_switches_count ,
         idle_switches_count ,
         failed_to_create_worker
FROM     sys.dm_os_schedulers
WHERE    scheduler_id < 255
```

Listing 7.19: Investigating context switching.

One-off queries of this sort, using the "History" columns, are not necessarily very useful. A large number of context switches, accumulated over a long period, may simply reflect the activity of scheduled nightly processes, where such context switching does not affect the users. In order to detect excessive context switching during normal OLTP operations caused, for example, by abnormally high user loads, we need to take a baseline measurement and then track and compare the results over time.

As noted during the earlier discussion on common wait types, hyper-threading (parallel execution) in OTLP systems can lead to context switching, and to CXPACKET and SOS_SCHEDULER_YIELD waits. Furthermore, certain hyper-threading implementations in older processors do not "play nicely" with the SQL Server engine and can exacerbate the issue. According to Zach Nichter, in his Technet Magazine article, *Optimizing SQL Server CPU performance*, at HTTP://TECHNET.MICROSOFT.COM/ EN-US/MAGAZINE/2007.10.SQLCPU.ASPX, if hyper-threading is enabled and you are seeing more than 5000 * (Number of Processors) context switches per second, it suggests that the scheduler is context switching between the same processor, yet thinking it is swapping to a different one, and you should consider turning hyper-threading off and retesting performance. However, new hyper-threading implementations on Intel's Nehalem processors work much more smoothly with SQL Server. For further details, see Joe Chang's blog, *Hyper-Threading from NetBurst to Nehalem*, at HTTP://SQLBLOG.COM/ BLOGS/JOE_CHANG/ARCHIVE/2010/03/23/HYPER-THREADING-COMMENTS.ASPX.

A large number of idle switches, indicating periods when the processor was idle with no requests to process, can indicate a poor distribution of workload across available processors. A low value on one scheduler, coupled with very high utilization on another one, might indicate that large operations that really could benefit from using parallel operations are not doing so. For example, if you have **MAXDOP** set to 1 on a server with 8 CPUs, then your CPU-intensive nightly reports will run on only one of the CPUs, while all the others sit idle.

Is NUMA enabled?

A final useful query against the **sys.dm_os_schedulers** DMV is one that indicates whether or not NUMA (Non-Uniform Memory Access) is enabled on a given SQL Server instance, as shown in Listing 7.20.

```
-- Is NUMA enabled
SELECT  CASE COUNT(DISTINCT parent_node_id)
            WHEN 1 THEN 'NUMA disabled'
            ELSE 'NUMA enabled'
        END
FROM    sys.dm_os_schedulers
WHERE   parent_node_id <> 32 ;
```

Listing 7.20: Is NUMA enabled?

AMD-based servers have supported hardware-based NUMA for several years, while Intel-based Xeon servers have added hardware-based NUMA with the Xeon 5500, 5600, and 7500 series.

CPU utilization history

This script uses the **sys.dm_os_ring_buffers** DMV which, according to Books Online, is:

Identified for informational purposes only. Not supported. Future compatibility is not guaranteed.

Ooh, that sounds scary! Well, despite the warning and lack of documentation in Books Online, there are multiple blog posts from Microsoft employees that show examples of using this DMV. The one shown in Listing 7.21 returns the CPU utilization history over the last 30 minutes, both in terms of CPU usage by the SQL Server process and total CPU usage by all other processes on your database server. This query only works on SQL Server 2008 and SQL Server 2008 R2.

```
-- Get CPU Utilization History for last 30 minutes (in one minute intervals)
-- This version works with SQL Server 2008 and SQL Server 2008 R2 only
DECLARE @ts_now BIGINT = ( SELECT   cpu_ticks / ( cpu_ticks / ms_ticks )
                           FROM     sys.dm_os_sys_info
                         ) ;

SELECT TOP ( 30 )
        SQLProcessUtilization AS [SQL Server Process CPU Utilization] ,
        SystemIdle AS [System Idle Process] ,
        100 - SystemIdle - SQLProcessUtilization
                             AS [Other Process CPU Utilization] ,
        DATEADD(ms, -1 * ( @ts_now - [timestamp] ), GETDATE())
                             AS [Event Time]
FROM      ( SELECT   record.value('(./Record/@id)[1]', 'int') AS record_id ,
                     record.value('(./Record/SchedulerMonitorEvent/
                                   SystemHealth/SystemIdle)[1]', 'int')
                                          AS [SystemIdle] ,
                     record.value('(./Record/SchedulerMonitorEvent/
                                   SystemHealth/ProcessUtilization)[1]',
                                   'int')
                                          AS [SQLProcessUtilization] ,
                  [timestamp]
            FROM      ( SELECT    [timestamp] ,
```

```
                                CONVERT(XML, record) AS [record]
                FROM            sys.dm_os_ring_buffers
                WHERE           ring_buffer_type =
                                        N'RING_BUFFER_SCHEDULER_MONITOR'
                                AND record LIKE N'%<SystemHealth>%'
                        ) AS x
            ) AS y
    ORDER BY record_id DESC ;
```

Listing 7.21: Recent CPU utilization.

The query subtracts the `SystemIdle` value and the `SQL Server Process` value from 100 to arrive at the value for all other processes on the server. The results provide a handy way to see your recent CPU utilization history for the server as a whole, for SQL Server, and for other processes that are running on your database server (such as management software). Even though the granularity is only one minute, it's very useful to be able to see this from T-SQL rather than having to look at PerfMon or use WMI to get CPU utilization information. In our experimentation, it's only been possible to retrieve 256 minutes-worth of data from this query.

Investigating Memory Usage

In this section, we'll discuss the DMVs that allow us to investigate how SQL Server is using memory, and provide useful indicators of possible memory pressure.

Memory pressure in SQL Server is often a little harder to spot and diagnose than CPU pressure. High CPU usage will immediately make itself known via that fact that one or more of the CPUs will be pegged at 90+ percent for long periods of time. However, in basic terms, SQL Server will use as much memory as you give it. SQL Server uses a central memory broker mechanism to efficiently distribute memory across all components that need it. Any memory that is not currently required by another component remains in the buffer pool (in the form of 8-KB pages), and is used to cache pages read from disk.

So efficient is SQL Server at using any memory that is available to it that we often have to limit the amount of memory that SQL Server has access to (using the `max server memory` server configuration.) In fact, about the only way to give SQL Server more memory than it needs is to have more RAM than data, a condition that is pretty rare unless planned that way.

The first evidence of memory pressure usually comes from PerfMon counters relating to memory paging (such as `Memory: Pages/sec` and `Memory: Page Faults/sec`), or to disk utilization resulting from memory paging (since all data is accessed through memory after it is read from disk), as well as SQL Server counters such as the `SQL Server: Memory Manager` and `SQL Server: Buffer Manager` sets of counters. In the Memory Manager set of counters, it's useful to check that the value for the `Total Server Memory (KB)` counter, which is the amount of memory in the buffer pool that is currently in use, is generally well below the value for the `Target Server Memory (KB)` counter, which indicates the maximum amount of memory that the SQL Server process can use. Other interesting counters in this set include those relating to memory grants, where a long queue of processes waiting for a workspace memory grant could be indicative of memory pressure (this issue can be investigated further using the `sys.dm_exec_query_memory_grants` DMV).

In the `Buffer Manager` set of counters, the `Page Life Expectancy` counter is especially useful for detecting memory pressure. This value should generally be 300 or greater, indicating that pages stay in RAM for an average of 300 seconds, or 5 minutes. If it is significantly lower for sustained periods, it indicates that SQL Server is being forced to flush the cache to free up memory.

If you do detect possible memory issues, you can investigate further using the DMVs covered in this section, and find out exactly where and why the issue is occurring, rather than just reporting to your system administrator that a problem exists.

System-wide memory use

There are a few ways to get a picture of the memory use in SQL Server using the DMVs but, new to SQL Server 2008, there is an excellent DMV called **sys.dm_os_sys_memory** that provides a summarization of the memory condition of the system. It shows the current levels of memory in the system, the cache, and so on. Amongst the columns this view returns are:

- **total_physical_memory_kb** – the total amount of non-virtual memory available to the OS in kilobytes

- **available_physical_memory_kb** – the amount of non-virtual memory currently available to the OS

- **total_page_file_kb** – the current size of the OS's virtual memory/page file

- **available_page_file_kb** – the amount of virtual memory currently available to the OS

- **system_memory_state_desc** – calculated value based on two other columns (system_high_memory_signal_state and system_low_memory_signal_state) that indicates if available memory is high, low, steady, or transitioning from one state to another.

- The final column in this list, **system_memory_state_desc**, requires a little more explanation. When you start the server, this value will likely be "Available physical memory is high," while a value of "Available physical memory is low" is an indicator of external memory pressure, since it means that the OS has little available memory and so may require SQL Server to reduce its memory usage. This will result in SQL Server reducing the size of all of its memory caches, and means that plans will get flushed from the plan cache, and so on.

When memory utilization is just right, the value will be "Physical memory state is steady." For short periods, you may very occasionally see a third value of "Physical memory state is transitioning," indicating that the memory state is changing from high to low, or vice versa.

Using these five columns, as shown in Listing 7.22, we can get an overview of how much RAM is available to the operating system in total, and how much of it is currently not in use. The first and second values correspond to the Task Manager Physical Memory (MB) values for total and available memory.

```
SELECT  total_physical_memory_kb / 1024 AS total_physical_memory_mb ,
        available_physical_memory_kb / 1024 AS available_physical_memory_mb ,
        total_page_file_kb / 1024 AS total_page_file_mb ,
        available_page_file_kb / 1024 AS available_page_file_mb ,
        system_memory_state_desc
FROM    sys.dm_os_sys_memory
```

Listing 7.22: System memory usage.

The following results were taken from my writing laptop with just under 2 GB of RAM (some allocated to video RAM).

total_physical_memory_mb	available_physical_memory_mb	total_page_file_kb
1912	912	3825

available_page_file_kb	system_memory_state_desc
2265	Available physical memory is high

This DMV also provides additional columns to get information about the memory assigned to the system cache and the kernel if, for some reason, you need to determine these individual values.

Process memory use

Also, for SQL Server 2008, there is another DMV pertaining to memory, `sys.dm_os_process_memory`, which returns a single row summarizing memory usage from the point of view of the SQL Server process. This DMV has the following columns (and more), all of which give you the current status of memory on the server:

- **physical_memory_in_use_kb** – all physical memory in use on the server by the SQL Server processes, in kilobytes

- **virtual_address_space_committed_kb** – amount of virtual address space committed to the SQL Server process

- **virtual_address_space_available_kb** – amount of virtual address space that is committed but not currently in use

- **page_fault_count** – number of times data needed was not found in process memory, causing a physical read to disk

- **process_physical_memory_low** – when the SQL Server process is needing more RAM than is physically available, this value is set to 1

- **process_virtual_memory_low** – when the SQL Server process is needing more virtual RAM than is currently available, this value is set to 1.

The query in Listing 7.23 is about as simple as it gets, but nevertheless summarizes some useful memory data for your SQL Server instance.

```
SELECT    physical_memory_in_use_kb ,
          virtual_address_space_committed_kb ,
          virtual_address_space_available_kb ,
          page_fault_count ,
          process_physical_memory_low ,
          process_virtual_memory_low
FROM      sys.dm_os_process_memory
```

Listing 7.23: Memory usage by the SQL Server process.

Using these values, along with those from **sys.dm_os_sys_memory** (plus a few of the counters, such as **Buffer Manager:Page Life Expectancy** from the performance counters) you can get a good feeling for how your SQL Server 2008 server is using memory.

Particularly useful are the two columns, **process_physical_memory_low** and **process_virtual_memory_low**. If these values return 1, you will know that you have a good indication of a memory problem, even if you are not an expert in SQL Server memory.

Memory use in the buffer pool

When a data page is read from disk, the page is copied into the SQL Server buffer pool and cached for reuse. Each cached data page has one buffer descriptor. Buffer descriptors uniquely identify each data page that is currently cached in an instance of SQL Server. The **sys.dm_os_buffer_descriptors** DMV returns cached pages for all user and system databases, including pages that are associated with the Resource database.

As stated by Books Online:

Returns information about all the data pages that are currently in the SQL Server buffer pool. The output of this view can be used to determine the distribution of database pages in the buffer pool according to database, object, or type.

Listing 7.24 shows that this DMV can tell how your buffer pool memory is being used, i.e. which databases and which indexes are using the most memory in the buffer pool.

```
-- Get total buffer usage by database
SELECT  DB_NAME(database_id) AS [Database Name] ,
        COUNT(*) * 8 / 1024.0 AS [Cached Size (MB)]
FROM    sys.dm_os_buffer_descriptors
WHERE   database_id > 4 -- exclude system databases
        AND database_id <> 32767 -- exclude ResourceDB
GROUP BY DB_NAME(database_id)
ORDER BY [Cached Size (MB)] DESC ;


-- Breaks down buffers by object (table, index) in the buffer pool
SELECT  OBJECT_NAME(p.[object_id]) AS [ObjectName] ,
        p.index_id ,
        COUNT(*) / 128 AS [Buffer size(MB)] ,
        COUNT(*) AS [Buffer_count]
FROM    sys.allocation_units AS a
        INNER JOIN sys.dm_os_buffer_descriptors
                AS b ON a.allocation_unit_id = b.allocation_unit_id
        INNER JOIN sys.partitions AS p ON a.container_id = p.hobt_id
WHERE   b.database_id = DB_ID()
        AND p.[object_id] > 100 -- exclude system objects
GROUP BY p.[object_id] ,
        p.index_id
ORDER BY buffer_count DESC ;
```

Listing 7.24: Memory allocation in the buffer pool.

The first query rolls up buffer pool usage by database. It allows you to determine how much memory each database is using in the buffer pool. It could help you to decide how to deploy databases in a consolidation or scale-out effort.

The second query tells you which objects are using the most memory in your buffer pool, and is filtered by the current database. It shows the table or indexed view name, the index ID (which will be zero for a heap table), and the amount of memory used in the buffer pool for that object. It is also a good way to see the effectiveness of data compression in SQL Server 2008 Enterprise Edition and SQL Server 2008 R2 Enterprise Edition.

Memory clerks and memory grants

Each of the various components in SQL Server has its own memory clerk, responsible for allocating memory for that component. This DMV provides a high level, point-in-time picture of the memory clerk processes that manage SQL Server memory. We won't cover this DMV in detail but, as an example, Listing 7.25 will provide a useful, quick overview of buffer pool usage for a given instance.

```
-- Buffer Pool Usage for instance
SELECT TOP(20) [type], SUM(single_pages_kb) AS [SPA Mem, Kb]
FROM sys.dm_os_memory_clerks
GROUP BY [type]
ORDER BY SUM(single_pages_kb) DESC;
```

Listing 7.25: Buffer pool usage.

Typically, you'll see most memory usage associated such memory clerk types as CACHE-STORE_SQLCP (the cached query plan store for ad hoc SQL) or CACHESTORE_OBJCP (the store for objects such as triggers, stored procedures, functions, and so on).

Some of the more obscure memory clerks are not well documented, but an important one to watch out for when investigating memory issues is MEMORYCLERK_SQLQERESERVATIONS, which indicates that there may be insufficient memory in the buffer pool for certain queries to execute.

Such issues should be investigated further using an execution-related DMV, namely sys.dm_exec_query_memory_grants, which:

> *Returns information about the queries that have acquired a memory grant or that still require a memory grant to execute. Queries that do not have to wait on a memory grant will not appear in this view.*

This DMV allows you to check for queries that are waiting (or have recently had to wait) for a memory grant, as demonstrated in Listing 7.26. Although not used in this query, note that SQL Server 2008 added some new columns to this DMV.

```
-- Shows the memory required by both running (non-null grant_time)
-- and waiting queries (null grant_time)
-- SQL Server 2008 version
SELECT  DB_NAME(st.dbid) AS [DatabaseName] ,
        mg.requested_memory_kb ,
        mg.ideal_memory_kb ,
        mg.request_time ,
        mg.grant_time ,
        mg.query_cost ,
        mg.dop ,
        st.[text]
FROM    sys.dm_exec_query_memory_grants AS mg
        CROSS APPLY sys.dm_exec_sql_text(plan_handle) AS st
WHERE   mg.request_time < COALESCE(grant_time, '99991231')
ORDER BY mg.requested_memory_kb DESC ;

-- Shows the memory required by both running (non-null grant_time)
-- and waiting queries (null grant_time)
-- SQL Server 2005 version
SELECT  DB_NAME(st.dbid) AS [DatabaseName] ,
        mg.requested_memory_kb ,
        mg.request_time ,
        mg.grant_time ,
```

```
        mg.query_cost ,
        mg.dop ,
        st.[text]
FROM    sys.dm_exec_query_memory_grants AS mg
        CROSS APPLY sys.dm_exec_sql_text(plan_handle) AS st
WHERE   mg.request_time < COALESCE(grant_time, '99991231')
ORDER BY mg.requested_memory_kb DESC ;
```

Listing 7.26: Which queries have requested, or have had to wait for, large memory grants?

You should periodically run this query multiple times in succession; ideally, you would want to see few, if any, rows returned each time. If you do see a lot of rows returned each time, this could be an indication of internal memory pressure.

This query would also help you identify queries that are requesting relatively large memory grants, perhaps because they are poorly written or because there are missing indexes that make the query more expensive.

Investigate memory using cache counters

In the previous section, we took a brief look at how memory is allocated to our system via memory clerks. To get a bit deeper into the cache entries, we are going to look at `sys.dm_os_memory_cache_counters` which will give some more detailed statistics about how cache memory is currently being used by SQL Server across its various caches.

Essentially, this DMV provides a snapshot of cache-usage values, based on current reality. The column `single_pages_kb` is the amount of memory allocated via the single-page allocator. This refers to the 8-KB pages that are taken directly from the buffer pool, for the cache in question. The column `multi_pages_kb` is the amount of memory allocated by using the multiple-page allocator of the memory node. This memory is allocated outside the buffer pool and takes advantage of the virtual allocator of the memory nodes.

- **name** – the descriptive name given to the cache.

- **type** – the type of cache being reported on, such as the CACHESTORE_SQLCP plan for SQL cached plans. Type is more generic than name. For example, for type CACHESTORE_BROKERREADONLY, there are at least three different names listed: "Service broker routing cache," "Service broker configuration," and "Service broker dialog cache."

- **single_pages_kb** – the amount of memory allocated to the cache by the single-page allocator. Memory allocation will be in multiples of 8-KB pages, taken from the buffer pool.

- **multi_pages_kb** – the amount of memory allocated to the cache by the multipage allocator. This memory is allocated outside of the buffer pool using the virtual memory allocator.

- **single_pages_in_use_kb** – the number of the single pages allocated that are currently in use (not tracked for UserStore type entries).

- **multi_pages_in_use_kb** – the number of the multipages allocated that are currently in use (not tracked for UserStore type entries).

- **entries_count** – the number of distinct entries in the cache, regardless of whether they are single or multi pages.

- **entries_in_use_count** – number of entries that are actively being used by SQL Server.

A large number of multi_pages_kb for either of these cache types can lead to decreased performance on builds previous to SQL Server 2005 SP2 (Build 3042). Since SQL Server 2005 SP2 is no longer a supported service pack, this is yet another reason to get SQL Server 2005 SP3 (Build 4035) and, hopefully, SQL Server 2005 SP3 CU9 (Build 4294) applied.

To see all the cache counters, you can execute a simple query of the form shown in Listing 7.27.

```
SELECT  type ,
        name ,
        single_pages_kb ,
        multi_pages_kb ,
        single_pages_in_use_kb ,
        multi_pages_in_use_kb ,
        entries_count ,
        entries_in_use_count
FROM    sys.dm_os_memory_cache_counters
ORDER BY type,name;
```

Listing 7.27: Returning the cache counters.

This will return quite a few different types, including:

- **CACHESTORE_SQLCP** – cached query plan store for ad hoc SQL

- **CACHESTORE_OBJCP** – cached query plan store for objects such as triggers, stored procedures, functions, and so on

- **CACHESTORE_PHDR** – cache query trees for objects that do not maintain query plans, such as views and constraints

- **CACHESTORE_TEMPTABLES** – temporary tables

- **USERSTORE_TOKENPERM** – cache security information

- **USERSTORE_DBMETADATA** – caches the metadata for databases; each database has its own entry denoted in the name column.

Using these and other types of cache counter, you can get a good idea of how much cache memory is being used, plus you can see how much of the memory is currently being used (and hence held in memory) by SQL Server processes. As an example usage, to see how active your cache is for SQL plans, we can filter on type, either **CACHESTORE_SQLCP** or **CACHESTORE_OBJCP**, as shown in Listing 7.28.

```
SELECT   name ,
         type ,
         entries_count ,
         entries_in_use_count
FROM     sys.dm_os_memory_cache_counters
WHERE    type IN ( 'CACHESTORE_SQLCP', 'CACHESTORE_OBJCP' )
             --ad hoc plans and object plans
ORDER BY name ,
         type
```

Listing 7.28: Investigating the use of the plan cache.

On my test laptop, this returns the following output:

name	type	entries_count	entries_in_use_count
Object Plans	CACHESTORE_OBJCP	22	0
SQL Plans	CACHESTORE_SQLCP	44	2

We can run some ad hoc SQL, such as **select *from sys.objects**, and then rerun Listing 7.18, in order to see a new entry added to the SQL Plans cache:

name	type	entries_count	entries_in_use_count
Object Plans	CACHESTORE_OBJCP	22	0
SQL Plans	CACHESTORE_SQLCP	46	7

Notice that the `entries_count` for SQL Plans has increased by two, one for the counters query, and one for the ad hoc SQL (it might increase more due to other background processes) but the use count was not incremented. This, of course, is because the query will have finished prior to us rechecking the cache. Note, too, that if we run the ad hoc statement again, exactly as before, the entries count will not change. However, if we add even a single space, it will increase. To see this in action, we can create a procedure that will take some time to execute, using the handy **WAITFOR** command, as shown in Listing 7.29.

```
--in a different connection, execute this all at once:
USE tempdb
go
CREATE PROCEDURE test
AS
    WAITFOR DELAY '00:00:30'
    SELECT  *
    FROM    sys.sysobjects
go
EXECUTE test
```

Listing 7.29: Investigating plan reuse counts.

Then, while it is executing, you will see that at least one new entry has been created, and it is in use.

name	type	entries_count	entries_in_use_count
Object Plans	CACHESTORE_OBJCP	23	0
SQL Plans	CACHESTORE_SQLCP	46	7

Once it has finished, you will see the cache entry is no longer in use. Clearly, this is a micro-example of what is rarely such a small amount of memory. You will have far more queries in cache in your busy system, and the same goes for all of the many other types of cache memory that are available.

Note that, while the `sys.dm_os_memory_cache_counters` DMV provides detailed information about cache memory, it's still fairly high level and it's possible to drill even deeper using, for example, the following DMVs:

- `sys.dm_os_memory_cache_entries` to investigate individual cache entries and trace them back to their associated objects

- `sys.dm_os_memory_cache_hash_tables` to find out about the actual hash tables where the cache entries are placed

- `sys.dm_os_memory_cache_clock_hands` to find out about internal and external memory pressure at the cache level.

Keep in mind, though, that curiosity killed the cat, mostly because he spent so much time digging around looking at all the data that he forgot to eat.

Investigating Latching

As discussed in *Chapter 4,* locking is an integral and normal part of the operation of an RDBMS when mediating concurrent access to shared database resources. Generally speaking, this refers to the shared, exclusive, and update locks acquired on specific database rows, in order to avoid interference between transactions that are reading or writing that data simultaneously. However, in addition to these locks, SQL Server has to acquire further "lightweight locks," known as latches, in order to coordinate access to other resources implicitly required to execute the query, such as a page/extent in memory, a file handle, a worktable in `tempdb`, or any such thing that the engine may need to access, which is not specifically and directly specified in the request that is issued.

In essence, latches are to locks what fields are to columns. In relational theory, a column is a logical representation of the data, managed completely by the SQL Server engine. A column doesn't have a physical location. A field, on the other hand, is a physical location in a record, where you can find the actual set of bits and bytes. So, whereas a lock is represented by a row of data in a system table and is used to lock access to a resource that a user wants, a latch is used by the query processor to lock physical memory or some internal structure, to ensure consistency.

As noted, latches are lightweight devices, designed to be held for very short periods of time and, as such, are supposed to be of minimal cost. Also, it's true that their acquisition is, to some extent, beyond the SQL programmer's control. Nevertheless, as discussed in *Chapter 2*, poorly designed SQL can and will cause more latches to be acquired than is necessary, thus limiting the overall scalability of the system.

The `sys.dm_os_latch_stats` DMV provides our window onto the world of latch statistics in SQL Server for the different types of latches that it provides, such as the BUFFER latch type that is acquired before reading or changing a database page. The `sys.dm_os_latch_stats` view can be used to see if any types of latches are being waited on excessively. For example, if you were getting 844 errors (buffer latch timeouts), particularly frequent ones, you can use this DMV to check to see if the BUFFER latch is constantly being waited on, possibly indicating a need to improve the I/O system, whether the memory and/or hard disk subsystems. Of course, it can simply mean that you have queries that need tuning but, in either case, your I/O system cannot handle the current load.

This view is based on a set of counters that are added to or set periodically (as in the max wait time for a given class). The data is reset at a reboot or it can be cleared with the command:

```
DBCC SQLPERF ('sys.dm_os_latch_stats', CLEAR);
```

Listing 7.30: Resetting the latch statistics.

The following columns are available:

- **latch_class** – the type of latch; a full list can be located in the Books Online topic for the `sys.dm_os_latch_stats`

- **waiting_requests_count** – a cumulative count of the number of times that a process has needed to wait on any latch of the latch type

- **wait_time_ms** – cumulative amount of time processes have spent waiting on any latch of the latch type

- **max_wait_time_ms** – the maximum amount of time a process has waited for a latch in this class.

As an example, try executing the query shown in Listing 7.31 on a busy system.

```
SELECT   latch_class ,
         waiting_requests_count AS waitCount ,
         wait_time_ms AS waitTime ,
         max_wait_time_ms AS maxWait
FROM     sys.dm_os_latch_stats
ORDER BY wait_time_ms DESC
```

Listing 7.31: Seeking out latch waits.

On my server, a very busy SQL Server that was rebooted just a few days previously, the results returned were as follows:

latch_class	waitCount	waitTime	maxWait
BUFFER	8222456	31717841	5172
ACCESS_METHODS_SCAN_RANGE_GENERATOR	3436520	4106876	484
DBCC_MULTIOBJECT_SCANNER	1759162	526480	187
ACCESS_METHODS_DATASET_PARENT	122981	241125	938
DBCC_OBJECT_METADATA	1394243	219441	31
DBCC_FILE_CHECK_OBJECT	629937	172415	16
DBCC_PFS_STATUS	381815	66465	16
DBCC_CHECK_AGGREGATE	112423	29574	16
NESTING_TRANSACTION_READONLY	147186	28869	47

Note that most of the latch waits have been for buffer latches, used to synchronize any access to the SQL Server pages. The average wait time for a buffer latch is 3.85 ms (31717841 / 8222456), but the maximum wait time of over 5 seconds is a bit worrisome. However, we can't really tell too much from this stat other than that you may need to do some more digging using `sys.dm_os_wait_stats`, which was covered earlier and includes values that differentiate between latches used for input and output.

The second largest wait type is `ACCESS_METHODS_SCAN_RANGE_GENERATOR`, which, according to Books Online is *used to synchronize access to a range generator during parallel scans*. This can indicate poor indexing for certain types of loads, particularly transaction processing loads that should be based on short-and-sweet queries. When a query is executed using parallelism, it indicates some form of large scan or hash/merge join that is fine for reports, but not for dealing with small sets of data that an OLTP system should be executing on. When you see this form of latch, you will likely see `CXPACKET` wait types showing up as well (see Listing 7.2). The `ACCESS_METHODS_DATASET_PARENT` is another latch class that pertains to parallel operations.

You will note that many of the latch types are documented as *internal use only*, which can be cold comfort at times. However, like the `DBCC_` classes, you can get generally get an idea of their purpose; in this case, many of them are used by the consistency checkers internally to hold access to certain objects as needed, as is the case for the `NESTING_TRANSACTION_` classes.

While you may not be able to get a tremendous amount of decipherable information from these latch classes as a first stop, there is still a good bit of low-level information that can be mined from the data, particularly when certain latch wait times are really large and represent an obvious problem.

Summary

The topic of OS DMVs is deep and wide; an entire book of material could be compiled just from the DMOs prefixed with `sys.dm_os_`.

All the DMOs provide data that is fairly "raw" in nature, often using measurements in units that are not that common to the average DBA. How often, for example, do you measure time in CPU ticks? ("*Honey, American Idol is on in 1.4 trillion CPU ticks. Are you coming?*")

Probably the most difficult part about a chapter like this is that the topic is so wide that we could not even begin to cover everything. For the `sys.dm_os_wait_stats` DMV alone, for example, there are 231 different wait types documented in Books Online. We covered a few very common ones, but still left 200+ untouched. In the end, we whittled the list down to higher-level objects that we feel DBAs will find most useful in investigating pressure points in their SQL Server systems and, hopefully, the chapter has at least managed to shine a light on some useful diagnostic data, such as:

- `sys.dm_os_wait_stats` – information about what types of things your SQL Server has been waiting on

- `sys.dm_os_performance_counters` – information from the SQL Server performance counters, with some formatting that is not widely documented

- `sys.dm_os_sys_info` – information about the overall configuration of your system

- `sys.dm_os_schedulers` – information on schedulers that handle spreading work out to the CPUs

- `sys.dm_os_sys_memory` – new DMV for 2008 that gives you an overview of how the server is managing memory

- `sys.dm_os_process_memory` – new DMV for 2008 that gives you an overview of how the SQL Server process is doing for memory

- **sys.dm_os_memory_cache_counters** – stats on how the cache memory is being utilized, including how much memory is actively being used

- **sys.dm_os_latch_stats** – stats on the low-level resource locks that SQL Server uses to lock physical pages in memory, and more.

And now, it is really up to you, as the reader, to take the information provided and expand upon it, based on the potential problems and bottlenecks that you are experiencing on your systems.

Index

SQL Server
and .NET Tools
from Red Gate Software

SQL Compare® Pro

$595

Compare and synchronize SQL Server database schemas

↗ Eliminate mistakes migrating database changes from dev, to test, to production
↗ Speed up the deployment of new databse schema updates
↗ Find and fix errors caused by differences between databases
↗ Compare and synchronize within SSMS

> **"Just purchased SQL Compare. With the productivity I'll get out of this tool, it's like buying time."**
> **Robert Sondles** Blueberry Island Media Ltd

SQL Data Compare Pro

$595

Compares and synchronizes SQL Server database contents

↗ Save time by automatically comparing and synchronizing your data
↗ Copy lookup data from development databases to staging or production
↗ Quickly fix problems by restoring damaged or missing data to a single row
↗ Compare and synchronize data within SSMS

> **"We use SQL Data Compare daily and it has become an indispensable part of delivering our service to our customers. It has also streamlined our daily update process and cut back literally a good solid hour per day."**
> **George Pantela** GPAnalysis.com

Visit **www.red-gate.com** for a 14-day, free trial

SQL Prompt Pro $295

Write, edit, and explore SQL effortlessly

↗ Write SQL smoothly, with code-completion and SQL snippets

↗ Reformat SQL to a preferred style

↗ Keep databases tidy by finding invalid objects automatically

↗ Save time and effort with script summaries, smart object renaming and more

> **"SQL Prompt is hands-down one of the coolest applications I've used. Makes querying/developing so much easier and faster."**
> **Jorge Segarra** University Community Hospital

SQL Source Control $295

Connect your existing source control system to SQL Server

↗ Bring all the benefits of source control to your database

↗ Source control schemas and data within SSMS, not with offline scripts

↗ Connect your databases to TFS, SVN, SourceGear Vault, Vault Pro, Mercurial,
Perforce, Git, Bazaar, and any source control system with a capable command line

↗ Work with shared development databases, or individual copies

↗ Track changes to follow who changed what, when, and why

↗ Keep teams in sync with easy access to the latest database version

↗ View database development history for easy retrieval of specific versions

> **"After using SQL Source Control for several months, I wondered how I got by before. Highly recommended, it has paid for itself several times over."**
> **Ben Ashley** Fast Floor

Visit **www.red-gate.com** for a 28-day, free trial

SQL Backup Pro $795

Compress, encrypt, and strengthen SQL Server backups

- ↗ Compress SQL Server database backups by up to 95% for faster, smaller backups

- ↗ Protect your data with up to 256-bit AES encryption

- ↗ Strengthen your backups with network resilience to enable a fault-tolerant transfer of backups across flaky networks

- ↗ Control your backup activities through an intuitive interface, with powerful job management and an interactive timeline

> **"SQL Backup is an amazing tool that lets us manage and monitor our backups in real time. Red Gate's SQL tools have saved us so much time and work that I am afraid my director will decide that we don't need a DBA anymore!"**
>
> **Mike Poole** Database Administrator, Human Kinetics

Visit **www.red-gate.com** for a 14-day, free trial

SQL Monitor

from **$795**

SQL Server performance monitoring and alerting

↗ Intuitive overviews at global, cluster, machine, SQL Server,
  and database levels for up-to-the-minute performance data

↗ Use SQL Monitor's web UI to keep an eye on server performance
  in real time on desktop machines and mobile devices

↗ Intelligent SQL Server alerts via email and an alert inbox in the
  UI, so you know about problems first

↗ Comprehensive historical data, so you can go back in time to
  identify the source of a problem

↗ Generate reports via the UI or with Red Gate's free SSRS Reporting Pack

↗ View the top 10 expensive queries for an instance or database
  based on CPU usage, duration, and reads and writes

↗ PagerDuty integration for phone and SMS alerting

↗ Fast, simple installation and administration

> **"Being web based, SQL Monitor is readily available to you, wherever you may be on your network. You can check on your servers from almost any location, via most mobile devices that support a web browser."**
>
> **Jonathan Allen** Senior DBA, Careers South West Ltd

Visit **www.red-gate.com** for a 14-day, free trial

SQL Virtual Restore $495

Rapidly mount live, fully functional databases direct from backups

- ↗ Virtually restoring a backup requires significantly less time and space than a regular physical restore
- ↗ Databases mounted with SQL Virtual Restore are fully functional and support both read/write operations
- ↗ SQL Virtual Restore is ACID compliant and gives you access to full, transactionally consistent data, with all objects visible and available
- ↗ Use SQL Virtual Restore to recover objects, verify your backups with DBCC CHECKDB, create a storage-efficient copy of your production database, and more.

> "We find occasions where someone has deleted data accidentally or dropped an index, etc., and with SQL Virtual Restore we can mount last night's backup quickly and easily to get access to the data or the original schema. It even works with all our backups being encrypted. This takes any extra load off our production server. SQL Virtual Restore is a great product."
>
> **Brent McCraken** Senior Database Administrator/Architect, Kiwibank Limited

SQL Storage Compress $1,595

Silent data compression to optimize SQL Server storage

- ↗ Reduce the storage footprint of live SQL Server databases by up to 90% to save on space and hardware costs
- ↗ Databases compressed with SQL Storage Compress are fully functional
- ↗ Prevent unauthorized access to your live databases with 256-bit AES encryption
- ↗ Integrates seamlessly with SQL Server and does not require any configuration changes

Visit **www.red-gate.com** for a 14-day, free trial

SQL Toolbelt $1,995

The essential SQL Server tools for database professionals

You can buy our acclaimed SQL Server tools individually or bundled. Our most popular deal is the SQL Toolbelt: fourteen of our SQL Server tools in a single installer, with **a combined value of $5,930 but an actual price of $1,995,** a saving of 66%.

Fully compatible with SQL Server 2000, 2005, and 2008.

SQL Toolbelt contains:

↗ **SQL Compare Pro**

↗ **SQL Data Compare Pro**

↗ **SQL Source Control**

↗ **SQL Backup Pro**

↗ **SQL Monitor**

↗ **SQL Prompt Pro**

↗ **SQL Data Generator**

↗ **SQL Doc**

↗ **SQL Dependency Tracker**

↗ **SQL Packager**

↗ **SQL Multi Script Unlimited**

↗ **SQL Search**

↗ **SQL Comparison SDK**

↗ **SQL Object Level Recovery Native**

> **"The SQL Toolbelt provides tools that database developers, as well as DBAs, should not live without."**
> **William Van Orden** Senior Database Developer, Lockheed Martin

Visit **www.red-gate.com** for a 14-day, free trial

Performance Tuning with SQL Server
Dynamic Management Views
Louis Davidson and Tim Ford

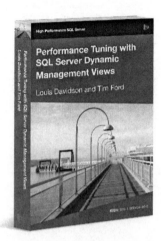

This is the book that will de-mystify the process of using Dynamic Management Views to collect the information you need to troubleshoot SQL Server problems. It will highlight the core techniques and "patterns" that you need to master, and will provide a core set of scripts that you can use and adapt for your own requirements.

ISBN: 978-1-906434-47-2
Published: October 2010

Defensive Database Programming
Alex Kuznetsov

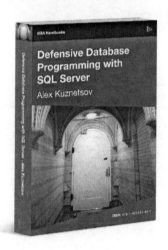

Inside this book, you will find dozens of practical, defensive programming techniques that will improve the quality of your T-SQL code and increase its resilience and robustness.

ISBN: 978-1-906434-49-6
Published: June 2010

Brad's Sure Guide to
SQL Server Maintenance Plans
Brad McGehee

Brad's Sure Guide to SQL Server Maintenance Plans shows you how to use the Maintenance Plan Wizard and Designer to configure and schedule eleven core database maintenance tasks, ranging from integrity checks, to database backups, to index reorganizations
and rebuilds.

ISBN: 978-1-906434-34-2
Published: December 2009

The Red Gate Guide to SQL Server
Team-based Development
Phil Factor, Grant Fritchey, Alex Kuznetsov, and Mladen Prajdić

This book shows how to use of mixture of home-grown scripts, native SQL Server tools, and tools from the Red Gate SQL Toolbelt, to successfully develop database applications in a team environment, and make database development as similar as possible to "normal" development.

ISBN: 978-1-906434-59-5
Published: November 2010

CPSIA information can be obtained at www.ICGtesting.com
Printed in the USA
LVOW051241230512

282902LV00002B/3/P